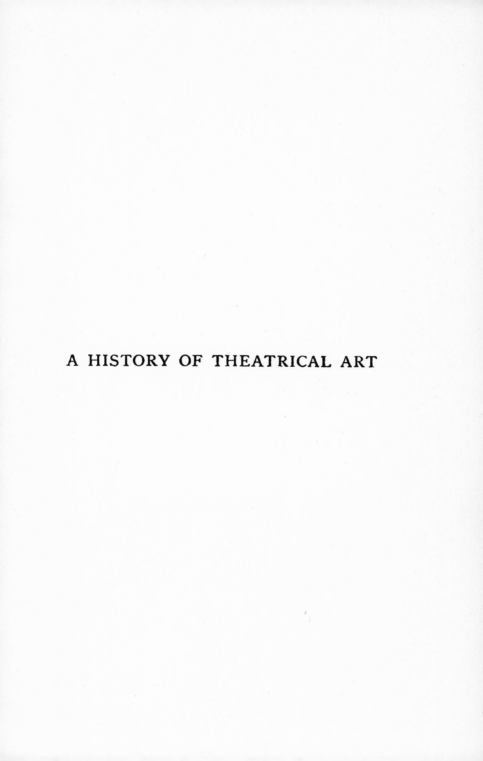

A HISTORY OF THEATRICAL ART

Garrick as Hamlet (p. 396).

Fig. **70**.

A History of Theatrical Art

In Ancient and Modern Times by

Karl Mantzius

Authorised Translation by

Louise von Cossel

Volume V

The Great Actors of the Eighteenth Century

GLOUCESTER, MASS.

PETER SMITH

1970

First Published, 1909
Reprinted, 1937
Reprinted, 1970

CONTENTS

CONTENTS

LIST OF ILLUSTRATIONS

*When not otherwise noted, the reproductions are made from originals
in the author's collection.*

INTRODUCTION

First Steps of Professional Dramatic Art in Germany—Literary and Social Conditions—Touring Companies—Hauptaktions—Hanswurst—Internal and External Conditions of the Troupes.

THE progress of German civilisation is distinguished from that of the other European countries by its lack of a national centre.

To France and England, Paris and London are like two enormous foci, which attract the rays of intellectual life in huge pencils of such intense heat and strength that they burn indelible marks into the tablets of history. In the annals of the theatre such marks are the names of Shakespeare and Molière, which the lapse of time has not been able to obliterate.

In the development of German civilisation nothing similar occurs. The prolonged horrors of the Thirty Years War and the prostration that followed it, spoiled, we may say, the whole seventeenth century for the German nation. The rising revolutionary wave, which had manifested itself in such movements as the Reformation, the peasant revolt and the folk-song, was beaten down. The foreign hordes of French, Swedes, Russians, Swiss, and adventurers of no country combined in destroying national life and customs, and left the country physically and mentally scorched and devastated.

In the many small autocratic principalities which had sprung up in consequence of the Peace of Westphalia, the Courts developed into caricatures of the Court of Versailles. They had their court-poets and *maîtres de plaisir*, without possessing sufficient money to act as patrons, or sufficient authority to allow art to manifest itself freely, or sufficient taste to choose the good and reject the bad. And, surrounding the Courts we see the more or less impoverished capitals, whose citizens were too cowed to entertain independent opinions, or to dare to enjoy anything before having cast shy glances at the castle for approval.

Amidst such surroundings, and in such an atmosphere, no art could thrive, least of all dramatic art, which more than any other requires liberty, order, and wealth. True, there was no lack of poets nor of actors either, but their art is of very slight value. The poets tried to consolidate their position by forming literary societies on the model of the Italian academies; such were the "Palm Order" or the "Fruitful Company" in Weimar, the "Pegnitz Shepherds" or the "Crowned Flower Order" in Nuremberg, the "German Patriotic League" in Hamburg, the "Elb-Swan Order" in Holstein. However, their well-intentioned efforts were practically lost in outward ceremonies and proceedings of mutual admiration, and no genius arose in their midst. And the scanty dramatic literature which the seventeenth century has to show is strangely dwarfed and stunted. As examples may be mentioned the cut and dried adaptations by Martin Opitz of antique and Italian plays, the equally dull imitations by Andreas Gryphius of Seneca's library dramas, his somewhat more important comedies *Horribiliscribrifax*, in which he introduces the Italian Capitanotype into German literature,[1] and *Absurda comica or Herr Peter Squenz*, in which some critics have seen traces of Shakespearean influence. Finally, we have the bloodthirsty dramas of Daniel Caspar von Lohenstein, the most typical of all in so far as, though they did not, properly speaking, form a school, they were quite in harmony with the taste, not only of their own time, but also with that of the following period. Right up to the middle of the eighteenth century, the best way of laying hold on the attention of the spectators was to heap horrors on horrors, crimes on crimes, and to make the performers express themselves in the mixture of coarse language and the " Ye Gods ! " style, which was characteristic of Lohenstein. Even his character as an author was somewhat typical. Himself a quiet, peaceful and modest scholar, the subjects he chooses for his plays are of the most revolting kind, such as the incestuous relations between Agrippina and her son Nero, appalling court-scandals from Turkey at the time of Sultan Ibrahim, and so forth. Within the four walls of his study he revels in bloodshed and lewdness, imprecations, lamentation, and invective. Though his style is a distinct imitation of Italian types, this arm-chair ferocity is an ever recurring phenomenon in German tragic art, and the name of Lohenstein indeed deserves to be remembered, if only as an example to be avoided.

A diametrical contrast to the Silesian Lohenstein was the North German pedagogue Christian Weisse, who made poetry serve practical purposes, and to whom posterity owes a number of practically useful, but shallow

[1] *Cf.* my *Theatrical Art*, vol. ii., *Middle Ages and Renaissance*, p. 250.

plays of all kinds ; tragedies, comedies, farces, all in the same dry and commonplace prose, beside which the artificial and stilted verse of Lohenstein appears doubly bombastic.

The seventeenth century had not much more to offer in the way of dramatic literature properly so called. Yet, however poor we may find it, it was still too good for the contemporary theatres and actors. None of the dramatists mentioned obtained any importance on the stage. Christian Weisse wrote for the pupils of his school ; one of Opitz's plays, an adaptation of an Italian opera, is known to have been performed at a court festival. As to the plays of Lohenstein and Gryphius, it has never been ascertained whether or not they were ever publicly performed. They became what their authors had probably meant them to be, closet dramas. With regard to Germany they mark the long schism between literature and the stage, a separation which was natural enough at the time, as there was no real theatre in existence.

Germany was overrun by English, French, Dutch, and Italian acting companies. Some of these obtained permanent court appointments, others toured from place to place. Some of them preserved their nationality, others gradually assimilated themselves to their German public. German elements mingled with the foreign actors and helped to make their plays understood by the uneducated public. At last independent German companies (" bands ") were formed.

The plays were of the most easily intelligible sort. English actors presented coarse and popular adaptations of famous plays from their own country, even of Shakespearean pieces, copiously intermixed with dances, music, and acrobatic tricks, things that everybody could understand ; Italians as a rule, gave operas, but also improvised plays with harlequins' *lazzi* ; the Dutch performed farces and pantomimes ; the French, the plays of their own great dramatists, Molière, Racine, Corneille, as well as lighter plays by Destouches, Dufresny, etc., and French ballets.

It was as a bastard child of these foreign races that German dramatic art made its first appearance, and like a queer vagabond mongrel roamed about for a long time, cutting its strange capers, hunted from town to town, everywhere exhibiting its peculiar mixed race-marks. To the English element was due its grotesque, bombastic and noisy tragic style—" King Cambyses' vein," as Shakespeare called it ; to Italian influence it owed its mechanical technique and the guild-like constitution which soon became a characteristic of German companies ; from Dutch patterns came its coarse pickle-herring drolleries, while the stiff dancing-master bearing and gestures were of French origin.

In the seventeenth century German dramatic art has no history but that of the wandering jugglers, quacks, musicians, and acrobats. It is impelled by no dominant thought, centred in no great genius ; it bears the stamp of no national poetry. Its history is limited to records stowed away here and there in town-hall registers, stating when such and such a company came to such and such a town, when such and such a " Principal " (leader) was to act in such and such a tennis-court.

Historians of the German theatre, when very industrious, may be able to give a dry report of the travels and sojourns of the different troupes, and not much more. For about a century there is no development to speak of in the German theatre. Though ever restless in its movements, figuratively speaking it remains stationary, always revolving in the same circle.

From time to time a solitary name obtains some note, such as that, for instance, of Johannes Velten. Perhaps in his case this was due to the fact that he was not, like so many of his colleagues, originally an artist's apprentice, a barber, a hernia-surgeon, or an oculist, but a worthy and well-to-do Bachelor and Master of Arts, who had studied at the universities of Wittenberg and Leipzig. There is a well-known theatrical tradition that as an undergraduate he took a fancy to dramatic art through acting in a university performance of Corneille's *Polyeucte*.[1] Indeed, it seems very probable that the young and well-educated man, after having abandoned the scientific career and joined the wandering folk, tried to raise both the *répertoire* and the style of acting of the company which he joined, and whose leader he afterwards became. In fact there is extant a *répertoire* of his time, which, besides a heterogeneous mixture of English, Dutch, French, German, and Italian adapta-

---

[1] In Schmidt's *Chronologie des deutschen Theaters*—one of the principal sources of the history of the old German theatre—and in quotations from this work in Devrient's *Geschichte der deutschen Schauspielkunst* we find accounts of this performance of *Polyeucte*, which is said to have taken place in 1669. But Velten was born in 1640, and became a B.A. in 1661, so he could not in 1669 have acted in this play as an undergraduate. He probably became an actor in the company of Carl Andreas Paulsen as early as 1665.

tions, contains a number of translations from Molière's plays, which we may safely suppose were introduced by Velten, even though he is now proved not to have translated them himself, as had been previously believed.

The company of which Velten became a member deserves to be mentioned in so far as it may be called the mother-troupe of a series of acting companies, that lead down in direct line to the celebrated Fr. L. Schröder. Its " Principal " was a Hamburger, Carl Andreas Paulsen, who since 1650 had been travelling about in Germany, and had also several times visited Copenhagen as manager of one of the earliest German troupes that came to that town.

Velten did not become an independent manager till about 1678, and at that time his company was called " The Electoral Saxon Comedians." This troupe on its long wanderings also visited Copenhagen, though not till after the death of Johannes Velten, which occurred about 1695. The leadership by that time had passed on to his wife Catharina Elisabeth Velten, who, we suppose, was the first of the series of sturdy female managers who became so frequent afterwards.

As mentioned above, a whole pedigree of noted and distinguished companies can be traced up to the Paulsen-Velten troupe ; their achievements will be treated in a later chapter of this work. The company of Frau Velten became that of Denner-Spiegelberg ; the latter changed into the Neuber company, then successively into the Schönemann, the Koch, and the Ackermann companies, which finally, in the year 1771, passed on to the leadership of the great Schröder.

These troupes formed, so to speak, the aristocracy of the wandering actors in Germany. Alongside of them a large number of other companies travelled about, who in wealth and momentary fame were not inferior to them, but who, nevertheless, by the style of their performances and by the lower degree of culture of their leaders, may be considered as having been of secondary rank.

As a typical manager of this class of company we may mention Johann Carl Eckenberg, or von Eckenberg, as he liked to call himself, the famous "strong man," "Samson the Invincible," "who could lift with one hand a cannon with a drummer and his drum on the top of it, and hold it there as long as it would take the drummer to empty a glass of wine comfortably." Eckenberg (born 1684 in Harzgerode) belongs to a later period than Velten, and represents the connecting link between the juggler of the fairs and the theatrical manager. He himself was an acrobat and his wife a rope-dancer, but he brought with him a large company of court comedians and acrobats, who acted jointly in their heterogeneous *répertoire*, which contained, besides acrobatic tricks, Italian magic lantern plays, etc., . comedies such as that concerning Dr Faustus, who is seen in the tortures of hell, tormented by black devils with red-hot tongs, and his valet Hanswurst, who, "*wegen alzugroszer Vexirung*," was taken up into the air by subterranean spirits and torn to pieces alive.[1] Eckenberg was by no means a common juggler. He was not only a man of great pretensions, but also a manager who possessed considerable means and com-

[1] G. F. Schütze, *Hamburgische Theatergeschichte*, Hamburg, 1774, p. 62.

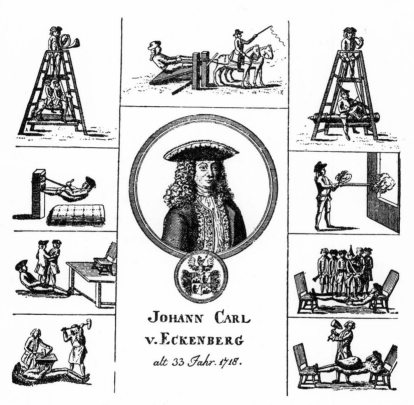

1—"The Strong Man," Eckenberg, and his Tricks (p. 8).

parative distinction. His company had obtained the patent of Royal Prussian Court Comedians, and for some years he occupied a prominent position, being a great favourite of King Frederick William, whose taste this *tour de force* comedy suited admirably.

After all, if within the world of strolling actors there was a distinction of rank, an aristocracy and a somewhat inferior class, it was not of extreme importance, by no means so great, no doubt, as that which exists now-adays between a well-established Metropolitan theatre and a touring provincial company.

The actors formed, so to speak, one large professional family. Though we do not pretend as yet to possess full knowledge on this subject—scientific research into theatrical history is still in its infancy, and many documents that might throw light on it no doubt lie still undiscovered in archives here and there—we may safely assume that at no time between the middle of the seventeenth and the middle of the eighteenth century was there any considerable number of touring companies. The same names recur constantly—now in the North, now in the South, in Stockholm, in Vienna, in Russia, on the Rhine; everywhere the same companies, the same actors. Braving the immense difficulties of travelling, they strolled about all the northern half of Europe, like the circus-companies of our own day, and also like them forming a large coalition, united, not by any outward bond, but by common interests, a common calling, and by the common contempt in which they were held.

They always married within their own class, or if

one of the parties did not originally belong to the profession, he or she had soon to join it, for no other trade could be pursued during their wandering life, and it would have been too expensive for the companies to go on long journeys with a totally useless member.

This is why we meet with so many families among the German comedians, whose members were all actors, such as the Veltens, the Denners, a family of harlequins, the large Elenson Haak family, the Spiegelbergs, the Ackermann-Schröders, and many others. In these families all members of both sexes, from fathers and mothers down to the infants of three years, had to share in the stage-work, to unite their efforts in what was mostly a hard fight to earn their bread.

Of what kind, then, were the work, the art, and the conditions of life of these troupes?

First of all, what did they act? It has been briefly mentioned that the pieces of the *répertoire*—that is to say, those of the plays which were not direct translations, such as at first were most frequently used—were the products of mixed influences from all surrounding countries.

In the *répertoires* of this period the expression "*Haupt - und - Staatsaktion*" (chief-and-state-play) constantly meets our eyes. In literary and theatrical history these "Chief-and-State-Plays" have come to signify a certain variety of representation, which conjures up before our imagination a stilted hero, who has to go through a number of absurd adventures in as many absurd changes of scene, fiery dragons, clowneries, and bombastic declamation. But originally the expression was not meant to convey the idea of a hodge-podge comedy; in fact, it was no qualification of kind, though the plays that came in under this heading frequently belonged to the category described.

The performances of those times generally consisted of two plays, a longer *pièce de résistance* and a short after-play. The first part of the representation, the *Aktion*, was the principal part, and so was naturally called *Hauptaktion* —chief play—whereas the little comic after-play was called *Nachkomödie*, or *Nachspiel*. This is very distinctly shown by the old play-bills, whose length and curious style give us an amusing insight into the manner of advertising in those days. One of the earliest, of 1702, dates from the Velten company, the most distinguished of the time; it runs as follows :—

"To-day, Saturday, on the 15th of July the Velthenian "band" as Royal Polish and Electoral Saxon Court-Comedians, will perform on their stage an uncommonly pleasing Scripture play, which by its magnificent theatrical scenery, but also particularly as an emotional subject, can scarcely be improved and cannot displease anybody.

" We omit to give a summary of its contents [as was frequently the custom], as the matter cannot be unknown to anyone. Only the principal events and noteworthy scenery are hereby indicated as follows : The *Aktion* is called *The Ascension of Elijah or The Storming of Naboth.* After the performance of this excellent " chief-action " a very pleasant after-play is to form the conclusion, the title of which is : *A School-*

master murdered by a Pickle-herring or The Bacon-thieves nicely taken in.

" The stage is in the Dutch Hogshead." [1]

We see that the *Hauptaktion* in this case simply means the principal play, the more important part of the performance ; it treats of a Scriptural subject, a relic of the mediæval Mysteries.   But it might as well be an ordinary comedy, such as the well-known play by Johann Rist,[2] *Peace-wishing Germany*; which was also acted by the Velten company in Hamburg at the beginning of the eighteenth century.   The play-bill calls it "an admirable comedy by the brilliant author Johannes Rist," and promises "after this incomparable moral *Aktion*, a short after-play which is exceedingly laughable."

The longer plays by Molière, too, such as *Tartufe* and *Le Bourgeois Gentilhomme*, which belonged to the *répertoire* of the old German companies, were described as *Hauptaktionen*,[3] whereas the smaller pieces, such as *Georg Tauntein* (*George Dandin*) and *Les Précieuses ridicules*, were used as after-plays.   The word *Staats-aktion* (state or parade-action), which we meet less frequently on the play-bills, no doubt alludes to mag-nificent scenery, such as is indicated in the programmes quoted above ; it conveys the same idea as the expression *gala performance* in a modern circus or music-hall.

So it is obviously a mistake if writers of theatrical

---

[1] This play-bill comes from Hamburg.

[2] Play-bill from Hamburg, without date, lent by Schütze, *op. cit.* p. 43.

[3] In an undated play-bill of 1719, also due to Schütze, *Tartufe* is called "a noteworthy and modest *Hauptaktion*."

history consider *Haupt-und-Staatsaktionen* as a particular kind of play; and whether they hailed from Spain or elsewhere, or grew out of German soil, naturally becomes an idle question.

A totally distinct fact is, that the *répertoires* of the old German companies contained a number of home-made pieces, which, though differing widely as to their subjects, may, for the sake of convenience, be classed together and termed *Haupt-und-Staatsaktionen*, though we are incapable of drawing parallels between their form and construction, as they were not printed, scarcely written, and though we know the text of only one, and nothing but the title of many of them. They are of the following kind:—*L'Ecole des Filoux or The School for Rascals*—viz., *The vicious life of the ill-famed rogue John Sheppard in London, his extraordinary practices and shameful end, with Harlequin, a merry, faint-hearted, and luckily hanged assistant in the thieves' guild.* Or the famous piece, *The Asiatic Banise*, with its full title: *The bloody yet brave Pegu or The Sun of the Realm brilliantly rising on the Asiatic horizon in the praiseworthy person of the Asiatic Banise.* Or the more modern, *The World's great Monster or The Life and Death of the late Imperial General Wallenstein, Duke of Friedland, with Hanswurst.* Further, the great spectacular drama on Tamerlane, known already in the time of Shakespeare, which on the German stage bore the following complicated title: *The strangely victorious Tamerlan or Fortune playing with the person of Bajazet, who was precipitated from the summit of happiness down into the*

abyss of despair, a formerly very proud, but finally humi-
liated Turkish Emperor or The female Harlequin.[1]

All possible subjects were arranged and adapted for
the use of the companies, beginning with the earliest
imaginable, such as *Adam and Eve*, a very popular
Aktion, in which even Hanswurst was introduced, down
to the most recent political events, such as the *Feats and
Death of Charles XII.* Of this last equally popular
subject, which was represented in a puppet - show in
Hamburg as late as the middle of the eighteenth
century,[2] we still possess a text used for a performance in 1720—a few years after the death of Charles
XII. before Frederikshall.

It is written in the scantiest outline. A few scenes
only are worked out—serious monologues and versified
speeches for singing ; the remainder is merely indicated,
like the *imbroglios* of an Italian improvised comedy,
especially in the comic parts, where Harlequin and his
partner, *Plapperlieschen* (Prating Lizzie) are the leaders.

The style is absolutely rough, without a vestige of
artistic form or a spark of poetic inspiration ; it is an
undigested mixture of utterly crude historic facts and
bombastic speeches, put together in the most confused
and disorderly way. Let us take a sample. The play,
which is in four acts and has an epilogue, begins as
follows : Charles XII. is sitting at a table explaining
to the audience the situation in which he finds himself,
in a lengthy monologue, beginning thus :—

1 The female Harlequin, whom we should not have expected to have
anything to do with this subject, is Manch, the bride of Bajazet, who,
disguised as Harlequin, accompanies him to the war.

2 Comp. Schütze, *op. cit.* p. 100.

"Almighty Ruler of this immense Earth! Hand that drives fortune and misfortune by the reins of Thy Will, that tempers [!] the plots of mortals. Who am I? Lord, Thy slave. Thou who hast hitherto carried me safe through the breakers of my awful fate. Permit me, impartial Europe, in this quiet solitude to give you a short summary of my life, which has been spent hitherto in bloodshed, amid corpses, in good and bad fortune. Charles XI., a son of Charles Gustavus (to whom the Swedish throne had been bequeathed by Queen Christina of world-wide fame), was my father, and my mamma was Ulrica Eleonora, daughter of King Frederick III. of Denmark, whom he begat by Sophia Amelia, Princess of Brunswick-Lüneburg, who on the 19th of June 1682 gave me birth between 7-8 in the morning, to the joy of the whole Swedish Kingdom. My education was very careful, but the years of my youth were full of calamities, as my life from my twentieth year till now may be considered as a constant campaign," etc.

The catastrophe itself, the fall of Charles, is not developed at all, only indicated in a summary way, as follows. After a comical scene between Harlequin and Prating Lizzie, in which the former takes leave of beer and brandy, a curtain is dropped across the middle of the stage, and we witness—

Scene 10.

Charles XII., Friedrich [hereditary Prince of Hesse-Cassel], Carl Friedrich [of Holstein Gottorp], Sicker (adjutant-general), Soldiers.

"While vigorous firing is going on, Charles orders

everything to be kept ready for the bombardment.   He
encourages his people to the assault ; at last a ball hits
him, and he falls."

Then the death of the hero occasions the following
outbursts of feeling :—

SICKER.

Good heavens !   The King is killed.
> *[Covers him with a mantle.]*

CARL FRIEDRICH.

Miserable siege !

FRIEDRICH.

O ! fatal day !

SICKER.

A sad end of the campaign !

FRIEDRICH.

Let the Royal body at once be taken away and
transported to Stockholm.   There is nothing for us to
do here, but to raise the siege and try to save our army
as well as we can.

Upon which the Swedes leave the stage and give
place to the Danes, who come from Frederickshall, and
the final scene of the play is enacted as follows :—

Scene II.

Budde [major-general], The Commander [of
Frederickssten].

THE COMMANDER.

This sudden quiet of the Swedes gives me much

to think of; could there possibly be some design beneath it?

BUDDE.

No, sir; I will reveal it to you. The King has been hit by a falconet ball.

THE COMMANDER.

To others, then, this day most fatal is of all,
Now Charles the Twelfth indeed lies before Frederickshall.

BUDDE.

I for the hero grieve; however, it had to be.
Of enemies now our town itself relieved can see.

[*Omnes abeunt.*]

There is nothing to prove that all the plays of this class were as void of talent and spirit as this. Possibly some of these home-made *Hauptaktionen* were conceived and written with some dramatic power and taste; however, it does not seem likely; all the evidence tends to show that these massive German productions were nearly all prepared after the same recipe. The authors, by the bye, concealed their identity under an anonymity so dense that we do not know whether it was due to modesty or to shame. Probably most of these plays were the result of domestic industry within the companies. As the managers can hardly be supposed to have possessed sufficient means to pay a distinguished author to adapt the subjects that were best qualified to attract the public, this work may have been done by the manager, his wife, or some comedian who could wield the pen; and out of the indispensable sensational ingredients—among which murder, fireworks, cannon-shots, processions, and music were the stock supply—he or she concocted the strange mental food which could be digested by none but the ostrich stomachs of the German citizens of those times.

One spice, however, was never to be left out, and it may have been just this ingredient which made the audience swallow the dish so easily, namely, the comic element. It is the popular humour, inseparable from every scenic performance of the time, which forms the only bright spot and the only *raison d'être* of this utterly debased period in the history of theatrical art.

It is clear that in plays of the ordinary *Hauptaktion* style, of which we have seen a few samples, it was absolutely impossible to produce any kind of dramatic art ; but in the comic parts there was no restraint at all. In them, at any rate, a possibility was open to art, and in them, indeed, it grew into real power, though its domain continued to be in the lower spheres.

This comic art never developed into the sublime *imperishable* humour of Shakespeare, still less into the keen and elevated satire of Molière ; it was more akin to the wit of Holberg, in his *Jeppe paa Bjerget* (*Jack on the Mountain*) ; it was like the revenge of the oppressed people on the scourge of the oppressor, deriding everything, itself in particular. It contains no vigorous satire on certain social conditions, it does not go to the bottom of human follies; it contents itself with aiming its wit at them and mimicking their foibles ; and, therefore, it does not create comedy, but only comic actors. Dangerous satire and deep humour in the mouth of the comic

2—Hanswurst (p. 19).

actor, the half-irresponsible jester, become mere jokes and fooleries.

This merry jester, fool, or clown, whose different phases we have had an opportunity of treating in an earlier chapter of this work, in his German guise was originally called " Hanswurst." The name is of ancient date. It is introduced into the written language of Martin Luther, who says that it is generally applied to "coarse boorish persons, who pretend to be wise, and yet speak and act in an unreasonable and clumsy way." But, a favourite as he always was on the stage, Hans soon got many names. " Pickelherring," borrowed from the Dutch farce-player, was for a long time the name most used in the little after-plays, whereas the inevitable comic person in the *Haupt-aktion* was generally called *Courtisan.* Later the Italian influence became predominant, and *Harlequin*, introduced by the comic actor, Bastiari, of the Velten company, made his entrance on the German stage, whence he was but reluctantly expelled.

However, under the different names and disguises, the old typically German Hanswurst showed his broad, "beery-phiz," and his coarse and jolly humour main-tained originality in the face of the grotesque gloom of English drollery, and the Franco-Italian nimble vivacity. Hanswurst became the national type during the first feeble period of young German dramatic art, and those among the actors who won any fame during that time were, so to speak, all of them Hanswurst players. Especially in South Germany, and more particularly in Vienna, this popular type throve and became almost a feature in the physiognomy of the Austrian capital, which even to this day has not entirely vanished. Under the popular names of Kasperl and Jackerl, who originally were nothing but variations of Hanswurst, the old jester still amuses the merry Viennese in the Prater, though it must be admitted that his theatre has dwindled down into a puppet-show, and his company into a number of little dolls.

In Vienna the typical Hanswurst won his special popular character through Joseph Anton Stranitzky, who had originally been a member of the Velten company, but had afterwards (in 1708) settled down in Vienna, and, so to speak, founded the popular stage there. He transformed the jester, who had hitherto been represented without any particular national stamp, into a Salzburg peasant, adopted the green Tyrolese hat, which subsequently became as inseparable from the typical Hanswurst as the fox-brush and the wand, made him talk the Bavarian dialect, which always sounded droll to Viennese ears, and, though his *répertoire* was doubtless for the most part borrowed from the Franco-Italian theatre,[1] the foundation was laid of a kind of popular comedy, which might possibly have developed into something better, if the new spirit of the time had not mercilessly crushed it.

[1] Stranitzky had received a tolerably good education, and knew foreign languages. He published a number of humorous writings, among which is a collection of comic scenes under the title of *Olla potrida des durchgetriebenen Fuchs mundi*. I have not had access to the very rare original of this book, but it seems to have been a selection from Gherardi's *Théâtre Italien*. At any rate, the sample given by Flögel in his *Geschichte des Groteskekomischen* (pp. 126 ff.), is a direct, though not a good, translation of *Arlequin empereur de la lune*.

However, other champions of the "green hat" continued the work of Stranitzky, for instance Gottfried Prehausen, who was a native of Vienna, and worked chiefly there ; Franz Schuch, the leader of a distinguished German company that travelled all over Germany ; and Felix von Kurz, also a Viennese, who somewhat varied the type, and called it " Bernardon."

The *Hanswurstiade* became indispensable to the public and to theatrical managers. In Vienna it received its distinctive stamp, but its reign spread all over Germany, and while the amiable and graceful Austrian humour carried it across the stage with ease, without giving it time to drop into the deepest pitfalls of tastelessness, the North Germans tramped about in all its pools, splashing the mud up and down, so that at last people found the performance unbearable.[1]

But what finally rendered Hanswurst intolerable on the stage was that he appeared in everything. Whether Hanswurst, Pickelherring, or Harlequin—in the eighteenth century the last name was the most commonly used—he poked his nose in everywhere. First he went on through all the acts of the *Hauptaktion* as a prattling commentator on all that the serious persons did, and then had his independent and leading part in the after-play, which always, so to speak, formed a frame to the harlequinade.

Though the merry-maker, the comic actor, was the most indispensable man in a German travelling com-

---

[1] As late as the middle of the eighteenth century, Flögel—the author of *Geschichte des Groteskekomischen*—saw Schönemann, one of the most refined theatrical managers, as Harlequin, enter upon the stage in his night-shirt, which was besmeared with glue at the back.

pany, his branch of art enjoyed no consideration, not even among actors.   If he was not himself the leader —which indeed was not seldom the case, harlequinade being the speciality of the company—he was looked upon as far beneath the tragic hero, the "chief agent," as he was called.

On the whole, there was a very marked distinction of rank in the companies, a detailed ceremonial; and the elders exercised a good deal of tyranny over the younger members, who retaliated by teasing and making fun of their elders.   Such a band of actors was like a travelling work-shop, with a master, a foreman, older and younger apprentices, and boys ; its constitution was strictly like that of a guild.   It was as if the actors tried to make up for the lack of general esteem from without, by leading their lives within their own domain according to the strictest, most snobbish, and most mechanical rules possible.

The companies were mostly very large—much larger, for instance, than the French strolling companies, and even than the stationary ones in Paris.   They might contain as many as forty members, though probably half this number was the general rule.   But a company even of twenty persons was large compared with that of Molière, which at times did not contain more than ten or eleven.   In Germany it was the *répertoire* which necessitated so numerous a staff.   The heterogeneous list of characters in the *Hauptaktion* required a large supply of working power.   On the other hand, most of the actors were badly trained and miserably paid.   The first steps of the young in the theatrical career were mostly treated with the utmost indifference by the other members. Even in later and more advanced times such things might happen as the popular actress Karoline Kummerfeld, *née* Schulze, relates in her *Memoirs* about her *début*.

It was in 1758 that, as quite a young girl, she joined the Ackermann company, who were playing in Switzerland. Frau Schröder-Ackermann, the masterful lady principal, mother of Fr. L. Schröder, chose Iphigénie in Racine's tragedy of that name for her *début*. Karoline Schulze did not know the piece, but she learned her own part as well as she could from the manuscript copy of it, as it was in vain to try to get hold of the entire play. When she dropped a word about rehearsals there was an outcry among the elders who acted in the piece. Rehearsals of an old play, and for the sake of a *débutante*! That was entirely out of the question. Then she suggested to Ackermann to give her another part with which she was familiar and which she knew better, Chimène in the *Cid* of Corneille. But he answered : " The thing is not so easy as you fancy. We can act no plays here except those of which the play-bills are printed ; there is no printing office in this town." So Karoline Schulze made her *début* as Iphigénie, after having gone through the two first acts with Frau Schröder-Ackermann, knowing nothing of the rest of the piece, and having had no rehearsal with her fellow-actors, guided in her movements and exits only by the long forefinger of the female prompter.

It is possible, however, that such a thing would not have happened during the *Haupt-und-Staatsaktion* period properly so called,[1] during which, though the beginner was treated with contempt and without any friendly help, the plays seem to have been very carefully prepared. We know the golden saying by the old Hanswurst Stranitzky : " The theatre is as holy as the altar and the rehearsal as the vestry," and, indeed, the many *jeux de théâtre* that constituted the *Hanswurstiades* seem to have been prepared with the greatest minuteness till they went off with the same infallible accuracy as the acrobatic performances. The whole *genre* was calculated upon this, and, no doubt, in Germany as in Italy and France, much professional work was done in order to produce the striking effect which is always the consequence of rapid and flashing exchange of speeches and comic changes of attitude.

But in the serious *Staatsaktion* as well there was much to rehearse ; there were many rules to learn, many ceremonies to observe, before reaching the goal of being a perfect *Hauptagent*. The persons represented on the stage were strictly divided according to their rank, and those who stood highest had always to be saluted with the honours due to their position, just as they themselves had certain sublime movements to execute, which required a good deal of practice. Thus the kings had a series of

---

[1] Our sources for the internal conditions of this time are but scanty. One of the most important is found in the souvenirs and scattered observations which Iffland has given in his *Almanach fürs Theater* (1807) under the title *Über den Vortrag in der höheren Tragödie*. This article has frequently been utilised, among others, by Eduard Devrient, in a somewhat unjustifiable way, by quoting long passages as if they were the writer's own thoughts, without stating his source. However, the information we gather from the article must be used with some discretion, as it is partly cast in a humorous form, and does not pretend to furnish strictly accurate historical data.

curving gestures with their sceptre, an attribute that never left them, all of which a professional actor had to know ; and no novice was accepted in a company without having passed an examination in his "sceptre action."

When the principal persons were assembled on the stage they were always — according to the French pattern—arranged in a semicircle, and there were fixed rules for the manner in which they had to join and to leave this semi-circle, which invariably fronted the audience ; no secondary characters were allowed to enter it ; they had their places further back, behind the gaps, so as to be fully visible to the spectators without intruding too much on their attention.

Delivery in the serious style was not to resemble ordinary human speech. The object was to render it sublime, and this, then as now, consisted in speaking as slowly as possible, in drawing out the vowels to the utmost length and speaking with an ever recurring excessive *crescendo*, beginning in an ominous murmur, and in the end raising the voice to inarticulate roars.

With such utterance the conventional movements harmonise well : a slow walk, with one leg dragging behind the other, the elbows either held tight against the body or widespread like wings, and the feet in the fourth position. The hands were on no account to be lifted above the head.

Distinction, sublime carriage, were the aim and end of the efforts of these actors, and since, coming as they generally did from the lower classes, they could not possess these advantages through education, and since, on the whole, ease and natural grace were not common in the nation, they formed for themselves this code of rigid rules, which in the eyes of foreigners gave the *Staatsaktion* a stilted and affected appearance.

This solemn ceremoniousness was introduced even into the intercourse of private life. The actors did not associate much with any but their own class, for the houses of the citizens were mostly closed to them ; in some towns they were even forbidden to seek lodgings in private houses. But within their own narrow circle they treated each other with extreme formality. The " chief agent," for instance, was never the first to greet any other ; he only acknowledged the respectful salutation of his inferiors ; in public places the leading actors had their own particular seats, and no apprentice could approach them without having received a condescending invitation to do so. An observation of one of the younger on the acting of an older " agent " was considered as an outburst of madness, and deprecatory remarks about the plays that were performed might lead to instantaneous dismissal from the company.

As we said above, their economic condition was miserable. The managers sometimes made a great deal of money, but that was an exception, and in those cases, as a rule, they had athletic and acrobatic performances on their programme, which allowed them to charge somewhat higher fees. Otherwise the admission fees were exceedingly low. As late as 1724 the well-known manager ("Principal"), Johann Spiegelberg— according to the play-bill — did not ask much more than 14d. for the most expensive seats and 3½d.

for the cheapest. The rhymned advertisement runs as
follows :—

Hier in der Fuhlentwiet, dem Bremer Schlüssel über
Da giebt man 16, 8, 4 *Schilling und nichts drüber.*
Es wird präcis fünf Uhr bei uns gefangen an,
Das ist allzeit gewiss und hiemit kund gethan.[1]

For the front rows the fee was sometimes higher, but
the total of the proceeds can never have become considerable in the small theatres. It is true, there was no
great expenditure either. The scenery was exceedingly
poor ; three scenes were considered sufficient : a wood
for all open-air representations, a hall for all festive
interiors in royal or other great houses, and a cottage
room to represent simple homes. The celebrated Ekhof,
to whose pen we owe a strongly coloured picture of the
bad state of things before the theatrical reform, tells us
that when staying at Kiel during the *Umschlag* [annual
fair] he had to content himself with scenery made out
of coloured wall-paper—a yellow scene for all indoor
purposes and a green one for woods and fields. On
the whole, we know very little of the scenic conditions
of this period. However, it was a natural consequence
of the wandering life of the actors and the lack of permanent, properly constructed playhouses, that the scenery
differed very much according to circumstances—that it

[1] Here in the Fuhlentwiet, opposite to the " Bremen Key,"
You pay 16-8-4 *Schilling* [about 14d., 7d., 3½d.] and nothing more.
We begin punctually at five o'clock.
This is always certain, and hereby made known.
 In the Little Fuhlentwiete, a small crooked street in Hamburg, there
existed in the seventeenth century a " Comedy-Booth," which was much used
by travelling companies. In Great Fuhlentwiete as well plays were acted
in the public-house " Hof von Holland."

was at times modest, to say the least, at times very luxurious.   The stage might consist of "barrels or similar foundations with boards nailed on ; front curtain, back and side walls, might be formed of counterpanes, tablecloths, or, at most, of a piece of worn-out wall-paper."[1]   Or it might be established in a dainty little court-theatre, arranged according to Italian pattern, with many nice scenic appointments, for the use of court-operas and Italian magic plays.   So it is quite impossible to form a distinct idea of the outward theatrical conditions of the time.   So much, however, may be said for certain, that they were without style, taste, art, or sense.

With respect to costumes, the case was equally bad ; certainly the managers did not ruin themselves on this score.   The most important articles of dress for an actor were a pair of black velvet knickerbockers, a brown cloth coat, and a light silk waistcoat.   The two last-mentioned garments were provided by the manager, the knickerbockers by the actor himself, and he had great difficulty in finding an engagement unless he possessed a pair.   This costume, with slight varieties, had to do for all parts.   The king's attribute was a sceptre ; he wore a fine gold-embroidered waistcoat, and a hat with feathers on the top of his full-bottomed wig.   Heroes of prehistoric times were characterised by a scarf tied across the brown cloth coat, and wore a helmet instead of a hat.[2] The sword, which of course was indispensable, hung at the side in a belt covered with sham jewels of various

---

[1] Schütze, *op. cit.* p. 29.
[2] Iffland, *Alm. fürs Theater*, 1807, p. 146.

colours. At the best, old Greek and Assyrian heroes were attired according to French fashion, in a kind of armour of sham gold; they wore pouches, had their hair hanging down in a long pig-tail, and wore a high head-gear of feathers. The black velvet knickerbockers were never absent.

In the poorer companies, of course, the state of things was much worse. Lace collars and cuffs were cut out of white paper; the gold embroideries were cut out of gold paper and sewn on the stuff; the princesses wore no stockings in their shoes, and the heroes had to content themselves with old worn-out wigs.

On the question of actors' salaries during the *Hauptaktion* period, we have no means of obtaining information, as no regulations or accounts are left from those times; but the salaries are not likely to have been higher than in the time immediately following, during which they were exceedingly low. Thus, in 1740, the budget of weekly salaries which the manager Schönemann had to pay to a tolerably large company was 16 *Thalers* 8 *Groschen* (about £2, 13s.). Frau Schröder, afterwards Frau Ackermann, who had been very successful, left the said company in 1741 because she could not get her weekly salary increased to the 7 *Marks* 8 *Schillings* (about 9s. English) for which she asked. Ekhof, who, it is true, at that time was only a beginner, had 1 *Thaler* 16 *Groschen* (about 5s.), which was even lowered to 1 *Thaler* 8 *Groschen*.

However, if the budget for scenery, costumes, and salaries was low, one item of expenditure was exceedingly large, that of travelling expenses.

Long journeys were a necessity for the companies, as it was impossible for them to maintain themselves, on an average, for more than a few months in one town ; at the same time, these journeys were ruinous to the managers, as the small proceeds went to pay for expensive transport and post-horses.   Journeys were one of the few things that cost much more in those times than nowadays.   As a good example of the absurd relation between this item of the working expenses and the proceeds of the acting, we may state that the manager Ackermann, stepfather of the great Fr. L. Schröder, when, at the outbreak of the Seven Years War, he left Königsberg and went to Leipzig with his troupe, paid 2000 *Thalers* for these 117 German miles by post, whereas the first five weeks' performances in Leipzig brought him in no more than 409 *Thalers* gross receipts.

Moreover, the journeys were often very troublesome, sometimes dangerous, and always detrimental to work, as these frequent changes of residence almost entirely prevented the companies from studying new plays, and forced them to go on with the old hackneyed pieces, which, of course, had a relaxing and deteriorating effect on the actors.

Even in early times German companies travelled far and wide, not merely within the extensive territory of their own language ; they frequently visited Denmark, Norway, and Sweden, and in later times Russia became a favourite resort, where they braved great hardships in order to gain the Russian *roubles*, that were easier to get hold of than the German *Schillings*.   Naturally, these journeys to the far North, especially in winter, were fraught with the utmost difficulty. In Russia at times each single person and each single box had to be drawn in a small sledge across the unsafe ice of the frozen rivers, the guide preceding them at a distance of about 12 feet.[1] Old German writers of theatrical history give an account of a journey in Denmark by the Spiegelberg (or Velten) company during the hard winter of 1710. It is true that their reports do not quite agree, and the story has never been entirely cleared up. They say that the company had been acting in Copenhagen part of the winter, but during Lent the actors wanted to go to a fair across the Sound,[2] which, owing to the severe frost, was covered with ice. So it was decided to make the journey, about 18 English miles, by sledge. But a snowstorm came on, the guide lost his way, and after spending the whole day on the ice, the party arrived in the evening at a short distance from Copenhagen. The men, who had been sensible enough to walk, escaped unhurt from the hard journey, but all the ladies had their feet frost-bitten, and young Mlle. Denner (afterwards Frau Spiegelberg) so badly that the big toes of both her feet had to be amputated, in consequence of which she always had a rolling gait on the stage.

The object of this chapter has been to give a short account of this long theatrical period in as broad and

---

[1] Fr. L. Meyer gives an account of this in his long biography of Schröder. Hamburg, 1819, i. 13, about Ackermann's Journey from St Petersburg to Danzig.

[2] Löwe : *Geschichte des deutschen Theaters*, and C. H. Schmidt : *Chronologie des deutschen Theaters*, give very different accounts of this adventure, which is afterwards varied both by Overskou [a Danish author], in his *History of the Danish Theatre* (i. 127), and by Devrient (i. 344). Of these the report of Schmidt is by far the most trustworthy.

distinct outline as possible.   Against the background
of the highly developed and flourishing theatrical
conditions of other civilised countries, the years of
apprenticeship and the wanderings of German histrionic art appear the more miserable.   Even the outwardly very modest foundation of a national theatre
in our little Denmark possessed a brilliant wealth of its
own in the great comic author [Holberg] who was its
centre and intellectual leader.

Yet, though these wandering folk, who were much
more jugglers than artists, have no history, though no
poet wrote for them, no censor criticised them, no great
man patronised them, no highly educated people came
to see them, though they were nothing but the despised
pastime of the crowd, here and there among their number there must have been some one or other who had
higher aspirations, whose inward eye saw an image of
the art he cultivated, very different from the sights
which everyday life showed him—a beautiful, inspiring
image.   For, after all, the seed of all the good that was
to come was present, though unseen, in this ludicrous
and anything but beautiful chaos.

What was wanted was an energetic effort, a firm
purpose, to bring about a change.

CAROLINA NEUBER

I

Leipzig as the Intellectual Centre of Germany—Gottsched as a Reformer and the Neuber Family as his Instruments—French Tendency of the Drama—Carolina Neuber, her Character as an Actress and as a Woman—Her Husband and her Company.

WHILE German theatrical art was still roaming about homeless and unnoticed, literature succeeded in finding a centre in the university town of Leipzig. This town, which was at the same time a seat of learning, of gallantry, and of light living, had already witnessed the powerful and courageous struggle of Chr. Thomasius for the honour of the German language and for liberality in all intellectual domains ; it had heard young Günther —in his time the most original among the poets—sing his songs ; it had its " Poetic Society," its critical reviews and periodicals. Its public possessed literary interests, and was eager to promote national intellectual culture ; and during the first decades of the eighteenth century, Leipzig had reached the standpoint of being the centre of taste which ruled all Germany.

At about the same period the strong literary movement of this town found a prominent organiser in a young man named Johann Christoph Gottsched, who had come to Leipzig as a tutor in the house of Menke, the founder of the " Poetic Society."

There are few men of whom so much good and so much evil have been said as this " Pope of literature," as he was afterwards called.   He was one of those who are chastised with one hand and stroked with the other by historians of literature and of the theatre.   However, the blows fall heavier than the caresses.   His secret was, perhaps, that the caprice of fate had placed him in a *milieu*, where he might indeed assert himself, but for which his natural gifts and disposition had not suited him.

Gottsched was a Prussian, but as a young man he had fled from home, as his tall, stalwart figure rendered him a coveted object for the recruiting officers of Frederick William I.   Perhaps this was where he missed his real opportunity.   No doubt his sense of order, his punctuality, his tendency to discipline, and his energetic ambition would have well fitted him for the military career.   He went to Saxony and threw himself into literature and art, without possessing any genuine artistic sense or literary capacity.   But his very limited gifts were combined with an extraordinary talent for organisation and an uncommonly persistent and enterprising character.   The goal of his ambition was to organise German literature, and the means he found to this end was to arrange it entirely after the French pattern.   Having made up his mind on this point, he set to work to fulfil his task with great tenacity.   He wrote a book on poetics, which was to teach the Germans the right method of composing verse, and a book of rhetoric ; he also published a series of periodicals.   He soon became President of the " Leipzig

3

4

3—Gottsched (p. 34).   **4**—Carolina Neuber (p. 39).

Poetic Society," a kind of academy with correspondents all over the country, who kept him informed of all literary events, and reported to him about his adherents, whether they were keeping up or falling off. He meant to be the supreme judge of taste in Germany, its Boileau ; but, entirely lacking the artistic disposition, and the deep, though limited, sense of art of his prototype, he marched at the head of German poetry, not as a real chief, but as a kind of regimental drummer, with an air of importance, obstinate in his adherence to the time once set for him to beat, though unable to understand the music that was being played behind his back.

Among the things that were to be organised was, of course, the German Theatre. A tragedy, according to French rules, in French alexandrines, was soon written, but this—Gottsched saw perfectly well—was not all. It was the performers themselves that had to be brought under control, to be reorganised, and to be subjected to the French, or rather to the Gottschedian regularity, order, and decency.

A happy chance of attaining this end soon came to his assistance. It gained for him two enthusiastic adherents in the Neubers, husband and wife, who came to Leipzig in 1727 with their recently established company. They at once sought the rising star—Gottsched at that time was only twenty-seven years old—and concluded a kind of alliance with him, an alliance which became of great importance, which, indeed, is usually regarded as a turning point in the history of the German Theatre.

Of the two Neubers, the wife, Frederika Carolina,

née Weissenborn,[1] was by far the more distinguished. She was of good family, as her father occupied a respectable position as barrister and judicial inspector in Reichenbach, Saxony.   Left motherless at an early age, the fresh and clever young girl lived alone with her morbid, gouty father, who had given up part of his business, and now, in another little Saxon town, Zwickau, masterful and ill-tempered as he was, seems to have made it his principal concern to annoy everybody around him.   Only fourteen years of age, but very good looking and with a well-developed figure, Carolina entered upon a *liaison* with her father's clerk, a young law student, with whom she eloped from her dreary home.   The police were sent on the track of the juvenile lovers, who were arrested and brought before a law court.   The letters and the reports of the lawsuit, which have been preserved, show Carolina Weissenborn to have been a brave and high-minded girl, but at the same time they prove the cowardice of the young man on whom she had bestowed her love.   They never married, but each of them found comfort in their own way.

Carolina was reinstalled in the house of her harsh parent, where she persevered five years longer, before running away again, this time never to return.   Her second elopement was so thorough that she took two young students with her, one of whom was her future husband, Johann Neuber.   The three fugitives went to Weissenfels, where they sought refuge in the theatre, a haven which was the usual resort of young people whose life had been somehow turned out of its proper course.

[1] Born on 9th March 1697.

At that time—in 1717—the "Royal British and Electoral Brunswick-Lüneburg Court Comedians," under the management of Christian [Johann] Spiegelberg,[1] was acting in Weissenfels. This troupe, which also called itself "The High-German Company of world-wide fame," and which was an offspring of the Velten troupe, took up the three fugitives—Carolina Weissenborn, the pretty fair girl with the beautiful figure, no doubt with pleasure. Johann Neuber probably did not possess much dramatic talent—at any rate he never distinguished himself particularly as an actor—but he was a well-educated man of good breeding. About the third of the elopers, history tells us nothing.

How long the young couple — Neuber married Carolina Weissenborn the following year in Brunswick Cathedral—remained with Spiegelberg is not known. Some years later, however, they were members of the Haak company.[2] It was here that the new idea of raising the level of the company seems to have sprung up.

The mainstays of the company were Leipzig during the noted annual fair, and Brunswick. Besides the two Neubers it contained a few members who had raised themselves above the ordinary level of the *Haupt-und-Staatsaktion*, first of all Friedrich Kohlhardt, who, it seems, possessed great talent, and who was much com-

---

[1] In theatrical history we meet now with a Johann, now with a Christian Spiegelberg, but many circumstances seem to prove that they were one and the same man. He (Christian) travelled much in Scandinavia, and died in Bergen in 1732.

[2] Another offshoot of the Velten company, founded by its *pantalone* Elinson, whose widow, afterwards the wife of Haak, and after his death, of Hoffmann, held the leadership of the company for several years.

mended in his time, but about whom we possess very little information, and the intelligent Karl Ludwig Hoffmann, who married the widow Elinson-Haak and inherited the management of her company.

Young Gottsched noticed the comedians in Leipzig and, having by that time already conceived his reforming ideas, he wrote a kind of critique on them in one of his first pamphlets, *The Reasonable Censors* [1]—no doubt the first theatrical review which saw the light in Germany— in which he praised their attempts at playing regular comedies and tragedies.

This was in 1724. Next year, however, the clever manageress died, and the company was much weakened by continual quarrels between Hoffmann and his step children. The good actors left it, among others Neuber and his wife.

When at last Hoffmann threw up the game and went to St Petersburg, Neuber and his wife undertook the management of the company. In 1727 they succeeded in acquiring the privilege of calling their company the " Royal Polish and Electoral Saxon Court Comedians," which, for one thing, gave them a right " to act and play during the Leipzig fairs, as well as one week before and after them," but (otherwise) included no royal subvention.

By this time Carolina Neuber had become a fully matured actress. Thirty years of age, handsome, stately, with regular, prepossessing features and a majestic frame, which was shown off to great advantage by the many male disguises in which she liked to appear, she had all the outward qualifications of a great " leading lady."

[1] *Die vernünftigen Tadlerinnen.*

Nor were some of the inward conditions wanting. She was very impulsive, easily moved both to love and to anger, passionate and unrestrained. But she lacked taste as well as the power of losing herself in her art. As an actress, therefore, she fell out of fashion as quickly as the style of comedy which she had brought to the front. However, in her palmy days she was considered a great actress. Gottsched's pronouncement about her that "she is not behind any French or English woman in the art of acting" is of little consequence for, in the first place, Gottsched possessed no genuine theatrical sense at all, and secondly, he was no critic, only a literary politician, who praised his own adherents and blamed his opponents without regard to their actual value. But Lessing, whose judgments signify infinitely more, says of her: "We should be very unfair if we denied that this excellent actress possesses a thorough knowledge of her art. She has the intelligence of a man ; in one point only she reveals her sex ; she is too fond of trifling on the stage ; all plays of her own invention abound with disguises,[1] brilliant feasts, and wonderful shows. Perhaps, however, she knows her Leipzig people, and what I consider a weakness may be nothing but a stratagem with her."

Such as she was, however, and with her tenacious ambition, both personal and professional, she was an excellent instrument for the work which makes her a

---

[1] According to a play-bill of 1728, a piece was acted with the title *The Leather Seller of Bergamo*, in which Cathringen [no doubt Frau Neuber] appeared as *Pantolfo*, as *Fräulein Hohlnätgen*, as a learned philosopher, as *Fräulein Hausgrath*, as a bandit, and as a poor woman with many children.

conspicuous figure in theatrical history, that, namely, of exalting her art in the eyes of the world so as to render it the subject, not merely of common talk, but of written fame—in short, to bring it into contact with literature. She did not do this by a quiet movement of inward development. It was her gift to inspire people with a different view of dramatic art, though, indeed, this art had not been essentially improved, and she did it with as much noise, as much puff as possible. On that account she was able to co-operate with Gottsched, who, like herself, was neither able nor desirous to effect anything but an outward reform. Minds of a deeper and more sensitive artistic turn could scarcely have stood the toil of the pioneer work which these two stalwart natures combined in carrying out.

Her husband, Johann Neuber, is an obscure figure in theatrical history, chiefly because he was of no importance as an actor, but also because his quiet and modest appearance necessarily caused him to be overshadowed by his wife, who, so to speak, always marched with the band playing. However, the historians who have represented Neuber as a mere simpleton, of no consequence either in his family or in the company, are quite mistaken. His many letters —it was he who conducted the correspondence, and who, in the main, was entrusted with the administrative management of the company—bear testimony to his having been a sensible, well-educated man of good breeding.

Rumours of Gottsched's reforming ideas had already

spread widely in Germany. He had also applied personally to the " Principal," Hoffmann, trying to persuade him to give up the old-fashioned plays with the harlequinades that were his particular aversion, and take up regular French tragedies and comedies instead. Some translations of such plays were already in hand, and several of them had been attempted successfully on the stage, especially *Regulus* by Pradon, *The Cid* of Corneille, and *Iphigénie* by Racine; but to the direct question of Gottsched, why he did not produce more plays of the same kind, Hoffmann replied that the public could not do without the fool in the serious plays. As soon, however, as Mrs Neuber had taken the lead in her company, she saw that if she wanted to give something new and better than the earlier companies, if she wanted to raise the level of her profession and her art—and this was indeed her purpose—Gottsched would be the man to help her.

The Neubers had no sooner come to Leipzig for the Easter fair in 1727, than they sought Gottsched, and offered the young Master of Arts their respectful adherence. A formal alliance was concluded between the two parties, which aimed at nothing less than a complete reformation of the German stage. Gottsched was a methodical man, and he knew what he meant to do. The first important thing was to purify the stage of all that could be called improvised comedy and *hanswurstiades*. No *Haupt-und-Staat-aktions*, no burlesque after-plays! However, as almost the whole *répertoire* consisted of such pieces, a new one had to be produced; but whence? German dramatic authors

were practically non-existent; therefore, thought Gottsched, we must take refuge in the French, and
translate them till we have learned their art, which
cannot take very long.

As to the art of acting, the natural consequence
of introducing a *répertoire* of regular plays would be
the abolition of improvisation and the necessity for
actors to learn their parts thoroughly, and to reproduce
the Franco-German alexandrines with accuracy. The
costumes likewise had to be reformed. In classical
tragedy Gottsched would have preferred the genuine
Greek and Roman styles of dress, but this reform,
which was one of his most advanced and sensible
suggestions, was so thoroughly radical, and went so
dead against not only all German, but all international
convention, that he could not find approval for it
anywhere. Nay, afterwards, when with his usual
tenacity he persevered in advocating it, he was received with ridicule, and it very nearly caused his fall,
which we shall have an opportunity of mentioning in
a later chapter.

To Gottsched, therefore, the question appeared very
simple; he and his friends translated and adapted some
more French plays of both kinds. The actors played
them in the regular way, without improvisation or
clowning. Thus the German theatre would be reformed, and within a few years the Germans would
have overtaken the French and perhaps outstripped
the English, both in writing and in acting dramas.
There can scarcely be any doubt that Gottsched was
absolutely in earnest, and under the firm conviction

that art and literature could be "arranged" in such a way, if the thing were managed with the proper energy, and if he, Gottsched, led the way.

It may be doubted, however, whether the matter appeared quite as simple to the Neubers, who for ten years had been travelling about in Germany with the Spiegelberg and Haak-Elinson companies, and who knew the public of the small German towns well. At any rate it could not be—as has been sometimes suggested—a propensity for financial speculation that induced the young people to take up Gottsched's ideas with pleasure and enthusiasm, for they could not help seeing at once that it would entail great sacrifices to convert the general public from its taste for show-pieces, full of Hanswurst clowneries and jokes, to the monotonous recitals of the sublime, but not very amusing, French classics. That this was so appears clearly from the letters which the couple afterwards send to their "distinguished friend and patron," Gottsched, to inform him of the progress of his reforms in other towns. Thus on one occasion Johann Neuber writes quite pathetically from Nuremberg: ". . . to begin with, most people did not care to hear of a comedy entirely in verse. But now, indeed, I think the upper class are won over, and many of them have begun to like reading some of the new Leipzig books. . . . Perhaps (though it is not certain) we might earn more *thalers* if we acted merely old, tasteless, homely, native, popular plays; however, as we have started a good thing, I will not stop as long as I have a *groschen* to spend on it. In any case, what is good must remain

good, and I go on hoping that with your valuable assistance we shall win the day in the end, even though it
may take longer than a year. . . ." [1]

What we also learn from the correspondence which
was carried on between the Neuber company and the
ever mightier Leipzig professor [2] for several years is
the warm enthusiasm with which the couple, especially,
of course, the impulsive Frau Neuber, seize on the new
ideas, the eagerness with which they carry them out, and
their contempt for the fools who cannot understand the
value of the wonderful thing offered them in these
sublime plays.

To our eyes it does not appear a particularly
seductive ideal to play the French classical tragedies
in bad, clumsy translations or barren German imitations,
nor could German classical art be directly promoted by
them. Yet, indirectly it was of great importance that
the leaders of a company should be impressed with the
idea of having a vocation to work for, and one which
tended to raise them, not only in their own minds, but
also in those of other people, who had never thought of
troubling themselves about theatrical affairs. It brought
about an intercourse between literary, even university
men and the hitherto entirely ostracised class of wandering artists, of which twenty years previously nobody
would have ever dreamed.

---

[1] The whole letter is reprinted in Reden-Esbeck : *Carolina Neuber und
ihre Zeitgenossen* (p. 101), a book which contains copies of several interesting documents of the time, but which, otherwise, is quite worthless and
unreadable.

[2] He became *extraordinary* Professor in 1730, *ordinary* (in logic and
metaphysics) in 1734.

Moreover, it imposed a new method of work on the performing actors. The versified plays with their rhymed alexandrines forced the performers to take up their parts in a manner that differed very much from the earlier method. Even though it was not merely improvised comedy that had been acted previously, and even if the former work had also required preparation,[1] the new regular plays necessitated much accuracy in committing their parts to memory, and a depth of character-study hitherto unknown. And, it must be said, this new method of working caused the greatest difficulties to the actors, especially the study of their parts. Whereas the new task of penetrating into a character, to form and develop it, could not but interest and fill the mind of a really talented actor, the mere work of learning by heart was an immense toil, especially to those somewhat advanced in age, whose memories could not easily be trained after an entirely new fashion. Even to Frau Neuber, though she was only thirty years old when the alliance with Gottsched was concluded, learning by heart always remained a stumbling block, and in general many years passed before the actors altogether abandoned improvised comedy. Fr. L. Schröder, though belonging to the following generation, confessed that in his youth he had never learned his part in a comedy by heart, but had contented himself with studying the character and the situations, and otherwise said just what occurred to him.

After all, those who adhered to Carolina Neuber

[1] *Cf.* my *Theatrical Art*, vol. ii., in *Middle Ages and Renaissance*, for the study of Improvised Comedy.

mostly belonged to the younger generation ; they gladly accepted the new ideas and the new method of working, though perhaps in many cases they were more willing than able to carry them out.   Even the older supporters of the new fashion, the excellent Kohlhardt, for instance, and Lorenz and his wife were only in their thirties ; besides these a number of new men eagerly and enthusi- astically took up the new tasks.   The most distinguished members of the company were Koch, Schönemann, and Suppig.

The first mentioned, Gottfried Heinrich Koch, who afterwards played an important part in theatrical history, was a young lawyer of twenty-eight when he joined the Neuber company in 1728.   He was an intelligent, precise young man of quiet habits and many capabilities, but probably without special or great dramatic talent.   He could paint, write verse and act, and was a valuable addition to the young company.   He painted scenery, wrote and translated plays, and acted all kinds of parts. He had no difficulty in adapting himself to the new school ; the graceful style and regular diction came easy to him.   In the course of time he became a very popular actor, especially in the Franco-classical comedy, the style of which his assimilative nature had picked up from French actors, especially on one occasion when his com- pany was visiting Strassburg.   He was also successful in tragic parts as long as the Neuber style was in fashion ; but he was incapable of rising beyond it, and at a later period he figured as a somewhat ludicrous relic of a taste that had passed out of fashion.   In serious parts especially, his affectedly refined gestures were ridiculed, and it was asserted that whenever he put his hand inside his open waistcoat he moved it in a semi-circle, and always back to his pocket again in the same way. Nevertheless, though no genius, he became a very able theatrical hand, and in his time was one of the most useful members of the Neuber company.

Johann Friedrich Schönemann, who joined the Neubers in 1730, was about the same age as Koch,[1] but while the latter came as a beginner, Schönemann had been acting for at least six years, chiefly with the discredited Förster company. Originally he was a harlequin, but when with the Neubers he acted a little of everything, more particularly the valets in the French plays. He was a practical and a serviceable man. He married the charming Anna Rachel Weigler, and these two became the chief pillars of the company during the subsequent years, she as a female lover, he partly in comic, partly afterwards also in serious parts, in which, however, he was unsuccessful.

" Little " or " handsome " Suppig[2] was a native of Dresden and joined the company about 1731. He was a very dainty, elegant, little man, clever at French, who played the piano as well as billiards, was nimble of movement like a dancing-master, and spoke in a clear treble voice. He soon became the first lover of the company— some reporters say, even of the manageress—and played

---

[1] Koch was born in Gera, 1703, and became an undergraduate at Leipzig ; Schönemann in 1704 in Crossen-on-the-Oder.

[2] This characterisation is taken from a libellous pamphlet on Carolina Neuber, entitled *Leben und Thaten der weltberüchtigten, etc., Frederica Carolina Neuberin, etc.* From its gross witticisms and accusations may be drawn a few items of information, for example about Suppig, about whom it is difficult to learn anything elsewhere.

heroes in tragedy and young men in comedy.   In particular, he was the first who represented the *élégant*, the
dandy, the *Stutzer*, as this character is called in German
theatrical language.   His talent, cut after the French
fashion, was admirably suited for the new style ; besides,
he had greater facility than most others in studying the
clumsy rhymed verses.   He became the faithful friend
of Frau Neuber both in good and evil days, and did not
forsake her even when everything went against her.
Of the details of his life very little is known ; but it is
certain that he died before her.

The whole company probably consisted of a score
of members, and they led a very patriarchal life under
the leadership of the masterful but lively and amiable
Carolina Neuber.   The young unmarried actresses lived
in her house, and the unmarried actors boarded with
her.   She talked to them about the new art and the
new plays, and thus gained their warm adherence to
her principles.   At the same time she turned them to
practical use, as the young women had to work at their
dresses, the men to write play-bills and paint scenery,
like Koch.   Rehearsals and performances were attended
to with a seriousness hitherto unknown.   And as to the
virtue and morals of her female charges, the experienced
mistress kept her eyes open and did not allow any
escapades that might lower the company in the esteem
of good society.   For the same reason she kept watch
also on the tendency of the young men to frequent
public-houses, though it was not in her power to prevent
such visits altogether.   Those among the actors who
were good hands at cards and billiards used to improve

their miserable salaries by such little accomplishments as could only be turned to account in public places.

II

Struggle for the New Ideas—The Neuber Company in Hamburg—The Movement Culminates in the Banishment of Harlequin from the Stage—The Rupture between Carolina Neuber and Gottsched—The Fall of Both.

AND now the little band, eager and courageous, started on its tour through Germany to carry out all the innovations which were to raise the level of the German stage and German dramatic art, while the "most learned and most noble" Professor Gottsched remained quietly in Leipzig and received information about the progress of his undertaking.

Matters, however, did not proceed quite in accordance with his ideas. For one thing, it proved impracticable to leave out altogether the merry after-plays with Hanswurst or Harlequin, which the public insisted on seeing ; for another, the number of regular tragedies in hand was not sufficient, and Neuber always complained that the promised translations were not forthcoming. However, a glance at the *répertoire* which gradually became the stock of the company [1] shows an immense difference between these productions and the appalling dramatic rubbish - heaps of the preceding period. Comedy, in particular, is well represented, almost entirely by French pieces; but it was just this that was the order of the day. Molière, indeed, was not in

[1] In Reden-Esbeck's book, p. 107 ff., will be found a list of plays from a season in Hamburg in 1735.

favour with Gottsched, who found him too coarse, not quite exempt from Hanswurst jokes, but Destouches was entirely to his taste, and this fashionable author was very prominent in the Neuber *répertoire*, besides Marivaux and Regnard.   However, several of Molière's plays were contained in the list, among them *L'Avare*, which became one of Koch's best parts, *Le Malade imaginaire*, and *Tartufe*, besides *Les Précieuses ridicules*, which must have been a thorn in the flesh to Gottsched, especially as it was acted by the Neuber company under the title *Harlequin as Marquis Mascarilias or The Laughable Maidens*.   On the other hand, he had reason to be pleased with several of the tragedies, such as Racine's *Iphigénie*, *Alexander* (in German : *Der Streit des Vorzugs in der Grossmutter zwischen Alexander dem Grossen und Porus*) and *Bérénice*, Corneille's *Cid* and *Cinna*, Pradon's *Régulus*, Voltaire's *Brutus*, and, last but not least, *The Dying Cato*,[1] a fearful original tragedy by the reformer himself, with Kohlhardt shining in the title *rôle*.

Yet, besides these regular and in part excellent pieces we find several with very suspicious titles, such as *Harlequin as Living Clock and Sham Mummy*, *The Merry Jewellers' Apprentices or The Feigned Count October and Baron November* ; and even quite undisguised *Hauptaktions*, such as the ill-famed *Asiatic*

---

[1] Its originality, certainly, was not great, as Gottsched's malicious Swiss enemies soon discovered that Addison's *Cato*, which nobody knew at the time, strikingly resembled the *Cato* of Gottsched, and that with the help of scissors and paste the former had been amalgamated with parts of *Caton d'Utique* by Deschamps, so as to form the " original " which was to introduce the new era.

Banise and *The Enchanting Princess or The Living Skeleton*, in the latter of which, according to the play-bill, "the knights would be adorned with full armour from top to toe, as well as with helmet, shield and plumes."

Frau Neuber, it is true, purified the harlequinades of their coarsest jokes in an attempt to cultivate and refine the old merry-maker, but in doing so she only deprived him of all pith and substance, and he became what he had never been before—dull. And, no doubt, it was this spirit of compromise and half measures—which otherwise was not in her nature, but was probably due to her more prudent husband and to the influence of members of her company, especially of the over-sagacious Koch—that laid the seeds of her subsequent misfortunes, for it brought her into conflict both with the general public and with the critic, Gottsched.

The young reforming company considered Leipzig as its headquarters, but between the great fairs other towns had to be visited, and among the best of these was the large and wealthy city of Hamburg.

Though the large population of Hamburg was chiefly engrossed in mercantile and other practical interests, at the beginning of the eighteenth century this old Hanseatic town was the seat of a powerful intellectual life. It was rich and had suffered less than any other German town from the devastations of the Thirty Years War. The constant intercourse with other countries, chiefly England, gave it an international importance. Literary societies and periodicals in the style of the famous English *Spectator* were flourishing; people took

lively interest in theatrical and musical affairs; the opera
had a long and glorious career in Hamburg, and it produced dramatic authors, some of whom stood under the
command of Gottsched, such as Fr. G. Behrmann, who
wrote the "classical" tragedies *Timoleon* and *The
Horatii* for the Neuber company, and Peter Stüven, a
very industrious German adapter of French tragedies.
Others were more independent; Heinrich Borkenstein,
for instance, whose local comedy, *Der Bookesbeutel*,
became one of the most popular successes of the
time.

It was only natural that this lively town full of
foreigners, English, Dutch, French and Danish, with a
more international stamp than any other in the whole
country, should tempt every acting company, and very
soon after its foundation the Neuber company found its
way there and kept returning.

To begin with, matters went pretty well. The time
was favourable. The opera, which had passed through
an uncommonly brilliant period, was just declining in
favour, and the Hamburg public always liked novelties.
So in one of his bulletins to Gottsched Neuber could
write the following hopeful lines : "The operas here are
very bad and their proceeds are low, but we have as
many spectators as circumstances allow and as many
patrons as there are here."

However, the patrons of the "classical" plays were,
unfortunately, not sufficient in number to uphold the
company, though they did their best — the wealthy
patrician Behrmann, in particular, repeatedly assisted
the Neubers with direct subventions—and the general

public did not see the obligation for the sake of art to go and listen through five acts to the declamation of verses so involved that they were scarcely intelligible. It was, moreover, the favourite habit of Frau Neuber to invoke the reverence of the audience for the new art in many small versified prologues or introductions of her own. But the practical Hamburghers did not want to be admonished, they wanted to be amused for their money; and at last, after many visits with ever-decreasing receipts, the hot-tempered lady's blood was up, and in 1735, after a season, during which she had actually suffered privation and run into debt, she concluded her performances in a way which created the greatest sensation far and wide, and became very detrimental to her reputation.

In our days, when the public is quite accustomed to being the scape-goat, when it is almost essential to good literary breeding that every poet and every critic should load the public with abuse, Carolina Neuber's sarcasm appears very tame, and we can scarcely understand the offence it created. But in those days, when no author or actor approached his public without bowing low and humbly to "the courteous reader" or the "highly honoured" assembly, people were taken aback and insulted when a mere manageress of a theatrical company not only forgot all humility, but even ventured to take free citizens to task.

Carolina Neuber's offence [1] was that before the fare-

[1] The play-bill was signed Johann Neuber, but everybody seemed to take it for granted that his proud and hot-tempered wife was at the bottom of it.

well performance in Hamburg she issued the following playbill : " In honour of and in deep gratitude to those who have seen us frequently and with pleasure, of those who have not been able to see us, who have not ventured to see us or not been willing to see us, this day at parting a German introductory play will be performed, as well as a comedy, by the Royal Polish Electoral Saxon and also High-Princely Brunswick-Lüneburg-Wolfenbüttel Court Comedians.[1]   The introductory play is entitled *Conditions of Dramatic Art during all four Seasons.*   The scenery has been made expressly for this play.   The title of the comedy is *Britannicus,* and is a translation of the same play by M. Racine.   The conclusion is a farce.   Last performance on Monday, Dec. 5th, 1735."

"JOHANN NEUBER."

This foolhardiness in upbraiding the very high and honoured public proved fatal to the Neubers.   The play-bills had no sooner been circulated through the town, than the chief burgomaster prohibited the performance, and the indignant actress had to leave Hamburg without telling its inhabitants the truths that were burning on the tip of her tongue.

Besides this the company had annoyances of an even more serious nature.   For a time they were deprived of their headquarters, Leipzig, and Frau Neuber even had the humiliation of knowing that it was a harlequin player, Joseph Ferdinand Müller, son-in-law of old Elinson, who after a long struggle gained possession

[1] In 1733 the Neubers had acquired the Brunswick-Lüneberg patent.

of the Saxon patent, and even of the theatre—the Butchers' guild-hall—where the young company, with its enthusiasm for the new ideas, had won its first victories.

In compensation for the ingratitude of Saxony Duke Charles Frederick of Schleswig-Holstein showed great interest in the new art; he gave the "Neuber stage" the title of Schleswig-Holstein,[1] and offered it an annual subvention of a thousand *Thalers* to play at the "Kieler Umschlag," the great fair at Kiel, which was the Duke's residence. His enthusiasm for the drama was so great that he would sometimes even act in it himself.[2]

This, of course, was a comfort. However, the name of Leipzig, the town of learning and gallantry, was written in Carolina Neuber's heart, and her only desire was to return thither. In her characteristic style, which in the original knows neither of commas nor of capitals, she writes as follows to her "High-bred, highly learned, most honoured Lord and Patron, Gottsched": "I am pining to death. It is just like a kind of magic which dominates me, that I must continually think of Leipzig, or else I must be in love with it. In spite of all the bad hours and of my loss, I think with more pleasure of the good hours, and particularly of those which I spent in Your Worship's

[1] The patent is reprinted in Reden-Esbeck, p. 191 f., and clearly shows that it was the new efforts to raise dramatic art and the *répertoire* which gained the Duke's favour for the troupe.

[2] This, at any rate, is asserted by Schmidt in his *Chronologie* (p. 50), and after him by many others. Of course it could not be in the public theatre, but at the Court-performances. The "Kieler Umschlag" was held from 6th January to the beginning of Lent.

sagacious company and in that of my other worthy
friends." [1]

And she actually succeeded in coming back, as,
after several efforts, Neuber was allowed to build a
" comedy booth" in front of the Grimmai Gate near
Rose's Garden.   The reform was now to be firmly
established in a conspicuous way.   It was no secret
to Gottsched that on the long journeys through Germany the *répertoire* had not always been kept quite
pure, and that Harlequin or Hanswurst had carried
on his game freely enough, in company with the regular
tragedians.   The important thing now was to reveal at
one blow the difference between the old and the new,
and the plan was formally to banish from the stage
Harlequin or Hanswurst, who was considered as the
representative of the old style.   Carolina Neuber herself
wrote one of her admonishing fore-pieces, and with great
solemnity the old jester and his variegated costume were
exiled from the German stage. [2]

Gottsched's heart was won, and the theatrical
beheading of Harlequin—which Lessing afterwards
described as a genuine harlequinade in itself—roused
quite an astonishing sensation in the literary world, astonishing because the very act was a childish trick in
itself—on Gottsched's part a stroke in the air, on the
Neubers' a blow against their rival Müller, who lived on
harlequin-plays.

[1] Letter from Carolina Neuber to Gottsched, of 15th February 1735
(Brunswick) ; reproduced by Reden-Esbeck, p. 170 ff.

[2] It is a myth that on this occasion a doll representing Harlequin was
burnt and Hanswurst abolished by a regular *auto-da-fé*, though the story is
repeated in nearly all histories of the theatre from the *Chronologie* to Reden-
Esbeck.

Now, if by this stroke the jester had actually been abolished, if not from the German stage, at least from the Neuber performances—and if not from the farces, at any rate from the principal plays—the affair would have been something of a feat; the banishment of Harlequin would to some extent have signified the turning-point, which many German historians of the theatre have represented it to be. But not a year later the Neuber play-bill again announced one of the good old Haupt-aktions with Hanswurst and his whole train, *The profligate Life and terrible End of the Arch-Magician of world-wide fame, Dr Johann Faust*, in which, among other things, "Charon was seen sailing in his boat, and Pluto approaching him on a fire-spitting dragon followed by his entire subterranean court and spirits." And in spite of his banishment, the audience sees " Hanswurst who chances to witness the enchantment of Dr Faustus. He must stop and is unable to stir from the spot until he has taken off his shoes.   The shoes dance with each other in a very amusing way."[1]

It would probably be a mistake to say that the ludicrous scene of banishment was nothing but a sham on the part of the Neubers, got up only to throw dust into the eyes of the mighty patron. No doubt, they

---

[1] The play-bill, which is dated Hamburg, July 1738, is reprinted in two places in v. Reden-Esbeck's book. It is strange, therefore, that this author, whose work on Carolina Neuber is otherwise entirely a mosaic of plagiarisms, should also, with regard to the banishment of Harlequin, copy word for word the statement of Devrient that it is untrue to say that soon afterwards she again took refuge in Harlequin in Hamburg. Comp. Reden-Esbeck, p. 211, and Devrient, ii. 36 f. Other authors as well deny that she reintroduced Harlequin directly. It is true that the above-quoted play shows us a Hanswurst, but this figure was considered only as a lower kind of Harlequin.

were perfectly honest, and nothing but the utmost need could induce them to resort to the old *hanswurstiades* in order to stop the ebb in the treasury.

Nevertheless, these apostacies from obligations solemnly incurred did not look well, and the great Leipzig critic had some reason to feel disappointed. There were other circumstances besides, which increased the resentment and disturbed the alliance that had hitherto been so cordial.

In Hamburg, which, in spite of the strained relations between the public and the hot-tempered Frau Neuber, continued to be the best resort of the company between the Leipzig fairs. *Alzire* by Voltaire had been performed in a translation by Peter Stüven, a merchant's son, who had already adapted several French tragedies [1] for the Neuber company. Now, when in the same year, 1739, the troupe came to the Leipzig fair, Gottsched suddenly was unreasonable enough to request the Neubers to give up Stüven's translation and study a new one produced by his "clever friend," viz. his wife, Louise Adelgunde Victorine, late Kulmus. It then appeared that this adaptation by the prolific Adelgunde was very bad, and the actors, especially Koch and Suppig, who had had some difficulty in learning the verses of Stüven, refused to undertake the new and perfectly unnecessary labour. The consequence was that the Neubers refused Gottsched's request, and *Alzire* was performed in the Hamburg translation.

This was wounding Gottsched in his tenderest spot.

---

[1] Voltaire's *Brutus*, Racine's *Britannicus* and *Phædra*, Corneille's *Earl of Essex*.

Vain and ambitious men are, as a rule, most sensitive where their wives are concerned, and at a period when translations ranked almost with originals, this slight on the part of the Neubers meant nothing less than a rupture. Though hostilities did not break out openly at once, we may take it for granted that from this day forward Gottsched no longer considered Carolina Neuber as a willing instrument for carrying out his principles, and that, consequently, he had lost all interest in her.

The alliance was broken, and whether it was mere chance or a sign of the great power of Gottsched, from this moment matters went down-hill with Frau Neuber, uninterruptedly and at full speed.

First, she again roamed about for a while and returned to Hamburg, where all went wrong with her a second time, and where, to her great grief, she was the loser in a competition with "the strong man," Eckenberg. Then—no doubt through her patron, Duke Charles Frederick—she received an offer to go to St Petersburg with her company. In her overweening pride, at her parting performance in Hamburg, she rated the audience so roundly that henceforth the free-town was for ever closed to her.

She went to Russia, but only with the remnants of the dissolved company. First and foremost, among those who remained behind were Schönemann and his beautiful wife, and this practical comedian at once understood how to profit by events. He ingratiated himself with Gottsched, to whom he introduced himself as Carolina Neuber's successor and as the man who desired to propagate his ideas in the world.

Schönemann was nothing but a man of business, with no deeper interest in art, and he was an utterly worthless actor in the serious drama favoured by Gottsched.   But he had a keen sense of the taste of his time and great astuteness in finding actors of prominent talent for his company.   The interest Gottsched took in him rapidly brought him forward.   Meanwhile poor Frau Neuber had to leave Russia after a year.   Her visit there had brought her nothing but failure.   At first she had had a hard competition with the Italian Opera, which was patronised by the Court-Marshal of the Russian Court. Then, when she had partially succeeded in gaining a position, the Empress Anna died suddenly, and the Neuber company lost the support of her favourite Biron, who was overthrown and exiled to Siberia.   Amid these political disturbances the foreign company could do nothing, and the Neubers had to leave Russia without even receiving the full amount of the salary due to them.

On their return home—in 1741—they at once went to the Easter-fair in Leipzig, but the Schönemanns had supplanted them in Gottsched's favour, and the almighty critic worked against his former friends both by word and pen.

Then Carolina Neuber did what many greater minds had done before her : she turned her weapons against her enemy from the stage, and a battle was fought—one of these battles which are always particularly bitter and unpleasant, when former friends stand opposed to each other, but which in this case was more ludicrous than anything else.

In his critical pamphlets Gottsched constantly depreciated the Neuber performances, though, indeed, their *répertoire* was remarkably pure,[1] and it was his old grievance, the costumes, that he especially attacked. In this point he demanded a strict imitation of the antique, besides recommending accentuations and attitudes which would make the classical subjects appear in the correct style. Thus one of Gottsched's journalists[2] wrote: "What would the spirit of Cato think at the sight of the strange three-cornered hats with their high plumes? the detestable powdered wigs, the over-ornamented folds of the garments, the shiny gloves, the stiff, wide skirt, the white stockings and artificial shoes, and last, but not least, the Parisian dagger never seen in Rome? Would he not accuse our time of great ignorance of the Roman antiquity? Would he not consider it most absurd to represent the Roman hero thus, as indeed [in this guise] the actor does not resemble him at all. None better than he would be able to convince the obstinate admirers and advocates of this kind of mixed pseudo-classical performance, that a gold-bordered hat, a pigtail, cuffs and shiny gloves, white silk stockings and a fashionable Parisian dagger, may be suitable enough for a German dandy, but not for Cato, the Roman."

[1] In the monthly periodical: *Belustigungen des Verstandes und des Witzes* of the year 1741, we find practically the daily *répertoire* of the Neuber company during this period, and it consists, with few exceptions, of the French classics recommended by Gottsched, though sometimes in the translations by Stüven which he disliked, sometimes also in his own or in those of " his able friend."

[2] Christopher Mylius, a cousin of Lessing's. As a poor young student of natural history and as a journalist, he put himself in Gottsched's pay, though afterwards he became his bitter adversary. The attack dates from 1742, as will be seen, after the struggle above mentioned had come to a close. Evidently Gottsched did not mean to give up his cause.

As we said before, this demand for a costume correct in style, at the time of which we are speaking, appeared pedantic and ludicrous to everybody, and another fifty years had to pass before the demand was satisfied,[1] and even then the satisfaction was only partial.

Carolina Neuber, therefore, might indeed be sure of general approval when, irritated at the constant censure and depreciation of her performances, she conceived the idea that the best way of showing the absurdity of the "literary pope's" assertions would be to test them on the stage. So one day, instead of the usual farce, the Neuber play-bill announced the third act of Gottsched's *Dying Cato*, in which costumes, attitudes and diction were presented according to the author's own critical demands ; the correctness was even carried so far as to simulate the naked skin of the feet by covering them with flesh-coloured linen, and to abolish the high red heels, all of which was pronounced by contemporary writers a ridiculous exaggeration. The consequence was that the whole performance struck the audience as a wild farce, and when Neuber, who himself acted the part of Pharnaces, laid particular stress on the final speech : "This, then, was the attempt!" he was greeted by a storm of applause, which proved that the audience understood the joke, but which was particularly offensive to Gottsched.

Naturally this ingenious, but not very tasteful, revenge did not calm the feelings of Gottsched towards the Neuber company, and henceforth his criticism of their performances became more personally rancorous

[1] By the French actor Talma.

than ever; human enough, indeed, but not excusable in a critic who has placed himself on so sublime a height as he had. However, the revenge of an actor or an actress who hits the mark is always worse than that of the most caustic critic, and Carolina Neuber was not a person to spare those who had roused her indignation.

In the heat of the battle she composed one of her many allegorical fore-plays, which was entitled, *The Most Precious Treasure*. The piece itself is lost, but in the list of characters represented, which reads as if it belonged to an old Morality, we see that the scene was laid in rather sublime spheres. This was part of the cast:

"Reason, as Apollo in a laurel wreath, holds instead of the lyre, the image of wisdom," represented by Suppig; "Art, as a female pilgrim, carries instead of a staff a measure and compass," played by Carolina Neuber; and finally there was—probably the principal character—"The Censor, as night, in a garment covered with stars, with bat's wings, bearing a dark-lantern and a sun of brass-foil on his head."

Everybody knew, before the play was performed, that the censor with the bat's wings, who was to be personated by the young comic actor Fabricius, was none other than Gottsched, and that Carolina Neuber was now going to deal him the decisive blow.

Gottsched knew this himself and did all in his power to prevent this performance. However, at the Court, which was now in Leipzig, he had a powerful enemy in Count Brühl, who, far from intending to forbid the play, went in person to one of its performances to enjoy the revenge of the actress on the arrogant professor.

The gist of this revenge, in other words, the subject of Carolina Neuber's play, we do not know ; its satire, however, must have been very sharp, since after its first performance Gottsched repeated his protest.   His remonstrances, however, ,were useless.

After all, these scandalous quarrels, though detrimental to Gottsched, did not help Frau Neuber.   The new theatrical movement, that had begun in such warm friendship and with the highest aspirations, had already exhausted itself.   The well-meaning attempt of Gottsched to raise the German theatre had no national foundation, and his personal vanity and partiality had procured him many adversaries, who took cruel advantage of the breach which the bold actress had made in his fame.[1]   Crowds of enemies rushed forward, and though Gottsched never formally surrendered, his absolute power, which had lasted for about fourteen years —from 1727 to 1741—was broken.   Not long after his wittier and much more dexterous enemies represented him to public opinion with considerable injustice as nothing but a ludicrous, conceited pedant, without the slightest importance.

---

[1] That it was Carolina Neuber's attack which had made Gottsched's other enemies taste blood, and that it created a very considerable sensation, is clear from the satiric epic, *The Fore-play*, which was issued in 1743 by Rost, the secretary of Count Brühl—who had also written *The Hidden Sheep*, a very popular pastoral play—against Gottsched, and was afterwards reprinted by Gottsched's bitter antagonists, the two Swiss writers Bodmer and Breitinger, together with the parodies *Cato Castrated* and *Iphigenia Violated*.   This book begins with a dedication to Carolina Neuber, in which we read among other things : "We consider the time when she broke with the Professor as distinctly marking the period when the wretched sublime style of the Gottschedian school was banished from the stage, and when, on the other hand, the natural and accurate style was introduced."

If Carolina Neuber tired of the struggle, it was chiefly on account of economic difficulties. She had always had to fight with financial troubles, but now she was struck by one misfortune after another. Kohlhardt, who acted the leading parts both in tragedy and comedy, died rather suddenly; she had annoyance from the Leipzig Consistory, and an attempt to try her luck in Frankfurt-on-Main proved a complete failure. Depressed and tired of all these mishaps, the Neubers made up their minds to dissolve their company, and Johann Neuber hoped to obtain a civil post which would enable them to leave the stage for ever. When this hope also failed, Carolina Neuber began afresh with her old energy, and it must be said in favour of her earlier leadership that the chief pillars of her old company at once responded to her summons. Among the number was Koch, as leading character actor; the ever faithful Suppig; the stately, well educated actor, Heydrich; the two charming actresses, young Fräulein Lorenz (afterwards Frau Huber), and Katharina Magdalene Kleefelder (afterwards Frau Brückner); besides the married couples Lorenz and Antusch, the comic actors Bruck and Schuberth, and others.

Not a bad company, on the whole; but perhaps the manageress lacked her old buoyancy; anyhow success deserted her. No doubt, also, Gottsched continued to pursue her with his hatred. We find his correspondents in different towns sending him with evident relish bulletins concerning the decadence of Carolina Neuber. Thus the well-known author, Grimm,[1] the originator of

[1] Grimm, who won his fame as a French writer in Paris, was an undergraduate from Leipzig, and a protégé of Gottsched's.

light society journalism, writes from Frankfurt-on-Main on 11th October 1745 : " Frau Neuber always carries on her business very cunningly.   She has been staying here now for quite three weeks with her whole company, and has not yet played a single piece.   I have just heard that she is going to open her theatre to-day with *Britannicus*, and in six days the Court and all the ambassadors are gone ; thus there is money to be made. She has built a play-booth, which she was unable to finish before, though her husband came some weeks previously to make arrangements.   I fear it will be a great loss to her."

Matters went wrong everywhere, and if it had not been for a little episode which brought the company into contact with something higher, this period would only have been remarkable as showing the certain and steady decadence of this woman, who had once been animated by the highest aspirations.

At that time there lived in Leipzig a small clique of literary Bohemians, poor young fellows who studied science, literature, and art, among others Mylius and his cousin Gotthold Ephraim Lessing, Ossenfelder, and Naumann, all of them gay journalists and light-living lyric poets, who had to struggle for their bread.   Besides these there was a respectable young man, Christian Felix Weisse, who took a great interest in art.   Though what these young men saw of the Neuber company was only a vanishing glimpse of its former glory, its stage was an admirable resort, which helped them to foster their dreams of the future and kindled their enthusiasm of the moment.   They admired the fine tragic art of

Fräulein Kleefelder, the gay music and songs of Fräulein Lorenz, as well as the beauty of her feet when she danced; they looked with respect at the stout and mature manageress herself, and at the "great Koch," whom they admired enthusiastically, both in tragedy as Essex and The Cid, and in comedy as the Miser. They greatly appreciated Heydrich's fine bearing, Suppig's dandified manners, and Bruck's gay comic art.

They wrote and translated pieces for the Neuber company, and in return obtained free admission to both the stage and the auditorium; they had familiar intercourse with the actors and actresses, which led to animated exchange of ideas with these lively people. This was of importance to both parties, and several of the undergraduates who were studying at the Leipzig University in those days became fertile dramatic authors. But to none of them did this intercourse become more significant than to young Lessing, who horrified his parents by the eagerness with which he cultivated his friendship with the wicked theatrical people. During these few years [1] Lessing gathered from the Neuber troupe a store of observations, of practical theatrical knowledge, of the exigencies of the stage, and of the essence of dramatic art, which afterwards in his double career as dramatic critic and as playwright became of incalculable value to him. He devoted himself entirely to the theatre, which certainly did not further his theological studies, but was so much the more beneficial to

---

[1] At the age of seventeen, in 1746, Lessing went to study at the Leipzig University, and his connection with the company lasted till 1748. Very likely his infatuation for Fräulein Lorenz was not of a purely artistic nature.

posterity.   With his friend Chr. Fr. Weisse he translated
a number of French and English pieces : Regnard's
Le Joueur, L'Etourdi, Thomson's *Sophonisba,* Voltaire's
Mariane, etc., and out of his own desk he took a comedy,
written during his schooldays in Meissen, which, by the
advice of his mathematical master, Kästner, the witty
epigrammatist, he offered to Frau Neuber, who at once
had it performed.   Its title was *The Young Scholar,* and
it was a satire on the conceit and pedantry of the young
Saxon undergraduates.

The play proved a success, and moreover brought
out the acting powers of George Friedrich Wolffram,
who hitherto had been very unsuccessful, but who in
the title-part of " The Young Scholar " had been fortunate
enough to hit off the typical Leipzig stamp, which as
a living picture of real life was bound to strike an
audience that had never been accustomed to such
life-like representations.

So Frau Neuber had the honour of introducing
Lessing on the German stage.   But this indeed was the
last sunbeam of vanishing fortune which for a moment
brightened up her theatrical career.   Her perseverance,
energy, and the proud defiance with which she had faced
constant adversity, had changed into unconcerned indifference, which considered that sufficient for the day
was the art thereof, and never thought of laying plans
for the future.   She lost the power of properly super-
intending her business, and no longer knew which way
to choose, a state of things that is always fatal to a
theatrical manager.

The company must have felt this, for members who

5

6

5—Carolina Neuber in her mature age (p. 69).
6—The Monument over Carolina Neuber (p. 71).

had hitherto been faithful and zealous now began to fall off. In the year when Lessing made his *début* with *The Young Scholar*, both his best friends in the company, Koch and Heydrich, left Frau Neuber and went to Vienna.

A general dissolution set in. It is painful to follow the leader through her last few years of desperate struggle to keep above water by supplications, complaints, petitions, begging letters in prose or in verse of her own composition, always in excited and disconnected terms—missives which she sent to magistrates, ministers, even to the king himself. Schönemann, her old actor, takes away her theatre, her landlord refuses to keep either herself or the other actors in his house, partly because they do not pay, partly because they are always smoking when they are not acting. The officers of justice put seals on her furniture; she and her staff must remain, for their creditors will not release them till they have paid. The death-blow came from Koch, her friend and pupil, who owed his professional training to her, and who had stayed with her throughout his career. He returned to Vienna, collected a troupe and acquired the Saxon patent by alleging that Carolina Neuber was no longer capable of managing a respectable company. That Koch and Schönemann, the two serpents whom she had nourished in her bosom, quarrelled with each other, was no consolation to her. In one of her many complaints she writes : " So everything is planned with a view to my complete ruin, and as I have spent on the theatre all my fortune, as well as the money I have made in foreign countries and brought home with me, they want to drive me away, and as a reward for all my bitter toil with the comedians, to make me a beggar, and, as begging is forbidden, to see me starve to death." As time after time she was rebuffed by the authorities— probably not from hardness of heart, but because they knew that in this case help would be useless—she had to lay down her arms and resign her post as manageress.

Then she made an attempt to exploit herself as an actress, and in 1753 even obtained an engagement in Vienna.   But time had outrun her.   She was far on in the fifties ; people thought her affected, her declamation stiff, and her costumes ludicrous.   On 27th June 1753, one of Gottsched's reporters, von Scheyb, could send the following account of one fallen star to the other : "Frau Neuber has been called hither from Frankfurt, and her appearance on the stage, it is true, was that of a sensible actress, but her voice was so weak that she could scarcely be understood.   At times she screamed and raged so violently that her voice failed.   Nor does she comply with Viennese taste in her costumes. As *nescio qualis* queen she was decked out as a Neapolitan princess.   Her head looked like the collar of a sleigh-horse."

The same year Frau Neuber had to leave Vienna. She and her husband scraped together a wretched little company, and made a fresh attempt to gain their living by roaming about in small towns for a few years. However, the outbreak of the Seven Years War in 1756 crushed every hope of being able to continue even this miserable existence.   They were now absolutely destitute, old and worn out, and Frau Neuber's prophecy of being starved to death might, indeed, have come true, if old friends and admirers had not rallied to the assistance of the poor couple by giving them bread and shelter until death carried them to their last haven. Frau Neuber survived her husband about a year; in spite of degrading poverty she kept up to the last her innate proud dignity, sent well-written letters in rhyme to her friends, and inspired the humble people among whom she lived with respect by the unshaken calmness with which she bore the misfortunes of her old age. She died in 1760 in a small farmhouse in the little village of Laubegast, near Dresden, where in 1776 a monument was raised to her—on the high-road, as its erection in the churchyard was forbidden—" by some persons who knew her merits, and were admirers of her art."

A few years later her good friend and bitter enemy Gottsched died also. He, too, had been defeated in the battle, mocked and ridiculed by the younger school of authors.

Time mercilessly cast away its instruments as soon as it had done with them. They erred in not adapting themselves to the new demands of public taste. But they deserved a brighter fate. At any rate it ought not to be forgotten that if, at their death, the German theatre had gained a position, if it had formed its place in the world of intellectual life, if clever men felt drawn to write for it and play in it, the pioneer work, which was the indispensable foundation of its reaching so far, was due to those two persevering, obstinate, one-sided people, Gottsched and Carolina Neuber.

KONRAD EKHOF

The First Steps of Sophia Schröder and Konrad Ekhof in their Artistic Career — The Schönemann Company — The Difference between Ekhof's Reform and that of the Neuber's—Ekhof as a Naturalist— His Ideas on Dramatic Art and His Academy.

ABOUT the year 1738 two young persons whom fate had turned out of their course, and who were brought together by their common admiration for dramatic art, were staying at Schwerin.

She was a charming young woman of twenty-four, married to an organist named Schröder, in Berlin, a clever and amiable man, but an incurable drunkard. After four years of matrimonial life, which the sad failing of the husband had rendered intolerable, the young wife, whose maiden name was Sophia Charlotta Biereichel, left husband and home and tried to fight her own way. Her father was a gold-drawer, and she herself had been taught gold-embroidery, which in those times was much used on costumes. So she hoped to be able to gain her own living by this work, and went to Schwerin to avoid the pursuit of her husband.

He was a young clerk of eighteen, born in Hamburg. Konrad Ekhof was his name, and his father was one of the city-guards. Originally he had served as a clerk in a post-office of his native town, and on account of his trustworthiness and his beautiful handwriting had been appointed to a position which was rather above his age. But when the postmaster requested that on Sundays he should act as footman to his wife, Ekhof took offence, and went to Schwerin, where he was engaged by a barrister, who was also something of a *bel-esprit* and possessed a good library, the dramatic portion of which was eagerly devoured by the young clerk.

How the two shipwrecked young people found each other, what were their mutual relations, and how they came to consider the theatre as their proper haven, we do not know. It seems, however, to have been Konrad Ekhof who most desired to break with the miserable life they were leading, and to try their luck with the tempting, unknown art, whereas Sophia Schröder, the child of a respectable artisan, had great scruples about starting on the uncertain, despised theatrical career. But when she found that gold embroidery procured her so poor a living that she had to leave Schwerin and try her good fortune in Hamburg, Ekhof very likely had not much difficulty in persuading her, when one day he brought her the news that the actor Schönemann, who had been with Frau Neuber, was now going to start a company of his own, and was looking out for actors with whom he might begin his work at Lüneburg. They went to Schönemann, and were at once accepted. No wonder that anyone starting a company for the first time should be glad to acquire such a member as Sophia Schröder; she was handsome, had a fine figure and bearing, and plastic movements. She was very intelligent and her education had been excellent. Her character—like that of her afterwards famous son — was passionate and enthusiastic, with a genuine artistic sense, and at the same time she was very business-like, practical, and

economical.   In her youth, probably, the former qualities
were predominant, but in later times it cannot be denied
that her practical sense decidedly took the upper hand,
converting the fresh, lively actress into a somewhat petty,
almost parsimonious, housewife.

The engagement of Konrad Ekhof could not be
considered as equally assured beforehand, but his fanatic
love of dramatic art pushed him on.   His outward appearance was not alluring.   He was low of stature,
rather ugly, bony and high-shouldered, and careless in
his bearing; but his face was expressive, and his small
eyes very intelligent.   At the first glance you would
scarcely have expected that this queer little fellow was
destined to develop German dramatic art by so mighty
a step that he may justly be called its true father.
Director Schönemann probably judged him more
leniently on hearing him, for he had a fine, sonorous
voice, though at that time it may not have reached the
perfect development which it acquired afterwards, and
which was thus described by Iffland : " In thundering
power, in delicacy and beauty, it never found its equal
on the German stage."

The salary offered to the two young people by
Schönemann was not large, but Frau Schröder received
almost double as much as Ekhof, namely 7 *Marks* 75
Pfennigs (about 8s.) a week, while he had to be content
with 4 *Marks* 60 *Pfennigs* (5s.).

The new Schönemann company, however, consisted
almost exclusively of young beginners, and none of them
received a higher salary than Frau Schröder.   One of
them was Uhlig, an undergraduate of twenty, typical of

those industrious, moderately-gifted young men, who, without possessing genuine dramatic talent, nevertheless make themselves useful by occasionally writing a play or a prologue, and bearing themselves decently through various parts. Another was Heydrich, who had greater talent, and who afterwards joined Frau Neuber, besides several other young people who were well-bred, had an academic education, and chose the theatrical career not merely because they could not get on elsewhere, but from real inclination and interest. Actors of this kind impressed on Schönemann's troupe a stamp of refinement of a somewhat higher standard than was usually met with, a character which the Principal appreciated and wished to maintain.

Of a somewhat different kind was Konrad Ernst Ackermann, who was destined to become of great importance to the theatre in Germany. Whether he went on the stage from inclination or necessity, we have no means of ascertaining. He was not very young—twenty-eight at his *début*—and he had already passed through a multitude of experiences. He was of good family, of fine and stately presence, knew a little of everything, was something of a painter, a dancer, a quack, an agriculturist, a splendid sportsman, horseman, skater, and fencer ; amiable, attractive and good-natured, though hot-tempered ; but he was an incorrigible vagabond and adventurer. As a young soldier this characteristic drove him hither and thither, travelling and fighting ; and afterwards, as the manager of an acting company, sent him roaming all over Europe, constantly making him lose his good chances by his restlessness. As an actor he soon became very serviceable by his various accomplishments and easy bearing on the stage, and by playing all kinds of parts he developed himself into a most excellent comic actor, whose pleasant naturalness never degenerated into exaggeration and bad taste.

The experienced members of the company included Frau Spiegelberg Denner, who had been so unfortunate in the sledge expedition on the Sound,[1] and who ever since had had an ugly, rolling gait. By this time she was a lady whom fate had knocked about a good deal ; most towns and countries had had opportunities of admiring her as Eve in the well-known *Staatsaktion, Adam and Eve.* She spoke a queer cosmopolitan jargon, and her acting was very affected, but she reaped success in the parts of elderly comic women, such as landladies and procuresses, in which her peculiarities were advantages. She brought her two daughters with her, the younger of whom—though not very young, being thirty-four when joining the company—afterwards became the wife of Ekhof, who trained her to become a good *soubrette,* though she was never quite able to throw off the old-fashioned *Hauptaktion* affectation.

Schönemann himself was also a man of experience. He was thirty-six when he started the company ; he had been acting for many years, and had enjoyed great popularity in the leading characters and comic valets of Molière. But in tragedy he was intolerable, ludicrous, stiff, and declamatory, an unswerving adherent of the Neuber-Gottsched principles. He was an able leader who lacked neither courage nor energy. Though far

[1] Comp. above, p. 31.

from being such an enthusiastic idealist as Frau Neuber, he was not without ambition and was eagerly desirous to bring his company to the front. Unfortunately he was also anxious to push himself forward in tragic parts, and persisted in playing them, even when shown distinctly enough that he did not please in them.

Thus, according to a reliable anecdote, the Duchess of Mecklenburg-Schwerin, who was a good judge of dramatic art, had long been annoyed at seeing Schöne-mann as Essex in the tragedy of that name by Thomas Corneille, a part which he acted almost throughout the play with closed eyes and an unspeakably stiff and grandiloquent declamation, acquired under the leadership of Frau Neuber. The artistic Duchess, who had noticed the progress of young Ekhof in the tragic line, one day expressed her astonishment to Schönemann that this actor was not more employed in tragedy. "Why, for instance," she added, "do you not try him in *Essex*?" "Essex," Schönemann replied, in great astonishment, "*he* play Essex, your Highness! Why, I would rather go through a month on bread and water in your prison than leave *my* Essex to Ekhof." "Very well," the Duchess replied, sharply, "then at least you will allow me never more to see *you* in that part." Schönemann, nevertheless, went on playing his Essex undisturbed for many years.

However, where his petty personal vanities were not concerned, Schönemann was a manageable and sensible man, an opportunist, a man of business rather than an artist; sincere and honest, with the gift of winning patrons and attracting poets and actors to his circle.

His wife was handsome and refined, and had a
pleasant voice, but she was not very important, and
her acting was still somewhat stiff and pedantic, though
afterwards it developed into a more natural style.

Such in outline was the company which on 15th
January 1740 gave its first performance in the riding-
school of Lüneburg, for the town had no theatre. The
play acted was Racine's *Mithridates*, in which Ackermann
had the title-*rôle*, Frau Schröder Monime, and Ekhof
Xifarez a secondary part.

Nobody would have expected that the bearers of
these three names, which then for the first time [1] appeared before the public, would in future become the
pillars of German dramatic art. The second of the three,
however, at once proved herself to belong to the front
rank. Frau Schröder from the very day of her *début*
might be looked upon as the leading lady of the Schönemann company, and there is no doubt that she felt herself
to be so. Ackermann won less favour, in spite of his fine
appearance—high tragedy never became his line—and,
as to Ekhof, nobody thought about him.

In fact, the signal success of Ekhof, his position in
German dramatic art and his influence on it, are very
remarkable.

The pompous reforms of Gottsched and Frau Neuber,
proclaimed with trumpets and drums, could not be mis-
understood. Its aim and end was daily blazoned forth
and hammered into people's heads; now the stage was

---

[1] Some authorities say that Ackermann had once before tried his powers
while forming one of a small, not particularly esteemed, company, whose
leader was Stolle, a brother-in-law of the harlequin-player Denner.

purified, art was raised, Germany had reached the level of the other nations. Even the two leaders of the movement, the bulky, overbearing professor and the exuberant, flushed, and gushing actress, necessarily forced themselves on the general attention. It was then, and is now, impossible not to take them into consideration; but the great clamour that surrounded them made, and still makes, people forget that in relation to the internal reform of dramatic art their work, after all, did not signify much. A number of French works, translated into German, had been introduced on the stage, and the mode of acting had been somewhat improved—somewhat, though far from sufficiently. In fact, Frau Neuber possessed no deep conception of the true nature of dramatic art, and Gottsched none at all.

The Neuber school was still clinging in a great measure to the Hauptaktion style. Its declamation was stiff, if not so regularly scanned as before, when this method was used also in prose.

Though Carolina Neuber did something to connect the too sharply divided and accented lines in reciting verse, declamation remained too unnaturally regular in modulation, without human life and without variation—a pedantic, affected and elaborate style, monotonous like the stiff French gardens with their artificially cut trees and hedges, a sham Versailles elegance, ill suited to the German soil.

The innovation which Ekhof introduced into the dramatic art of his country was of a very different kind indeed. The art of Frau Neuber was external; she mastered it, so to speak, by outward force: Ekhof's reform was in the deepest sense an internal one, which made art grow by a quiet development from within. Nor did it proclaim itself with noise and clamour as a new school and an epoch-making revolution. It grew slowly, just as muscles develop by daily training, and it was only by comparing it with the old school that one discovered how strong it had become.

Ekhof's outward life and appearance harmonised well with the character of his art. In the first place, he was nothing more than an actor, not a practical theatrical leader—at all events his work as independent manager is quite sporadic and insignificant ; he spent the first seventeen years of his professional career in the same company, and here it was that he received his first artistic training, or rather, he did not receive it, for no one in the company would have been able to teach him what he wanted—he acquired it by his own efforts. He gradually discovered that acting did not mean strutting about on the stage in more or less magnificent attire, pouring out a torrent of rhymed verse, or—in comedy—exhibiting a multitude of droll, but senseless fooleries. He discovered that the essence of dramatic art, what justifies it and makes it interesting, is the representation of human beings, their feelings, sufferings, and changing moods, through speech and gesture. And though this conception was by no means a secret in other countries, it was indeed perfectly new in Germany where this art of acting had hitherto been based on an absolutely erroneous theory, according to which tragedy consisted in being merely sublime, comedy merely droll, and nature, real human nature, was absent.

Later in the century Ekhof was called a naturalist,
which meant partly that he formed his characters from
direct observation of reality, copying accent, movement,
and facial play from life, not theoretically from precon-
ceived principles of tragic pathos, comic power, etc.;
partly that he became the great actor he really was,
without theoretical speculation properly so called, in
short, that his art was purely natural.

The first opinion is right but only in part, the second
is entirely wrong.

Though Ekhof was far from being a well-read man,
and though he was simple and plain in his intercourse
with others,[1] he reflected very much on his art, and was,
indeed, the first theorist on the German stage. When
his ideas were somewhat matured and he had come to
the front as an actor, which, however, took a number
of years, he wanted also to instil his views into his
companions. The Schönemann company had got on
well; its *répertoire* was full of variety and comparatively rich, and was no longer dominated exclusively by
French authors; the English mixed drama and Holberg [2]
had gained a firm footing in it; besides which native

[1] F. L. Schröder tells us (in *Meyer's Biography of Schröder*, p. 143) that
Ekhof, while staying in Hamburg, preferred to spend his free days in a little
wine shop, the landlord of which was named Klapmaier. Here he presided
over a small company of old citizens and militia officers, read the papers
and explained politics to them. The citizens listened reverently, and scarcely
anybody talked but himself.

[2] Among English plays the most popular were Lillo's *George Barnwell*
and Moore's *Gamester*, besides *The Devil to pay*, an operette by Coffey.
Holberg (in Detharding's translation) was a great favourite in Germany
during this period, and in some companies, that of Frau Schröder-Ackermann,
for instance, he for a long time even dominated his *répertoire*. The
Schönemann company acted the *Tinker Politician*, in which Ekhof played
Henry, *Jakob von Thybo*, *The Masquerade*, *Jean de France* and *Don Ranudo*.

literature was beginning to work its way by means of the plays of Borkenstein, Weisse and Elias Schlegel.[1]   In the later mixed drama there was more opportunity for studying real life, and this no doubt was a motive power to Ekhof.   After the lapse of from ten to twelve years he had quietly and by persevering work become the leading man in the company.   Ackermann and Frau Schröder had by this time left Schönemann, after being with him a year, and had formed a company of their own.   Somewhat later they had married and were now touring in the border countries of Germany, with varying success, but without as yet obtaining general recognition.

No doubt Ekhof was very superior to his companions, and as a fanatical advocate of his ideas, with an almost pedantic respect for the holiness and seriousness of dramatic art, he wanted to inspire his colleagues with the same feelings.   He conceived the plan of establishing an " Academy for Actors " within the company, which was to meet every alternate Saturday from two to four o'clock for the purpose of discussing parts, reading plays, talking over dramatic art in general, and so forth. Schönemann was quite indifferent to these theoretical discussions;   his interests inclined more and more to horses and horse-dealing; he had, however, a great respect for Ekhof, to whom by and by he left the whole management of stage matters, vain as he was, it pleased

---

[1] The Schönemann company itself included several fertile authors, among them especially Uhlig and Krüger.   The latter wrote a splendid part for Ekhof in his play *Duke Michael*, in which Ekhof made use of his excellent Low-German peasant dialect.   Ekhof himself was also an industrious adapter of foreign plays.   He translated Baron's *L'Homme à bonnes fortunes* under the title of *Der Mensch auf gut Glück, oder, Der Liebhaber von Profession.*

8

7

9

7—Konrad Ekhof (p. 83).   8—Heinr. Gottfr. Koch (p. 86).

9—Karoline Schulze (p. 106).

him much to see his company occupying a distinguished position in its art, so he willingly assented to the formation of the new Academy, and to the nomination of himself as its chairman. With one exception, Ekhof won the whole staff over to his plan. And so, with great ceremonial and very minute laws and precepts, this institution was started in the season of 1753.

Ekhof—the schoolmaster, as his companions called him—was now quite in his element, and had arranged everything with his usual pedantic minuteness. Though the company was not very numerous, the Academy had a number of officers: a president, a vice-president, a propositus, a vice-propositus, an inspector, two lectors, a vice-lector, a secretary, and a beadle. Of these fine titles Ekhof had invested himself with three.

At the second meeting of the Academy Ekhof, as propositus, made a few introductory remarks, which ran as follows: "To practise dramatic art or to be a comedian is not so easy a task as many consider it to be, who only look at the matter superficially and content themselves with the name of the thing, or who are only actors by accident, and whose advantages depend exclusively on chance circumstances. But neither is it the unsurmountable height that it is represented by others, who may perhaps possess some ability, but who, either from envy or pride, make it appear an impenetrable secret.

"No, it is an art which indeed seems unlimited, though it certainly has its limits, just as a desert seems endless to a wanderer, if he is so imprudent as to set out on a journey through it without previously inquiring the right way, so that he is likely to be misled by every side-path, and will consequently go astray and keep wandering to and fro without being able to reach his goal.   But he who knows his way, after having gone through the necessary troubles, will reach the end in due time. . . ."

"So it is indeed most necessary that those who practise dramatic art and want to be actors, seek the means which may ease their efforts and by which they may become more perfect in their art.   Dramatic art is copying nature by art and coming so near up to it that semblance is taken for reality, or to represent things of the past as if they were just happening.   In order to obtain some mastery of this art the following things are required : a vivid imagination, untired application, and a never idle practice.   These are the sure means by which all stray paths are avoided and all actors can reach the goal of their aspirations. . . ."

Konrad Ekhof had succeeded in finding the right way through the apparently endless desert of German dramatic art, and none was better able than he to be a guide to his more or less straying comrades.   Every one of his somewhat *naïve* words bear witness to the zeal and care with which he would have undertaken the leadership.   But to induce actors to take an interest in general artistic and professional questions without the prospect of pecuniary advantage or satisfaction of their vanity, is a task infinitely more difficult than to develop oneself into a great actor.   For the latter purpose you need only to be a genius ; for the former you need the long-suffering of a god, and Ekhof only had the patience of a human being.   After a year's torture from the secret mockery and open, surly resistance of his dull and foolish colleagues, he had to give up his noble but *naïve* plan of winning them over to higher aspirations.

This, however, did not slacken his zeal; in his mind burned a sacred fire which could not be extinguished, though it may have rendered him more eccentric than he was before. It was probably during this period that he wrote the following lines in an album :—

> *Es sind viel Vögel, die hassen mich,*
> *Ich bin ein Kauz und acht' es nicht.*

(There are many birds who hate me; I am a queer fellow and don't mind it.)

But, in particular, it made him more selfish, more eager always to act himself, and this tempted him to undertake many parts for which he was at least unsuited by age and appearance. This, together with his rather petulant temper, placed him, humanly speaking, in the eyes of his associates on a somewhat lower level than he deserved by his aspirations after the ideal.

II

Ruin of the Schönemann Company—Koch and Ekhof—Ekhof in the Prime of his Art—The Ackermann Company—Schröder as a Youth—Engagement of Ekhof by the Ackermanns and his First Meeting with Schröder.

MEANWHILE matters went rapidly downward with Schönemann. His original spirit of enterprise was entirely gone, or it had turned to horse-dealing, which had become a passion with him, but of which he understood nothing. He strolled about the country with a good-for-nothing son, swopping horses, but was perfectly indifferent to theatrical affairs. Ekhof kept the company together as well as he could, but the small proceeds were lost in the risky game of horse-dealing. The staff had to be diminished, and when, by way of economy, Schönemann even went so far as to dismiss Ekhof's sister-in-law, Frau Steinbrecher, *née* Spiegelberg (his wife's sister), matters became rather too bad for him, so he left the company and accepted an engagement with that of Schuch the harlequin-player.

His loss meant the dissolution of the Schönemann company. In the same year its chief, who at the beginning had been a tolerably able manager, retired for good into private life, and till his death held the position of Armourer to the Duke of Mecklenburg-Schwerin, in very modest circumstances.

The deserted company applied to Ekhof, desiring him to become its leader. To this he willingly assented, as, naturally enough, he did not feel on his proper level with his burlesque associates, whose sphere differed so very much from his own. His leadership, however, was of very short duration. It was evident that he felt no inclination for the business side of theatrical work. Art was everything to him ; for its sake he was able to work, venture, invent, and stimulate others, but in practical everyday life he was anxious, nervous, and rather petty. The exciting game of chance, as we might call the leadership of touring companies—chance, moreover, in which loss was almost a certainty—had no attraction for him, so he addressed himself to the able manager, Koch, who was just then disengaged, having dismissed his company on the outbreak of the Seven Years War, asking him to take up the reins. Koch was above all a man of business. Though originally endowed with considerable talent as an actor, an author, and a painter, the artistic side of his nature seems to have perished quickly in the hard struggle for existence, which in those days the life of a German stage manager undoubtedly was, making way for a very closely calculating, matter-of-fact, and order-loving spirit. So he became a leader who bowed low to high patrons and cared not a straw for exalted artistic principles. But with his appreciation of quiet and stability he helped in his own way to acquire for dramatic art better and more settled conditions than it had enjoyed before.

Though in his time he was considered an excellent actor—the young literary men in Leipzig even called him the *great* Koch—he does not seem, like Schöne-mann, to have preserved any personal vanity with regard to his art. In this respect he yielded to the eminent power which he considered Ekhof to possess.

Nevertheless, they did not get on at all well together. From the very beginning they were always at variance. The original cause of their dissensions has never been cleared up, but after six years Ekhof parted from Koch with great bitterness, and never forgot his grudge against him. Even in the very last year of his life he mentioned his former chief as " a man with a black and poisonous soul."

Ekhof, of course, on leaving Koch, was at no loss for an engagement. He at once came into connection with the old comrades of his youth, Ackermann and his wife, who at that time were staying with their company in

Hanover, and he accepted an engagement with them. This union created an artistic constellation, which was the most significant and interesting the German theatre had as yet exhibited.

When Ekhof passed from the company of Koch to that of Ackermann he was at the height of his power, and his reputation as the greatest German actor had spread far and wide. He understood everything : heroes, lovers, heavy fathers, comic valets, dialect-parts, even harlequin, though, of course, he did not act equally well in all.

First and foremost—to use the words of his younger colleague, Schröder—he was " the greatest master of theatrical language any nation ever possessed." Master of language, not elocutionist, for Ekhof did not use his splendid, powerful voice to produce musical harmony or empty sound, but always as a means of reflecting changing moods. He did not, like most actors who trade on a fine voice, play on one chord only ; the new, characteristic phenomenon in him was a manifold variety, an infinitely-shaded vivacity, a variegated diction which broke up the lines. And in harmony with all this, his facial play was thoroughly thought out and well calculated, and his gestures, in their apparent simplicity, were even more of a new creation than his diction. In their attempts to imitate the naturally graceful Italians and Frenchmen—attempts which, owing to their national characteristics, were bound to fail—the Germans had adopted a number of conventional gestures which irritated the experienced spectator by their lack of connection with their speeches, and gave the actors the air of puppets. In his annoyance at this, Lessing said : " In their opinion gesticulation only means, now with their right hand, now with the left moving away from the body, writing in the air half the figure of a stunted 8, or moving both hands simultaneously, as if they were rowing in the air." Ekhof, on the other hand, was very sparing of gestures, but he knew how to render each of them expressive, so that the slightest movement of his head, his hands, or his feet was as much noticed as his words, and to quite an equal degree formed a language of its own.

Just on account of this lifelike variety of his method, his best parts were those which at the time were qualified as *von gemischter Empfindung* (of mixed sentiments). It was these parts which had been brought into fashion by the new *genre* called the "mixed drama," and which, in contrast to the straightforward and rigid representation of character in the classical tragedy, allowed deep feeling, serious pathos, or pain to manifest themselves in everyday talk, even in comic art. In such comic-pathetic, rough-goodnatured, odd but noble characters, which now began to abound in dramatic literature, and which at this epoch of awakening sentimentality called forth tears and smiles at the same time, no doubt the art of Ekhof culminated. In the eyes of experts, therefore, such parts as Diderot's *Père de famille*, old Barnwell in Lillo's popular emotional play, and Odoardo in Lessing's *Emilia Galotti*, stood in the imperishable glory of perfection. Iffland, in describing a scene of Gotter's [1] *The*

[1] Friedrich Wilhelm Gotter (1746-1797) was a prolific dramatic author, influenced by contemporary French dramatic technique. His amusing

Hater of Marriage, where Ekhof represented Baron Sittmer, gives a graphic description of Ekhof's method in such parts.   This is how Iffland depicts the performance of the great actor : " What an amiable description of the married man he draws to the enemy of marriage. He is sitting with Terville, trying in a kind, affectionate way to impress him with the arguments that are to strike his selfishness.   Finally, the old man becomes more pathetic, more persuasive.   He describes the happiness of his own married life—speaks of his bereavements by death.   Here Ekhof stopped—his eyes seemed to be dimmed by tears, his lips trembled, his voice failed. Suddenly he rose and grasped Terville's arm with both hands, leaned over him, and then, with all the power of love and pain, in an indescribable, heart-rending tone, he said these words :—

" ' Unhappy man ! who dost not know that there is rapture even in nature's pain.'

" Rarely," Iffland adds, " did tears flow with such unanimous sympathy as at this scene.   The assembly were thrilled as if by an electric shock."

But though Ekhof was greatest in parts of this kind, he also had a number of strong characters in classical tragedy in which he was greatly admired.   It is true that his physique, which was anything but heroic, did not aid him, and he had some unfortunate, careless tavern

comedies, *Die Erbschleicher* (*The Heirs by Fraud*) and *Der schwarze Mann* (*The Black Man*) maintained themselves for a long time in the *répertoire.* I have not had access to the play mentioned above.   Ekhof did not play this part till 1777, much later, that is, than the period with which we are occupied at present.   Odoardo also belongs to a later period (*Emilia Galotti* was performed for the first time in 1772).

manners, such as coughing and spitting on the stage, which were indeed most unsuitable to the high and sublime spheres in which the plays moved. Nevertheless, his glorious, powerful and ardent diction bore him up in these parts, and such *rôles* as Orosman (in Voltaire's *Zaïre*), Richard III. (in Weisse's tragedy of that name), Canute (Canute the Great in Schlegel's drama) were among his most appreciated performances.

His appearance, which became prematurely old, was still less suited for lovers, such as Mellefont in Lessing's *Miss Sara Sampson*, yet he was much admired in these parts, though it was the general opinion that he continued playing them longer than was suitable for his years.

In comedy, too, he acted everything, from the subtle and refined to the most burlesque comic parts. Even here he did not like broad, coarse lines and traits. His characters were a mosaic of observation and oddities, which at times produced a picture of admirable effect, especially in parts of a discreetly comic nature, but which in coarse burlesque, where bolder strokes were required, appeared too studied and too artificial. Thus his Henry in *The Tinker Politician* was a failure ; it was thought too grimacing, too full of practical jokes. But his peasants were perfect, his low German dialect was nature itself; he knew his North-German peasant by heart and could hit him off in every detail. Fr. Nicolai,[1] the well-known bookseller and author, describes a visit to Ekhof in his home during the last years of his life. Nicolai made him read some serious scenes of Cronegk's *Codrus*

[1] In Iffland's *Almanach fürs Theater*, 1807.

and Voltaire's *Zaïre*. Ekhof's reading impressed him deeply, but after these the actor gave a sample of his comic *répertoire*, which Nicolai describes as follows : " As soon as he had finished reading the scene Ekhof jumped up from his chair like a boy, snapped the fingers of both hands, threw his dressing-gown on the floor and recited from memory a scene of the Low-German farce, *Der Bauer mit der Erbschaft*[1] (*The Peasant with the Legacy*) with so much originality and humour that several times we all burst out into loud laughter.   The former dignity and pathos were gone, and there was the peasant in every muscle of the face, the bent knees, the hunched shoulders ; down to the slightest movement of the hands, all was comic."

While Ekhof, small and plain, had developed himself under comparatively ordinary circumstances into an accomplished actor, the two stately associates of his youth, Frau Schröder and Ackermann, whom he was now again to join, had been undergoing vicissitudes of a somewhat different kind.

When Frau Schröder, with Ackermann and several others, left the Schönemann company in anger, she was a proud, enthusiastic young woman, who had immediately won a leading place on the stage.   But her attempts to create for herself a position as manageress did not turn out well, though she lacked neither courage nor zeal.   For some

---

[1] *Der Bauer mit der Erbschaft* was an adaptation by Krüger of Marivaux's *L'Héritier de Village*.   With Krüger's *Herzog Michel* it held a place among Ekhof's most celebrated peasant characters.   It was on seeing Ekhof in this character that a genuine peasant among the spectators exclaimed : " *Wo to'm Düwel hewwt de Lüde den Buern herrenohmen ?* " (" Where the devil have the people got hold of that peasant ? ")

years she acted in Hamburg and surrounding towns, but
without success. To us (Danes) her short independent
leadership is interesting, in so far as Holberg occupied a
very prominent place in her *répertoire*.[1] Otherwise the
period of her management was of no great importance,
except for the occurrence that—probably tempted by
the rumour of her theatrical feats—her husband, the
wreck of a genius, came from Berlin to see his formerly
much-loved wife as a celebrated actress. There was a
short blaze of reconciliation, after which the husband
again relapsed into the dark abyss of alcoholism, from
which he never again emerged. But this short meeting
of husband and wife had one important consequence :
Frau Schröder retired from the stage and again resumed
her art embroidery in Schwerin, until, on 2nd November
1744, she gave birth to a son, who received the name
which occupies the highest place in German theatrical
history, that of Friedrich Ludwig Schröder.

The theatre, however, continued to beckon her, and,
not long afterwards, she started afresh on its alluring but
deceptive career. Ackermann came to her side again,
and these two together shortly afterwards, as a married
couple, undertook the long adventurous expeditions, in
which they alternately reaped money and honours and
had to fight their way against creditors and misfortunes.
Russia and East Prussia had been their best resorts, but
from these countries they were driven away by the Seven
Years War, and they had been touring in Switzerland
and the Rhine countries with varying success, yet always

---

[1] She acted no less than fifteen of Holberg's plays, which made sixty-five
out of 250 performances in Hamburg.

maintaining outwardly the pompous style which Ackermann liked, even when their in-door circumstances were
miserable enough.

When Ekhof went to join them they were thriving
very well.   They had again ventured within the part of
Germany where there were good prospects for theatrical
companies, and in Hanover, where they were now staying—in 1764—they were very successful indeed.   People
liked their performances, which were rather unlike what
they were accustomed to see.   By generally staying in
out-of-the-way places the actors had developed independently without much intercourse with other companies.   They were not overworked, and had no severe
artistic principles to observe.   Ackermann, the fighter
and careless adventurer, had turned, in the course of
years, into a fat, somewhat indolent, but always stately,
amiable, and respectable man, who, living for his own
ever-varying private schemes and roaming inclinations,
preferred to leave the daily theatrical concerns alone,
and was very unwilling to take his dear pipe out of his
mouth.[1]

Frau Schröder-Ackermann, now a woman of fifty,
was no longer the hot-tempered leading lady, always
eager to act.   In fact, she did not care much for appearing on the stage, nor was there much left of her good
looks.   She was a sharp, rather masterful matron, who,
besides her marked sense of economy, possessed much
taste, and was a good teacher for the young.

[1] Even in the theatre he had it always at hand, and as soon as he came
off the stage he took it up, and was seen walking to and fro, part in hand,
pipe in mouth, studying the next scene.

Both were unswervingly natural and sound in their conception of art, and, though their direct influence was not great, as their wandering life prevented them from spending much care on rehearsals, the power of their example nevertheless created a kind of school in their company, a natural gay and healthy style, which only needed to be firmly established by quiet work to become of real importance.

Schröder, who was twenty years old when Ekhof joined the Ackermanns, was at a somewhat difficult age. His natural parts were splendid, but his education, if such a word can be used, and his childhood had been very irregular indeed. He had been tossed about in the most adventurous way, and had experienced more vicissitudes than usually fall to the lot of any but heroes of the most exciting novels.[1] He had appeared on the stage in his third year ; for his sake child-parts had been introduced in the plays ; when a little older he had acted young girls. Dragged about from place to place, in sledges across the Russian steppes, in canvas-covered waggons along the high roads, he had seen many people and many countries, but had not met with much tenderness from his mother, nor with much loving guidance from his step-father, since he had been hated by the evil spirit of his childhood, Clara Hoffmann, the prompter—*Einhelferin*, as it was called—who entirely possessed the ears of the parents.

[1] There is not space in this work for a detailed history of Schröder's childhood, but I can refer the interested reader to a large and very entertaining book about him by his first biographer Meyer, or to the excellent, though unfortunately still unfinished, work by Professor Litzmann, *F. L. Schröder.*

After staying at a college of Jesuits, in which he was very nearly caught for ever, and afterwards being in the hands of a private tutor, who was a remarkably eccentric free-thinker, he was placed in a very strict Protestant educational establishment at Königsberg, where Ackermann had built a new theatre, and a rather luxurious one for those times.   On the outbreak of the Seven Years War, and in fear of the Russians, the otherwise brave and honest Ackermann lost his head, and rashly abandoned his theatre as well as his stepson, both equally unprovided for and unprotected.

We now find the poor lad struggling for existence in the strange town for more than two years.   He had soon to leave the college, as his parents never sent money.   So he stood without relations or friends, without the slightest help or a farthing in his pocket, dependent on himself alone.

He sought refuge in the empty theatre, living there for more than a year, boarding with the family of a poor shoemaker, whom he helped in his trade.   Several times this queer, ragged, but self-asserting little landlord let the theatre to acrobats and conjurors, who taught him some of their accomplishments.   The deepest impression on his mind was produced by an eccentric English rope-dancer and acrobat, Michael Stuart, a man of literary and social education,[1] and especially by his

---

[1] The far-famed English acrobat Stuart gave performances in Copenhagen in May 1756, and was eminently successful, especially with the female sex.   On departing he eloped with a girl of sixteen, the daughter of a Copenhagen merchant.   She accompanied him for some years, bore him a daughter, and then vanished into obscurity.   This remarkable man, who professed to be of Royal blood, and who, when not drunk, was most fascinating, even appeared on the Royal stage in Copenhagen.

refined and charming mistress, with whom the fascinating artist had eloped from her home in Copenhagen.
At last, as a youth of fifteen, after manifold adventures,
young Schröder, like the prodigal son, returned to his
parents, clothed in rags, hardened by misery and
starvation, after having travelled partly on foot from
Lübeck to Basle, where his stepfather was stationed
at the time.

There was much friction between him and his
parents ; the young fellow had become proud and hard
in the bitter school through which life had already led
him. As we said above, when Ekhof joined the Ackermanns, Schröder was twenty years old. He was full
of unshakable self-confidence, and respected scarcely anything but physical accomplishments. His tall, slender
figure was trained in all sorts of acrobatic tricks, and, above
all, he was a superb and ingenious master of grotesque
dancing. Dramatic art, in which he particularly cultivated
the alert French valets, he treated with supreme, almost
disdainful nonchalance. It seemed to him too simple
and easy compared with the difficult art of tumbling,
in which he had become a master, and by no means
so lucrative as the elegant game of billiards, which was
the chief source of his income, and procured him the
means of indulging in the love adventures and extravagant tavern life, which were his recreation.

This momentous first meeting of Ekhof and Schröder
—of present art in its maturity and future art in its
germ—was the marriage of which the offspring was the
perfection of German dramatic art.

In its external aspect, the arrival of the great actor,

which had been anticipated with such great excitement by the Ackermann company, was both characteristic and grotesque.   On 24th April 1764,[1] just when the actors were returning home from their dancing practice, a canvas-covered van pulled up before Ackermann's house in Hanover.   Out of it crept a slip of a man with a bowed back and wrapped up in a kind of woman's cloak. Ackermann hurried up and welcomed his old friend, but Ekhof answered hurriedly : " By and by, by and by ! " Then there struck in a female voice from beneath the canvas : " Ekhof, take care of the dogs ! " after which two handsome little dogs made their appearance. Ekhof most deliberately pulled a pair of strings out of his pocket, fastened them to the collars of the dogs, and then placed them in the hands of his future chief with these words : " Take them up to your own room, Ackermann, when they have . . ." Ackermann left the honourable commission to a servant.

At length there emerged Ekhof's wife and his pupil, *Demoiselle* Sophie Schulz, who was also engaged for the company, both of them wrapped up in ugly cloaks, after which Frau Ackermann, Schröder's mother, led them into the house.   But Ekhof would not stir from the spot till all his belongings had come out and every wisp of straw had been ransacked.   Then he and the carrier went into the house and quarrelled for half an hour in the Low-German dialect, till at last Ackermann succeeded in settling the dispute.   At last Ekhof found time to

---

[1] The account which follows was taken down from the verbal description of Schröder by his friend and biographer F. L. W. Meyer, in his work *Friedrich Ludwig Schröder*, i. p. 125 f.

shake hands with his old comrade, then indulged in lengthy complaints on the troublesome journey, after which he rushed up to his room.

By and by at table he astonished Schröder by not in the least resembling the image he had formed of the great actor. He fidgetted during the whole meal, and scarcely allowed himself time to finish his food, before he hurried out into the town with the billposter to find lodgings.

How was it possible that this queer little man could be a great tragedian ? What would he look like as Œdipus ? for this was going to be his first part in the new company. Schröder and the other young scoffers looked forward to much fun from the *début* in their company of this deformed and fidgety little man.

The evening came without their having had an opportunity of hearing Ekhof, for it was not considered necessary to rehearse old plays. Schröder and his comrade Schulze were the two *choryphoi*,[1] who before the entry of Œdipus have to give expression alternately to the lamentations of the people over the avenging plague ; the high priest in the door of the temple has ordered silence, when Œdipus makes his appearance with Jocasta and his suite. The two *choryphoi* were laughing in their sleeves, for, indeed, the new guest did not look very imposing, though he differed exceedingly from the fidgety little man they knew. He now stood erect, and his bad figure had been improved by padding ;

[1] It was a version of the *Œdipus* of Sophocles made by Steffens, and this tragedy had already belonged to the *répertoire* of Ekhof while he was with Schönemann.

but no attempt had been made at hiding his immense flat feet, and his bony limbs were anything but fine and plastic.

But all of a sudden the following lines burst from the lips of Ekhof, with immense power and pathos :—

Ihr Völker, die der Schmerz in diesen Tempel führt
Bringt Thränenopfer her, vielleicht wird Gott gerührt !

(Ye peoples whom deep pain has to this temple brought, Bring sacrifice of tears ! God may perhaps be touched !)

—and all was forgotten : poor figure, ugly feet, all vanished in the enjoyment of this mighty heart-rending pathos, this passionate human feeling which rose from the bottom of his soul. Such depths of art had never been seen during the pleasant, easy-going leadership of Ackermann, and for the first time Schröder felt his heart swell with the conviction that art was not the same as gymnastics and volubility.

No doubt Ekhof's appearance on the stage marked a turning-point in the career of young Schröder, though, so far as I know, he has nowhere directly said so. But the vivid interest and no less vivid criticism with which he followed all the performances of Ekhof[1] during the five years they worked together, testify sufficiently to the fact that his art, in which he had hitherto lacked ambition, now appeared to him in a different light, and that he no longer regarded intelligence, reflection, and brain-work as superfluities.

If Schröder concealed from himself the effect which

[1] During this period Ekhof acted no less than 166 parts, to most of which Schröder has written short critical remarks.

the art and personality of Ekhof had produced on his mind, much less did he reveal it to his colleague in any kind of enthusiastic veneration.

The day after this performance of *Œdipus*, in which Ekhof had indeed touched Schröder so deeply, he sent for the young actor, desiring to rehearse with him his part in Regnard's *Gambler*, in which Ekhof was to act the title *rôle* at his second appearance with the company, while Schröder played Hector, the valet. But he met with a flat refusal from the young actor, who had been spoiled by the public; and at the rehearsal afterwards Schröder told Ekhof that on receiving his proposal he had thought that there must have been some mistake about it. He would soon show that he did not need any teaching; on the contrary, he might rather give than receive instruction. Ekhof replied soothingly that he had not thought of teaching, only of agreeing about the joint acting. "That can be done at the rehearsals," Schröder retorted. However, many of the precise traditional pieces of "business" which Ekhof proposed, and to which he had been accustomed for many years, did not find favour with Schröder. He was in the habit of acting with more freedom, of almost improvising in comedy, and he was sure of his audience, of its applauding his great facility and presence of mind on the stage, where he was always capable of letting his tongue run on, though his knowledge of the text of his part might be very superficial.

This was how Ekhof and Schröder first made acquaintance with each other, and thus the relations between them always remained. Schröder was overbearing and irritating in his manner towards his elder colleague, whom he even had the impudence to correct. He would stand between the wings and amuse himself with putting down in his note-book every conspicuous fault committed by the master, in order to annoy him afterwards by telling him of it to his face. Yet in his innermost heart he always felt a great admiration for the tragic genius of this man. Ekhof cautiously and politely avoided quarrelling with him, but inwardly he was tormented by the taunts of the young actor, which in the end rendered his life with the Ackermann company intolerable.

When Ekhof is reproached with not always sharing good and evil with Ackermann, but having at important crises sided with his rivals, it must not be forgotten that Schröder's insults may have embittered his life to such a degree that it might be natural enough for him to desire to leave the company.

III

Short History of the Hamburg "National Theatre"—The Chief Pillars of the Ackermann Theatre in Hamburg—Intrigues of Löwen and Frau Hensel—Foundation of the first German National Theatre—Lessing and his *Dramaturgy*—Ekhof's Wanderings with the Seyler Company —His Last Years as Leader of the Court Theatres in Weimar and Gotha.

EKHOF aged prematurely. As early as the end of the sixties he is several times mentioned as being too old for such and such a part, or we are told that his age forbade him this or that, though he was not yet fifty. This early physical decline was probably due partly to the excessive amount of work which he constantly undertook, and to his naturally weak constitution, and partly to the unhappy domestic circumstances of his later years. His wife was incurably insane, and as he kept her with him to his death—she died several years after him—and always carried her with him on his wanderings, his private life was both uncomfortable and exhausting.

Yet his artistic powers never declined. The only thing that could be urged against him was, that in his great eagerness to play and his lack of self-criticism—not uncommon faults even in persons of great talent—he persisted in acting youthful parts, comic as well as serious, in which his personal appearance prevented his creating any illusion.

Otherwise he retained his artistic vigour, and remained equal to himself even to the last, and shared in the many vicissitudes which still continued to agitate the German theatrical world. Of these the most important to posterity was, no doubt, the foundation of the first German National Theatre. This institution, it is true, lasted little more than two years, though it had been started with great expectations and considerable noise. In spite of its brief career, it raised itself an everlasting monument, not so much by its own intrinsic value as by the criticism of which it became the subject. It was the occasion of Lessing's *Hamburg Dramaturgy*, the cornerstone of all dramatic criticism.

The foundation of the Hamburg National Theatre came about in the following way. Ackermann, shortly after his successful sojourn in Hanover, went by Ekhof's advice to Hamburg, where he played in a theatre (Am Dragonerstall), which he had hired of Koch, who at the time was stationed in Leipzig. But as Koch would only let it for a short time, and Ackermann felt inclined to remain in Hamburg, still encouraged by Ekhof, who, naturally enough, preferred to stay in his native town, he —very rashly, as he possessed no capital at all—resolved to build a theatre of his own in the large and wealthy town, which he thought would be quite capable of making a permanent theatre pay. On the site of the old and long dilapidated opera house[1] he erected a building, neither very stately nor very convenient, but large enough for the time, and it was inaugurated on 31st July 1765, in the presence of a numerous and interested assembly of the Hamburg *beau monde.*

Ackermann had already won a public in the gay, free town, where novelties were always welcome. At that moment his company was doubtless the best in Germany.

Besides Ekhof, who was generally acknowledged to be the best German actor, and who rapidly acquired the same influence and quiet power in the Ackermann company as in those with which he had worked previously, we hear of Sophie Friederike Hensel (late Sparmann), a magnificent and domineering leading lady. Even as a very young girl she had led a most adventurous life, and at the age of seventeen—she was born on 23rd May 1738 —she had married the comedian Hensel, a somewhat indolent character, but not without talent, from whom, in spite of the attempts of Herr and Frau Ackermann to

---

[1] On the Gänsemarkt, where there is now a statue of Lessing.

mend her morals by bringing about a reconciliation, she now lived separated, leading a free and easy life, surrounded by a host of more or less distinguished admirers. As an actress Frau Hensel was in her way important. Her colossal form and commanding beauty fitted her admirably for the great heroines, and as long as she contented herself with playing such parts, there was in her acting both an outward and an inward beauty and power, which carried away the spectators and suited the national taste particularly well. Frau Hensel became the prototype of the mighty exuberant heroines, who for a long time dominated the stage. They may still be met with occasionally, especially in the classical German drama, and with their swelling bosoms and limbs, their ready tears and loud lamentations, they excite the great admiration of their countrymen, while to foreigners this massive and wholesale display of female sentiment causes more astonishment than pleasure.

However, Frau Hensel was also an intelligent woman. Lessing, with whom she began a quarrel soon after he started the *Hamburg Dramaturgy*, writes of her in a private letter : " Personally I am no friend of Frau Hensel's, but I am in justice bound to acknowledge that I have never yet found an actress who better understands what she has to say, or can better make others feel that she understands it."

Schröder, also, considered her excellent in certain parts, especially in those where there was no need of her dragoon-like strides, which suggested the Greek *cothurnus*, and her long-drawn " O-o-o-h ! " and " A-a-a-ch ! " but he was no doubt right in wondering that Lessing could compare Frau Hensel's leading lady tricks with Ekhof's true and serious art.

Frau Hensel's private character was dangerous and intriguing ; dangerous, because she used every means of attracting influential people, and using them for her private ends ; intriguing, because she hated every other actress who created a sensation, or was successful with the public, and tried every means to get her out of the way.

A particular thorn in her side was the pretty, bright and fascinating Karoline Schulze (afterwards Frau Kummerfeld), whose blue eyes, girlish appearance and charming talent had captivated the hearts of all the young men ; her dancing was the ideal of grace, and her acting of Juliet (in Weisse's *Romeo and Juliet*) appeared to the young the climax of dramatic art.   Just as a few years later she kindled the hearts of young Goethe and his associates in Leipzig, so the romantics of the Hamburg pit were at her feet, while the more solid mercantile class of men about town enrolled themselves under the standard of Frau Hensel.

Dorothea and Charlotte, Ackermann's two daughters, who were afterwards to appear as the best examples of their mother's excellent school, were already frequently employed in the *répertoire*, Charlotte, the younger, as yet only in children's parts ; Dorothea, though only twelve years old, also in those of young girls.   Her budding talent, however, could not make its mark in the presence of the two stars, each brilliant in her own sphere.

The company included a young and ardent lover in

Michael Boeck, who, though no genius and not even a man of great gifts, possessed a certain kind of deceptive talent, which was apt to carry away a not over-critical audience, and was useful as a substitute for the rare genius of a divinely gifted born lover, of which the company could not boast. It was Boeck who afterwards at the Mannheim theatre created Schiller's Karl Moor, thus in his way occupying a place in theatrical history. Indeed, he was only what the Germans call a *Macher* [Maker], who had a certain passionate style as hero but no soul. A *naïve* little remark of his characterises him better than anything we could say. When, after a year's absence, Schröder joined the company again and asked Boeck how he had got on in his art, the latter replied: "Oh, now I know all about it; I can make them applaud whenever I choose. Before my exit all I need do is to speak in an undertone and then suddenly break out into a thundering roar ; the applause will come at once."

He afterwards married Sophia Schulze (not to be confused with Karolina), who had formerly been with Schönemann, and thereafter had preserved a somewhat affected style, but was otherwise popular enough, especially in the so-called " breeches parts," those of women in male attire, a kind which was much to the taste of the time.

An actor of genuine talent was the young student David Borchers (born in 1744 in Hamburg), who joined the Ackermann company, and at his *début* at once roused great expectations, which, indeed, at the beginning were fully satisfied. With incredible ease and great imagination and boldness he accepted all kinds of character parts, at first mostly those of old men, becoming the successor of the old retired actor Schröter, whom he far surpassed. Later he undertook also a number of Ekhof's characters, which he played well enough not to let the great master be missed.   And all these tasks were accomplished as if they were mere trifles, without toil, anxiety, or study. But if he possessed the ease of genius, he also had its carelessness, its contempt of all ties and duties, combined with some vices, which in the long run ruined his talent. He was a great drinker and, above all, an ardent gambler.   He never thought of rehearsing, much less of studying his parts, and the consequence was that he never progressed beyond the auspicious beginnings of his youth, and rapidly degenerated till he lived only on the reminiscences of his former self.

But during the first years of his histrionic career he acted with Schröder, who was of the same age, and the two presented the very essence of fresh, youthful and gay dramatic art.   In popularity, however, Borchers scarcely equalled Schröder, who in his more popular characters, such as the merry French valets,[1] quite captivated Hamburg society ; they had scarcely ever, even in Frenchmen, found the equal of this young man with his quickness and elegance, his subtle, well-trained body and comic volubility.   His ballets, too, put on with magnificent luxury, were a novelty to the Hamburg public, and created an immense success.

To see Ackermann himself in his great comic parts,

---

[1] He acted them all in red stockings and braided coat, probably the customary livery of a lackey in those times ; so he did not wear the usual Zanni costume.

such as Bramarbas (in Holberg's *Jakob von Thybo*), *The Tinker Politician* (by the same author), Harpagon (in Molière's *l'Avare*), Grobian (in the characteristic Hamburg play *Der Bookesbeutel*), and later as Sergeant Paul Werner in Lessing's *Minna von Barnhelm*, was always a treat, for nobody equalled him in graceful, delicate and natural humour, which never degenerated into tasteless caricature.   His only drawback was that his memory had suffered so much—probably from constant smoking—that he had great difficulty even in remembering his old parts, which, though he might have played them a hundred times, he had to study over and over again.

His wife also was much appreciated on the stage, where, however, she appeared more and more rarely. Among her principal parts the Hamburgers reckoned her Susanne in *Der Bookesbeutel*, and afterwards Lady Rusport, in which everybody admired her sensible and correct playing.   But she gradually lost her taste for acting and preferred looking after the treasury and putting by a little money, which may indeed have been necessary enough, considering that the good-natured and liberal Ackermann, in spite of large receipts, kept involving himself in financial difficulties.

No wonder that this company, well provided in all branches, was received with enthusiasm by the Hamburg public.   It contained, however, some germs of dissension, which were soon to develop and lead to quite unexpected results.

Ekhof cannot be entirely exonerated from having helped to sow discord.   Being a native of Hamburg as well as a great actor, he of course gained even greater popularity in this town than elsewhere, and an almost fanatical Ekhof party came into existence, which admired all that he did, and after the usual way of fanatics, reviled all that was not Ekhof. This might be excusable enough as far as tragedy was concerned, in which Ekhof was the commonly acknowledged master. But in comedy it annoyed Ackermann, and Schröder even more, to see their colleague, himself very vain of his art, pushing forward and being exalted to the skies at their expense, and using such exaggerated burlesque means as were intolerable to themselves. Karoline Schulze, who must be considered an impartial witness in this theatrical controversy, being almost the only person who enjoyed the favour of the clique to the same degree as Ekhof, judges Ekhof very severely in her *Memoirs* for his exertions to please his fellow-townsmen by his exaggeration in the comic parts. She thought he lowered himself to the level of a " pickle-herring," and distorted his characters into an abominable caricature ; in such parts as Masuren (in *The Poetic Squire*), the apprentice Henry in *The Tinker Politician*, the *Malade imaginaire*, and the *Bourgeois Gentilhomme*, she describes him as "simply disgusting."

But even worse than Ekhof's grasping, indiscriminate avidity for parts was Frau Hensel's passionate mania for playing heroines, in so far as it made her more active, more intriguing, and more energetically determined to upset the ruling powers, and above all to get her captivating blue-eyed rival, Karoline Schulze, out of the way. And in her efforts to gain this end several circumstances and persons came to her assistance.

Shortly after the arrival of Ackermann in Hamburg a young man of letters, Johann Friedrich Löwen, called on him and offered to help him by word and deed. Löwen was the son-in-law of manager Schönemann, and his wife was a talented actress, but when, as early as 1757, Schönemann had dissolved his company and retired into private life, she was without an engagement, and her husband, who was a passionate lover of the theatre, had lost every opportunity of satisfying his craving. He now lived in straitened circumstances, holding a very modest civil office in Schwerin, and it was a desire for money as well as for work which prompted him to apply to Ackermann of whom he was a distant relative, but whose relations with the Schönemanns otherwise and in former times had not been of the most friendly kind.

However, the good-natured Ackermann received Löwen kindly, listened patiently to his advice and played his pieces and his translations. But very likely the persistency of the man became too troublesome, so Ackermann employed another "stage-poet," which made Löwen his bitter enemy and induced him to undermine Ackermann's management systematically by his critiques in a periodical published by himself.

It was very natural that such a man, struggling for bread as well as for the gratification of his theatrical passion, should become a willing instrument in the schemes of Frau Hensel. Besides this journalistic support, she succeeded in gaining even more effectual financial help. At this time her acknowledged and favoured admirer was Abel Seyler, a merchant of light

and luxurious life.   With his partner Tillemann he had
not long before suffered a sensational bankruptcy for an
enormous sum, out of which each of them had saved a
few thousands, but neither of them had lost his good
humour or his taste for light living.   Seyler's admiration for the fine actress was easily transferred to the
theatre in general, the theatre, that is, which formed a
frame round his favourite.

Thus a coalition of commerce, letters, and art was
formed in which each party had his own personal interests, but which outwardly was working towards the
sublime goal of abolishing the business-like leadership
that was detrimental to true art, and creating a new
National Theatre based on literary and patriotic
principles.

It was not difficult to weary out Ackermann, who
was already tired of the business.   Löwen easily accomplished the task by his theatrical articles, which, though
expressed in comparatively decent terms, were of a most
caustic effect, especially as at that time actors were
still quite unaccustomed to public criticism.   It was easy
enough also to induce the unstable man, who was always
planning new transactions, to let his recently built theatre,
especially as the terms offered, if they had been carried
out, would have been a sufficient compensation, and
have helped him over the financial difficulties, into which
his somewhat imprudent building enterprises had plunged
him.

Thus it happened that Seyler, Tillemann and Bubbers,
formerly an actor, now a wall-paper manufacturer,
entered into partnership and undertook the new theatre

on the Gänsemarkt, and that its artistic leadership was put into the hands of Löwen, who, besides choosing the *répertoire* and distributing the parts, was to attend to the technical and literary training of the actors, more especially through lectures and exercises. Changes, of course, were made in the staff. First of all the amiable and fascinating Karoline Schulze, the rival of Frau Hensel in public popularity, was dismissed, together with her brother, who was both actor and ballet-master. Both joined Koch's company in Leipzig. The new managers also wanted to get rid of Schröder, as they feared his sharp tongue and very independent way. It is true that they offered him an engagement, but in such a way that he refused it contemptuously and went off in search of adventures to join the merry company of v. Kurz (Bernardon) in Mainz. These were very considerable losses, and the new managers never found an actor capable of replacing Schröder. On the other hand, Frau Dorothea Löwen, late Schönemann, and Frau Susanna Mécour, late Preiszler, were very clever actresses, the former—born in 1732, and no longer very young—in the parts of gentle female lovers, the latter in *soubrettes*. The other newly engaged actors were numerous enough, but not very distinguished.

The most important of all the fresh engagements was that of Lessing. At first the new managers, who wished to announce their enterprise with great *éclat*, had wanted to engage him as permanent stage-poet. This, however, he declined at once and unconditionally. Then they conceived the remarkable plan of appointing him paid critic. He was to write all the theatrical notices of the Hamburg theatre, which the leaders were to publish at their own expense, paying Lessing a salary of 800 *Thalers* (about £120). And the result was *The Hamburg Dramaturgy*, a treasure of wit and learning— too noble a monument for a muddled and unsuccessful enterprise.

Lessing, who accepted the offer, partly because, as he said, he stood "idle in the marketplace and nobody would engage him," and partly because he thoroughly understood dramatic art, and took profound interest in it, soon saw that matters were not as they ought to be at this pretentious National Theatre, and that it would not last. As early as 22nd April 1767,[1] a month after its solemn opening, he wrote to his brother: "At our theatre many things are going on which I do not like. The managers are at variance, and nobody knows who is the cook and who the tapster."

This was precisely the case. Löwen, whose ambition was entirely disproportionate to his insignificance and superficial knowledge, had at once lost all his authority through his lectures, to which the actors did not care to listen, because he was no real expert, and he had to give them up very soon for want of auditors. As leader of the rehearsals on the stage he became a helpless prey to the impertinent questions of the performers, how such and such a speech was to be delivered, where they were to stand or to move. And this conceited writer, who in his books and periodicals had puffed himself up as a mighty authority

[1] The opening performance was *Olivet and Sophronia*, with a prologue delivered by Frau Löwen and an epilogue spoken by Frau Hensel, by which means the honours were equally divided between the two leading ladies.

10—Lessing (p. 115).

on the drama, on coming into contact with the practical requirements at once miserably collapsed.

Nor was Seyler, the careless bankrupt, likely to keep a tight hold of the economic reins. Frau Hensel displayed all her disagreeable leading lady caprices, broke with Lessing and persecuted him because of a very gallantly turned little reproach in his *Dramaturgy* [1] and sowed discord and disturbance everywhere. Ekhof worked for himself and his art, and the public was reserved and at a loss to understand what were the great things which Löwen had declared were going to happen but which never occurred. In short, a general dissolution set in even before things had had time to settle down. The *répertoire* was dull and indifferent; it had only one real treasure to boast of, Lessing's *Minna von Barnhelm*, which, however, was not so successful in Hamburg as it became shortly after in Berlin, although the acting was good.[2] But the management of the theatre was so inconsistent, that in spite of the high-flown proclamations about raising the German theatre

[1] In his review of Mme. de Graphigny's drama *Cénie*, Lessing wrote (20th article of *Hamb. Dram.*): "Frau Hensel is Cénie. Not one word from her mouth falls to the ground. What she says is not as if she had learned it; it comes from her own head, her own heart. She may speak or not speak; her acting goes on without interruption. I can only note one fault, but it is a very rare fault, a very enviable fault. The actress is too great for her part. I seem to see a giant handling the gun of a cadet. I should not mind doing anything if I could do it to perfection." The consequence of Frau Hensel's silly pride taking offence was that Lessing quite gave up expressing his opinions on the work of the actors, though he had always done it with as much politeness and prudence as in this instance, and had confined himself to their professional work.

[2] Ackermann's Sergeant Werner was universally admired, and though Ekhof was too old and too unattractive as Tellheim, there were excellent points in his acting. Borchers was much commended as the Landlord.

and abolishing the ballet, the leaders tried to attract
spectators by engaging artists who were to give an
acrobatic performance on the very evening when
Lessing's new play was to be acted for the first
time.

But under such a rule, with the literary amateur,
Löwen as standard-bearer of the ideal, and two bankrupt
merchants as financial guarantees, with confusion reigning
among the actors, the wisest of whom minded nothing
but their own business, matters were bound to go as
wrong as they did.   Only eight months after the opening
festivity the theatre had to close for the first time, and
though six months later a second attempt was made to
court success, it was only a short respite.   The proceeds
diminished day by day, and at last were so small that
the performances had to be stopped for several days.
Finally, on Nov. 25, 1768, the poor National Theatre
calmly breathed its last.   The person who had caused
both its birth and its death made a parting speech to the
public, and then with her lover and the remains of her
company went to Hanover, where the so-called " Seyler
Troupe "—Frau Hensel in the meantime had married
her friend—got on much better.

But Lessing wrote in the epilogue of his *Dramaturgy* :
" When the public asks, ' What has been accomplished ? '
and contemptuously replies, ' Nothing ! ' I ask in return,
' And what has the public done to bring about the
accomplishment of anything ? '   Nothing either, nay,
worse than nothing.   Not merely omitting to do anything to further the work, it has not even allowed it to
take its natural course.   What a *naïve* idea to give the

Germans a national theatre when we Germans are not yet a nation!"

No doubt Lessing was right. Nothing had been accomplished, and least of all by those who had boasted of their intention to create a national theatre. And very likely, if it had turned out otherwise, the Hamburg public would have shown no more sympathy with it. Nevertheless, something had indeed been done.

It was this : an opportunity had been given Lessing to publish his opinions on the drama and dramatic art, and these opinions were now spread all over Germany among the educated classes. The little pamphlets in which the *Dramaturgy* appeared created so much sensation, that to the author's annoyance they were at once pirated. All who were interested in dramatic art could now read them. Though the *Dramaturgy* neither is nor pretends to be a coherent and systematic work, and perhaps for the very reason that it consisted of short, occasional incursions, aiming its attacks just where they were wanted, it produced an immense and important revulsion in public taste regarding dramatic art, and in the public judgment on its essence.

First and foremost indeed, the work of Lessing was destructive. With bold strokes he demolished the clay feet of the idols which had so long been worshipped by the literary public of Germany. In those times it required much courage and great independence of mind to shake such an idol as Voltaire, and to show that he was by no means a great dramatic author. But in return for the French masters whom Lessing cheerfully massacred, he had no national celebrities to present.

He might have referred to his own dramas, but in his modest estimate of his own merit he did not take them into consideration.   But there was another man whom he constantly pointed out and ardently commended : Shakespeare.   To most people Shakespeare stood in the misty light of legendary vagueness.   Lessing asserted that the works of the great Englishman contained in abundance all that Voltaire and the other little French and German authors had blunted and diluted under the pretext of refining and modernising it.

To the development of the German drama Lessing's short critical articles were the pioneers of an important development, precisely because they were true criticism in the best and proper sense of the word. But with regard to the drama they were equally valuable, though the vanity of a hysterical actress soon wearied Lessing of criticising stage perform-ances, the dramaturgy contained a number of sparkling observations, which, in striking contrast to most things written by dramatic critics about the art of scenic repre-sentation, seem to be conceived by a professional actor. Lessing says of himself that he is neither an actor nor a poet,[1] but he criticises both dramatic poetry and dramatic art with an expert knowledge which, in the case of the latter, which he had never practised, was simply astounding.   And at a time when nobody had

[1] " Some people indeed now and then honour me by giving me the latter title, but that is only because they do not know me well.   They ought not to judge so generously from the few dramatic attempts I have ventured to make.   Not everybody who takes a brush in his hand and wastes colours is a painter. . . . I do not feel in myself the living source which works its way upward, and by its own power bursts forth in rich, fresh, pure jets ; I have to squeeze everything out by pressure." *Hamb. Dram.* : Epilogue.

ever been accustomed to see histrionic art made the object of critical treatment, much less by such a prominent authority, the effect of it was necessarily very great.

The *Hamburg Dramaturgy* also gave the impulse to the starting of many similar theatrical journals, periodicals, and so forth, and on the whole it may be considered as the mother of all German theatrical criticism.

Though in mentioning the individual actors Lessing always speaks of them with the greatest courtesy, it is easy enough to read between the lines that on the whole he was not satisfied with the mode of representation. "We have actors, but no dramatic art," he writes somewhere. "If in times long gone by such an art existed, we no longer possess it; it is lost, it has to be invented anew."

And this was precisely the fundamental defect of German dramatic art. There were individual actors of talent, but no really united acting, no leading principles, no inborn master-genius capable of combining the scattered elements of talent. Scenic art lived on a mixture of reminiscences of the Staatsaktion manner, Frau Neuber's method, the technique of Italian improvisation with a tincture of some genuine and strong ingredients due to Ekhof.

Ekhof indeed was still an isolated phenomenon. It is obvious enough from the *Hamburg Dramaturgy* that it was he who served as a model to Lessing, though from motives of policy he may have used equally commendatory terms about others. Nor can there be any doubt that the great critic received his conceptions of dramatic art through Ekhof.[1]

But Ekhof, though fond of commanding, did not naturally possess the mind of a great ruler. He was too cautious, too much afraid of outward responsibility, and too apt to go into details to be a good general leader. Otherwise it would have been natural if he had become the rescuer of the sinking National Theatre.

But this was not to be. Ekhof had still to roam about for years like a miserable juggler from one wretched stage to another till, when it had become too late for him to do anything in this direction, he found a secure haven worthy of him.

When the Seyler-Löwen enterprise had so pitiably failed, Ackermann had to come to the rescue and take up his theatre again. Young Schröder came back, and together with his mother seized the reins which he held so firmly and tightly that we can well understand why this state of things did not please Ekhof at all, and why he preferred, in spite of past experiences, to accompany Seyler and Frau Hensel to Hanover where they had succeeded in surreptitiously[2] acquiring a royal licence, a free theatre, and several other favours.

However, in spite of these most excellent terms,

[1] " What instruction the reader may find in this [Lessing's explanation of the mode of delivery in argumentative speech] is exclusively due to examples given by Herr Ekhof; I have attempted nothing but to make abstractions from what I have heard of him," Lessing says in *Hamburg Dramaturgy*, article iv.

[2] This is how Schröder afterwards justly qualified the Seyler-Hensel proceedings.

Frau Hensel succeeded in a remarkably short time in tiring the Hanoverians of her person by her incredible caprices and her rudeness to the public, because Ekhof's art was more enthusiastically admired than her own. So Ekhof had to travel about for some years with this badly managed company to small towns without suitable rooms, much less real theatres to play in, where the conditions were so miserable that the snow fell on the stage in winter, and in summer the sun shone in the actors' eyes through holes in the roof.

After two years Seyler was so reduced that it would have been impossible for him to go on if a relative of his had not offered to set the company on its feet again, on the express condition however, that Ekhof undertook the whole leadership and that Seyler abstained from all interference. The staff willingly assented to this arrangement, all except Frau Hensel, who sought and obtained an engagement in Vienna. Everyone, no doubt with the exception of poor Seyler, who was as infatuated as ever with his leading lady—was glad to see this troublesome woman take her struggles and victories to another arena, all the more so because the company possessed a talented substitute in grand tragic parts in Charlotte Henriette Brandes.[1]

By order and careful management Ekhof succeeded in tolerably restoring the affairs of the company, and just at this time he was lucky enough to receive an invitation for himself and his company from Anne

---

[1] Frau Brandes and her husband, a bad actor but an able author, had joined the Seyler company in Hamburg during the latter part of the National Theatre period.

Amelia, the clever and liberal Duchess-Regent of Saxe-Weimar, who engaged them to play in the Court Theatre at Weimar. Though this town was not yet what it was destined to become in the progress of German civilisation, it certainly must have appeared a paradise to the half-starved company. Here, apart from his domestic circumstances, which were as sad as ever, Ekhof spent some happy and comfortable years, which indeed he well deserved.

As a stage-manager,[1] however, he was far from being sufficiently large-minded and comprehensive in his views. He conducted the everyday work of the theatre with a pedantic and somewhat petty carefulness, but in the great outlines, especially in the choice of his *répertoire*, he lacked the spirit of enterprise and a just appreciation of the requirements of his time. He took up no important French or English novelties, not even the productions of his native soil; Lessing's last and Goethe's first play, the sensational adaptations from Shakespeare, if played at all, had to wait much too long and came lagging behind their appearance in the other theatres.

One reason of this over-cautious hesitation may have been that Ekhof, though his desire to play and to be the leader was quite unabated, had begun to lose his memory. He had difficulty in learning new parts, and even in old ones his memory might fail. The actor and author Brandes relates that one evening he

[1] According to the contract he managed the company during its stay in Weimar till 1772, when Seyler undertook the management. However, the above remarks about Ekhof's capacities as a manager apply also to his ater management of the Court Theatre in Gotha.

11

12

13

14

11—Charl. Henr. Brandes as Ariadne in Naxos (p. 121).
13—Fr. Ludw. Schröder as a young man (p. 131).

12—Joh. Chr. Brandes (p. 122).
14—Christiane Koch (p. 135).

broke down so completely in his part[1] that he lost all self-control and abused the prompter in face of the audience. Nevertheless, on this same occasion his art celebrated one of its greatest triumphs, for even when he had recovered, the audience naturally felt somewhat oppressed, and as Brandes says, "his fellow-actors also were put out. At this moment certainly Ekhof did not play *con amore*, but his pathetic accent, eloquent eyes and expressive face at once with magic power reawakened the warmest sympathy in the audience and called forth a flood of tears ; even his fellow-actors were touched, and it took them some time to recover from their emotion."

On the whole Ekhof was now considered old, though he was not so in years—on his arrival in Weimar he was only fifty-one. The wear and tear of life had told much on him, his health had always been delicate, and his physical qualities were often far from satisfactory, especially in the young lovers, whom he went on playing with undiminished predilection. Indeed, the critics, who used to exalt him above everybody else, were very hard on him in these characters. In Weimar, his Mellefont in *Miss Sara Sampson* was referred to in the following terms : "What foolish self-love and what slight judgment Ekhof must be possessed of, if he thinks he can convince us that he is the man for whose sake Miss Sara Sampson would commit a folly!" And the next year the same critic expressed his laconic criticism of

---

[1] It was a father's part in *The Duel*, a play by a clergyman Schlosser, which won fame in so far as it caused the great theological controversy between Schlosser and Goeze.

Ekhof's Tellheim in *Minna von Barnhelm* in the following words : " For shame, Miss Minna, what taste you have ! "

This critic, a certain Grossmann, who, by the bye, afterwards became an actor under Ekhof, who very kindly gave his assistance to his severe judge, acknowledged Ekhof as an incomparable actor of old men, but not of young dandies or passionate lovers, not of Nikander,[1] who travels about trading on his art of conquering women. " Nothing is more troublesome to Ekhof than kneeling, for which he has to make special preparations, for his knees are no longer flexible enough ; moreover, he does not stand firm on his legs, and therefore constantly stumbles in walking."

Ekhof, however, did not yield to these anything but flattering judgments, but went on playing his favourite parts, the seductive young men.   Even some years later he ventured upon the not very artistic *tour-de-force* of playing two parts in Voltaire's *Zaïre*, one of which was the ardent, passionate Orosman, thirty years of age, the other the octogenarian Lusignan ; this experiment, however, did not please the audience.

Strange to say, he was not very eager to keep his " old men " or " fathers " in the *répertoire*, though they always called forth the warmest applause.

Thus he did not care half so much to exhibit his Odoardo in *Emilia Galotti* as his Orosman or his *Gambler*, though contemporary experts cannot find words enough to express their admiration of his art in the former part.   With regard to Odoardo, he had a

---

[1] In Schlegel's *Triumph der guten Frauen.*

particularly flattering experience during the last period
of his theatrical life.

The pleasant stay in Weimar was suddenly broken
off by a fire which destroyed the theatre and part of the
castle (in 1774). The kindly Duchess, however, helped
the actors as well as she could, and sent them with a
warm recommendation to Duke Ernest of Coburg-Gotha,
who, to begin with, engaged them for three months.
From Gotha the company, conducted by Seyler, made
excursions to Leipzig, where Ekhof had acted in former
times with Koch's company, and where he met old and
new friends of his art.

Among the new ones was the well-known bookseller
Fr. Nicolai and his friend, the hot-tempered, capricious,
and somewhat rough J. J. Engel, author of *Ideen zu
einer Mimik* and other works. Afterwards he became
manager of the National Theatre in Berlin. It was
by acting Odoardo that Ekhof won the admiration of
this man, which happened in the following way. Engel
did not like *Emilia Galotti*, and had many arguments
with Nicolai about it. The latter maintained that if
only he saw Ekhof play it,[1] he would certainly be converted. At the first performance in Leipzig of this play
Nicolai persuaded Engel to go and see it, and at the
subsequent festivity, to which Ekhof was also invited, he
enjoyed the triumph of seeing Engel, who came later
than the others, rush up to him exclaiming: "I could
kill myself with annoyance that you are right after
all! . To understand *Emilia* entirely one must indeed
see Ekhof as Odoardo. What a devil of a

---

[1] Nicolai had seen Ekhof previously in Weimar.

fellow! He has set my blood boiling, I am in a ferment!"

The excited Engel was now told that the actor stood close by, upon which Engel embraced him most cordially. But immediately after he took a step backward, measured Ekhof from top to toe, and burst out, clasping his hands in amazement: "That little man never was Odoardo; he was eight inches taller, stout and strong!" upon which he again embraced the plain little man, and expressed his admiration of his thorough comprehension of Odoardo's character. Then Ekhof in the course of the conversation uttered these admirable words: "Most authors swim on the surface of the dramatic sea, because they have to gasp for breath so frequently. But Lessing dives deep, so the actor has to do the same if he wants to reach him." [1]

The vicissitudes of Ekhof's theatrical life were not yet quite at an end. "Principal" Seyler received an offer from the Saxon Court to make Dresden his permanent residence, and it was gladly accepted by him and Frau Hensel, who had by this time returned from Vienna. But Ekhof and several others much preferred to remain in Gotha with Duke Ernest, who, in order to retain them, promised to build a small permanent theatre at his Court—the first Court theatre properly so called. The Duke had been advised to take this step by the composer, Johann Friedrich Reichard, who was entrusted with the management of the theatre jointly with Ekhof. But the latter, of

[1] This episode is related by Nicolai in Iffland's *Almanach fürs Theater*, 1807.

course, became the stage manager, and it was he who in the main impressed his stamp on the theatre.

At this little playhouse Ekhof spent his last years as the highly respected and honoured manager of a Court Theatre. His circumstances were modest. His salary as actor-manager was only 12 *Thalers* (about £2) a week, and seven cords of fire-wood a year. But Ekhof was neither grasping nor extravagant; modest circumstances suited him very well. Though he achieved great things in his art, in private life he continued to be a humble citizen, contented with little, and comfortable without riches and luxuries.

During this period he wrote the following characteristic lines in an album :—

Lasz Garrick nur Guineen zählen ;
Mir wird es nie an Glücke fehlen—
So lang mein Fleisz gefällt, ich Zähren ernten kann,
Bin ich, obgleich nicht reich, doch ein glücksel'ger
    Mann.
Und wenn dereinst by meiner Gruft
Ein Kenner nur gerühret ruft ;
" Die Zähr, die er erzwang, soll hier freiwillig flieszen,"
So ehrt's mich mehr, als wenn mich Sammt und Stein'
    umschlieszen

(Let guineas roll as Garrick's fee,
I can without them happy be.
If my exertions pleasant seem and make tears in
    abundance stream,
Though I were never rich at all, you may indeed me
    happy call.

If by my simple grave some day
A friend of art be touched and say :
" The tears which oft he forced to flow, of free-will
   here I will bestow,"
A greater honour 'twere to me than velvet robe and
   gems would be.)

His leadership, indeed, bore the same unostentatious, somewhat narrow stamp.   He busied himself with great eagerness and accuracy on his little Court-stage, helped with his own hands to shift wings and scenes, instructed the young actors and conducted the rehearsals with much pedantry, but never exposed himself to the rising storm called forth by all the powerful voices of the new poets.   He created for himself and his circle a little world of art, where he worked like an old accomplished gardener with his pupils, under sheltering trees and within delicately ornamented walls ; but he never more ventured out into the great primeval forests.

Talented young men sought him, for his theatre was —next to that of Schröder—the best arranged and the most instructive.   Thus a year before his death no less than three of the best actors of the future, Beil, Iffland, and Beck, made their *début* on his stage.   He attached to his theatre such admirable actresses as Frau Starcke and Frau Hendel-Schütz.   And it was a great day in his life when the neighbouring Duchy of Weimar sent for him to play as guest in a private Court performance together with the Duke Karl August, with Goethe, Musäus, and other grand people.   Strangely enough, their choice had fallen on the fashionable English play,

Cumberland's *The West Indian.* Ekhof was the noble, somewhat lachrymose merchant Stockwell, father of the young West Indian scapegrace, Belcour, who was represented by no less a person than Goethe, in a white coat, blue silk waiscoat and silver-buttoned breeches, while the Duke had undertaken the young and gallant swordsman, O'Flaherty.

The worn and haggard actor, whose health was now far from good, was a guest in the house of Goethe, who treated him to his best wine, which was only offered on solemn occasions. He dined at the Duke's table, and was warmly greeted by his old patrons in this small and select assembly.

But this was indeed the last professional excursion of the actor who had been wont to travel so far and wide. His disease — probably phthisis — progressed rapidly, and though he tried to keep up his strength by all kinds of violent remedies, he succumbed to it about six months after his visit to Weimar, and died on 16th June 1778. He was only fifty-eight years of age, but as worn out and decrepit as an old man.

His last anxiety was about the foundation of a pension-fund for all German actors, a task which shortly before his death he recommended to the favour of his former enemy, Schröder ; and the last part he played was the Ghost in *Hamlet*, which he had after all introduced on his stage in Schröder's adaptation.

THE GREAT SCHRÖDER

I

Difference between Ekhof and Schröder—New Currents in Dramatic Literature—Important Companies in Germany—Koch and Döbbelin —The Vienna *Burgtheater*.

IF Schröder advanced so much further than Ekhof, both personally and generally, if he reached the climax of dramatic art in his country in the eighteenth century, this is not to be accounted for merely by the difference in their natural gifts and characters. They were indeed contrasts, even in their outward appearance ; beside Ekhof, the elderly little man with the almost deformed figure, the face prematurely furrowed and wrinkled by thought and grief, stood Schröder, with his tall, athletic and soldierlike figure, his elastic muscles well trained by all kinds of sport, his fair, smooth, ruddy complexion— the particular favourite of the gods ; and their characters showed corresponding differences.

Both were enterprising and almost passionate in their zeal. But while Ekhof in his eagerness and his love of work was apt to become petty, his thoroughness to turn into pedantry, and his aims to become too selfish, so that he lost the power of correctly judging his own capacities, Schröder showed a touch of greatness in his work, a power of concentration, the comprehensive view of a genius which, though he was conscious of his own value, showed him how to dispose himself without ever losing sight of the *ensemble*. Besides this he possessed a natural pride and courage which rendered him far fitter for leadership than Ekhof, who was not of a very daring disposition, and who in his outward life was contented with the circumstances of a humble citizen.

Nevertheless, Ekhof was, like Lessing, a pioneer ; he carried out the troublesome and insufficiently valued spade work, while Schröder, like Goethe, with the self-consciousness of a god, advanced on the well-paved road, and not merely because he was greater, but also because he stood on the shoulders of others, had a wider horizon and could reach more distant goals than his predecessors.

Outward circumstances, moreover, favoured him very much when it came to his turn to start on the great race for immortality.

In Germany there was just at that time a decided turning of the tide in poetic taste, and no less in men's views on the theatre. Lessing had broken the French idols and pointed to Shakespeare as the only true god for those who cultivated the theatre. Nobody had as yet ventured to present him on the stage in unadulterated form. He was too outlandish, too mighty and too puzzling for that. But the study of the great Englishman's dramas had become habitual with the young generation of poets, and had been a revelation to them. They drew a deep breath as they threw off the tight French stays, and cut the queerest dramatic capers, partly in their genuine and unbounded joy at escaping from the restrictions of the three unities, the stiff Alexandrines and other French refinements, partly in order to manifest at once their adherence to the dare-devil genius, which they thought was the distinguishing mark of Shakespeare.

The real pioneers of this "storm-and-stress" period were not of lasting importance either to the theatre or to literature, though some of their pieces were presented on the stage.   The very play, after which the period was named, *Sturm und Drang* by Max Klinger, appears ludicrous at the present time with its affected originality and absurd subject.

Indeed, the poet himself was quite aware that his efforts and those of his fellow-poets were only a transitory phase.   While Reinhold Lenz, the most violent, though also the most original of the "stormers," was ruined by dissipation and finally went mad, Max Klinger, the wisest of them, saw clearly that his work was only a struggle for emancipation, a search for a new national form of art.   With admirable clearsightedness he writes in the introduction to his *Theater* : "So far all the savagery has meant nothing but a search for a form agreeable to us! . . . Why model our theatre after French fashion, when we are Germans, and as the tinsel with which the heroes of Racine are loaded is so alien to our character?   Why after an English pattern, when we are very far from the exuberant, brilliant humour of this insular people?   A character full of simplicity, honesty, courage, perseverance, and obstinacy, goes home to the heart of the German people, whereas it does not know what to make of the gallant French, Greeks and Romans, nor the exaggerated caricatures of the English theatre. In short, the simplest form is probably the best."

The most important point was that a really artistic interest in the theatre was developing, that the eyes of all the young were fixed on it as the place where national art was to burst into bloom.   And the watchword on the stage was no longer, " Majestic bearing and the sacred rules ! " but *à la* Rousseau : " Liberty, truth and nature ! "

Young Schröder himself had practically experienced a *Sturm-und-Drang* period more wild and adventurous than anybody else's. The storm-tossed life and vicissitudes of his boyhood, the licentiousness of his youth, had left their marks on his character ; but his hot blood had an excellent regulator in the cool business instinct which he had inherited from his mother, though in him it never, as in her, degenerated into parsimony.

When the young, quick-witted actor and brilliant grotesque dancer contemptuously shook the dust of Hamburg off his feet and left the newly-established National Theatre, he at once turned his steps towards the place where he thought that his capacities would have the best chance of being appreciated. He sought and obtained an engagement with the well-to-do and popular, but not very refined company, which was travelling under the leadership of the far-famed—some people said : ill-famed— Viennese low comedian Joseph von Kurz, the creator of the Bernardon character, and author of the many burlesques in which this Hanswurst type was the chief personage, and which went by the title of *Bernardoniades.*

At that time Germany possessed very few theatres or companies which counted for anything. Besides the Hamburg National Theatre, which so soon dissolved into the Ackermann and Seyler companies, there were indeed only three which were considered good companies by experts,[1] viz. the Vienna Theatre and the companies of Koch and Döbbelin.

The name of Heinrich Gottfried Koch has been mentioned several times in these chapters. He was now an elderly man;[2] many years had passed since he was the factotum of Frau Neuber's company. As a manager he had followed a quiet and steady course and kept his head above water better than most others; always paying careful attention to the taste of the public and of the nobles, and conducting his company with strict economy and correctness, he had avoided the sharp crises through which most of his colleagues had passed during this difficult and disturbed period. His career had not been particularly brilliant, had shown no high ascents or deep falls; he had moved along the beaten track of simple esteem. Trained as he had been in the Neuber school, he had kept up in his company a certain pompous style and a Versailles daintiness in movement and costume which, though somewhat modified by the influence of Lessing, now at the beginning of the Rousseau-Lessing period, when naturalness was the watchword, appeared a little old-fashioned. On his stage Richard III.[3] dismounted from his horse in white silk stockings, and the anything but refined mediæval

---

[1] " Do you know any other which could come under consideration, with regard to which you could possibly have anything to communicate?" writes a correspondent (the publisher and *bel-esprit* Dyck of Leipzig) in a missive to Schmid's *Parterr*, p. 326.

[2] He was born in Gera in 1703.

[3] In Weisse's tragedy of that name; Shakespeare's tragedy was not on the *répertoire*.

women of the English court arrived from journeys in white hoop-skirts covered with gold embroidery, in low bodices and high powdered hair-dress.

But he had good actors, especially the excellent Johannes Brückner, who, educated in the school of Lessing[1] and Ekhof, may at that moment have been the best tragedian in Germany. His Mellefont in *Miss Sara Sampson* was even considered very superior to that of Ekhof. Afterwards Goethe's *Götz von Berlichingen* became his best character. In his wife, Christiane Henriette Koch, the old Director possessed an admirable, fresh, and powerful actress both in comedy and tragedy. Her splendid stage-appearance and sonorous voice were suited for *soubrettes* as well as for serious parts; among the latter, for instance, she was very successful as Marwood in *Miss Sara Sampson* and as the Queen in Weisse's *Richard III.*

However, the tragic leading lady *par excellence* was Frau Johanna Christine Starke (born in Breslau in 1732), a woman of a rich talent, particularly suited for emotional parts, which showed to especial advantage in mingled tragedy and tearful dramas. So long as the style of her time was still in fashion her reputation as the first *tragédienne* in Germany was disputed only by Frau Hensel; but both on the stage and in private life Frau Starke was more sympathetic; so while Frau Hensel reaped her greatest successes in female parts of a violent demoniac stamp, Frau Starke's strong point

---

[1] Originally Lessing had taken lessons of Brückner, but afterwards the relations were reversed, and Lessing cured his teacher of some of the Koch-Neuber pomposity to which he was addicted.

lay in sentimental characters, such as Cénie in the drama
of that name by Mme. de Graffigny, and as Miss Sara ;
later in maternal parts, such as Claudia Galotti, and
finally, when her tragic style became out of date, in
comic old women.

In light musical pieces, which were much cultivated
by the Koch troupe, Mademoiselle Steinbrecher was a
fine and elegant actress of the first rank.

Though Koch, like all contemporary German
" Directors,"[1] travelled about a good deal, he long
considered Leipzig as his headquarters. In this town,
however, which began to lose its reputation as the
centre of taste, he had to compete for popularity with
the newly-established Döbbelin company.

Karl Theophilus Döbbelin was a remarkable and
droll personage in the theatrical world.   He was the
prototype of the genuine German *Kulissenreisser*
("wing-splitter"), who for many years rendered the
German stage unsafe, and who only in quite recent
times seems to be dying out.   He was a tall, broad-
shouldered fellow with a bull-neck and a violent, roaring voice, and he made equal use of all these natural
"advantages" in all parts, without stint or distinction.
His mode of acting was invariably the same, whether
he played Richard III. or a comic peasant, and consisted chiefly in thundering out his speeches and rushing
incessantly about on the stage, filling the theatre with
noise and disturbance.   This boisterous acting was in-

---

[1] It had become old-fashioned to call the German theatrical managers
Principals, and the companies were no longer called *Bands*. A self-
respecting manager was called *Herr Schauspieldirektor*, a troupe was a
Gesellschaft and an actor a *Mitglied der Gesellschaft*.

15

16

17

18

15—K. Th. Döbbelin (p. 136).
17—Stephanie the younger (p. 144).

16—Mlle. Döbbelin (p. 138).
18—Joseph v. Kurz (p. 146).

tentional, and elicited much applause from the less refined part of the audience.

His character was good-natured, but he was stupid and an incredible braggart.[1] As an actor he had been travelling with various companies—originally with Frau Neuber during her declining period, afterwards with Ackermann and the harlequin-player Schuch. His public had always been among those whose applause is compelled by energetic and persistent noise and a running with sweat display of bodily strength. Having been fortunate enough to win a large sum of money at cards, he started a company of his own, with which, however, he was not successful to start with. But he gradually succeeded in working up the business by puffing advertisements and most reckless competition with his colleagues.[2] Döbbelin's productions in the way of advertisements, play-bills, addresses to the public, recall, nay almost exceed, the worst out-

[1] While he was staying with Ackermann, Schröder and the other young actors had much fun with him, both on and off the stage. They encouraged his boastfulness, and once egged him on to assert that he knew all the intricacies of the game of tarock, but not the cards. On another occasion he told them that one evening in playing Œdipus—in his usual way—he had kicked the heel off one of his shoes so hard that it flew up into a grand lady's lap, but she, carried away by his acting, did not find it till the next day in her pocket-handkerchief, which was wet with tears, and then sent it back to him.

[2] In Leipzig he went so far that when the Seyler company arrived there from Gotha (comp. above, p. 124), and was acting in a wooden theatre close to the Grimmai Gate, he spread the rumour that the theatre was tumbling down and dangerous to stay in ; and, this having no effect, he hired people to go secretly and cut to pieces some benches in the gallery. Afterwards, during the performance, they fell down and caused a panic among the audience and the actors, a panic which was stopped only by the coolness of Ekhof. A legal examination afterwards brought to light the real state of things. (Comp. J. C. Brandes : *Meine Lebensgeschichte*, ii. p. 179.)

rages of the *Staatsaktion* Principals.   Thus in advertising Weisse's *Romeo and Juliet* he wrote the following
amusing *Nachricht* (information) :—

"This tragedy without any doubt is one of the most
touching that have ever been acted on a stage, and in the
regularity of all details infinitely surpasses the same
tragedy by the English poet Shakespeare. . . . In fact,
all the parts in this piece are pathetic and well qualified
to procure honour for all actors.   The part of Juliet is
the most excellent.[1]   Her language is just like a fusion
of love and poetry (!) and betrays a very sensitive heart
and a mind nourished by all the flowery poets of Italy.
In the last act the scene represents the sepulchre of the
family of Kapellet, which is very elaborately painted."[2]

Döbbelin's staff was very defective, at any rate
during this period.   His best actress, and the only one
who distinguished herself from the rest of the company
by her taste and intelligence, was Frau Löwe, née Ling ;
but then she had been trained in the Koch company.
But the actress who figured as leading lady was Frau
Döbbelin, née Schulz, a handsome, charming and refined
woman, who was very ill-suited for the Döbbelin mode
of acting with wide-spread arms and screaming voice.

The other members were very inferior, and on the
whole this company was considerably beneath the contemporary companies of any note ; nevertheless it created
some sensation and found eager advocates among the
writers of pamphlets on the drama, who grew up like

---

[1] It was acted by Frau Döbbelin.
[2] Advertisement reprinted in a letter about the Döbbelin company to
Schmid's *Parterr*, p. 351 f.

mushrooms during this period. There exists a series of writings containing the whole literary controversy between the adherents of the Koch and those of the Döbbelin company,[1] and the partisans of Döbbelin, if not the cleverer, are by no means the less heated of the two sets. So he was allowed to the end of his days to stand as an appreciated and enthusiastic champion of the bad popular style. This, however, must be said in his favour, that he always aimed at high ideals, and therefore kept up a good *répertoire*, though it was not in his power to represent it artistically on the stage. When in 1765 he became an actor in the Schuch company in Berlin, which after the death of the respectable old Harlequin had become an utterly depraved band under the leadership of his coarse and dissipated sons, Döbbelin succeeded in a short time, though after a violent struggle, in getting proper plays acted, and in Berlin he was indeed considered as a purifier of taste and as the first serious actor that had been seen[2] there. Perhaps this was the reason why, later, when both he and Koch had settled permanently in the Prussian capital, he succeeded in keeping up the Berlin theatre undisturbed, and in doing so with a certain amount of ability.[3]

As to the Vienna theatre, its development differed

---

[1] A very sharp criticism in the letter to Schmid's *Parterr* quoted above called forth a whole series of extensive pamphlets, such as Contius's *Contributions to the Parterr*, a very badly written attack on Professor Schmid in Giessen, Hagen's much more important *Die Logen*, etc. These polemical pamphlets are now great rarities in the book world, and consequently not much known. However, they give many excellent contributions to the characterisation of Koch and Döbbelin, and ought to be quoted to a much greater extent than the scope of this work allows them to be.

[2] Comp. Hagen's defence of Döbbelin in his *Die Logen*, p. 44 f.

[3] He died a stage manager in Berlin at the age of sixty-six.

essentially from that of the other German theatres. A long time passed before the progressive movement from the old *Staatsaktion* and *Hanswurst* comedy to the regular play reached Vienna. It may have been on account of the close connection with Italy that the improvised comedy maintained itself quite unimpaired till about the middle of the eighteenth century, and acquired a peculiar national stamp through a most excellent and popular generation of comic actors, such as Stranitzky, Prehausen, Weiskern, and Joseph von Kurz, all of them champions of the "green hat," but each with his individual peculiarity.

Perhaps this jolly and genial popular theatre contained the germ of Austrian national dramatic art, but the outward conditions were not favourable to this popular comic style. The wind of the time came from another quarter, and finally in Vienna also mercilessly blew away the light thistle-down of improvisation, to make room for the more hardy shoots of the regular play.

The now celebrated Vienna Burgtheater dates from 1741. On the fourteenth of March in that year the Empress Maria Teresa gave permission for the use of a small tennis-court situated close to the Palace, as the Royal Theatre. It received the title of *Königliches Theater nächst der Burg*. But long before this there had existed another playhouse, the *Kärntnerthor Theater*. Both these theatres came under Royal supervision. This connection with the government, however, was by no means a sign of Royal favour. On the whole Maria Teresa took no interest in the theatre, and national popular comedy was in her eyes a horror and a disgrace.

Nor was she for many years present at the performance of any German play. Her first visit to such a play occurred as late as 1771.

In their administration the two Viennese theatres passed through a very stirring period. The leadership and the management was always changing. Now they were under magistrates and court-commissioners with endless appeals; now under the management of Italian adventurers; now under severe censorships and now under irresponsible actor-managers, and so forth. The history of the earliest period of the Burgtheater shows nothing but complications and confusion. At last a more solid organisation was established by the Emperor Joseph, who took much more interest in theatrical affairs than Maria Teresa had done. In the year 1776 the Burgtheater, from being a court enterprise under the crown, was changed into a national theatre, *i.e.* its financial arrangements came under the direct control of the crown, while the artistic leadership, after the pattern of the Comédie Française, was left to the actors themselves.[1] The Opera and the Ballet were abolished and exclusive attention was given to the German drama. The Vienna National Theatre was opened on 8th April 1776.

[1] Originally the leadership was put into the hands of a kind of general committee consisting of the older and more important members of the staff, who gave their votes on all questions concerning plays, cast, etc. The intermediate link between the general committee and the court superintendence was a so-called weekly manager or "*Wöchner*," one of the actors, who for a week was charged with the practical leadership, being subsequently relieved by one of his colleagues. This administration, however, was soon found unpractical, chiefly because the female members of the general committee were so troublesome that they had to be excluded from the meetings. Then a committee of five actors was established, chosen

With regard to its artistic development also, the Viennese stage had to pass through many trials, which began at the moment when regular dramatic art made its entry there.   This, however, did not happen till 1748, at the time when Koch and his wife, Heydrich and Mlle. Lorenz left Frau Neuber and went to Vienna ; but thenceforth a bitter and furious fight was carried on between the old champions of the improvised comedy and the new Leipzig school.   Both the administrative and the literary authorities sided with regular dramatic art and struggled against improvisation by means of the severest edicts of censure and punishment.[1]   However, the public and the lessees of the theatre favoured the old merry Hanswurst comedy, and the popular jesters scoffed at the new school *con amore* on the very stage.

Koch soon gave up the fight and returned to Leipzig with his wife to start a company of his own ; but Heydrich and Mlle. Lorenz remained in Vienna ; the latter obtained a first-class position at the Burgtheater as Frau Huber, afterwards Frau Weidner.

Vienna had its Gottsched in Professor Sonnenfels, who, as energetic and narrow-minded as his Leipzig

annually.   The members of this committee were originally called "Inspectors," afterwards stage-managers (*régisseurs*), and their domain included all the branches of stage leadership.   Under this form of rule the Burgtheater passed through its great artistic period, and the system still exists, though considerably modified by a bureaucratic literary committee of directors with many appeals, who again render the administration too complicated.

[1] To check the impudent sallies in which undeniably the Viennese comic actors were apt to indulge, a decree was issued in 1752 proclaiming that the first time an actor was guilty of uttering an indecorous jest, he was to receive a warning, the second time to suffer a fortnight's imprisonment, the third time lifelong incarceration.

predecessor, worked ardently for the regular play, and, taking advantage of his position as censor appointed by the Government, brought pressure to bear on the performers of improvised comedy. The latter retaliated by ridiculing the severe censor on the stage; but public opinion, of course, in the end declared in favour of the form of dramatic art which was now acknowledged in all other parts of Germany, and a new staff persistently refused to play in the old-fashioned *Hanswurstiades*.

The principal leaders of this new generation were the brothers Stephanie. Neither of them had considerable talent for acting, but both were well educated, possessed knowledge of the world, ability as authors, and the power of putting themselves in prominence. The elder brother, Christian Gottlob, was a tragedian, and his friends had made him believe that he resembled Lekain, the most celebrated tragic actor of the Théâtre français; so in his most sincere endeavour to reach his great prototype on the stage, he used to throw back his head, open his eyes unnaturally wide, and roar out his speeches always in the same manner. By exhausting himself in such furious acting he fancied he had attained the summit of art, and he succeeded in making part of the Viennese public share this belief. But judges of more experience and taste always found him artificial and rhetorical, though they acknowledged that he understood what he was saying, and had a certain command over the means which he had chosen to produce his effects.

On the whole, the tragic acting of the Burgtheater during these early times of the regular drama was very superficial, hollow, and declamatory, and at times taste-

less beyond measure.   Whereas in aftertimes the refined
Imperial and Royal Viennese Court Actors were celebrated for their exquisitely discreet, quiet, and delicate
acting, at the period of which we are speaking, Stephanie,
as the Prince in *Emilia Galotti*, after the death of Emilia
would seize the dagger and voluptuously suck her blood
in which it had been dipped.   Bergopzoomer, another
very popular tragedian, used to put soap into his mouth
before appearing on the stage, when he wanted to produce the highest effects of foaming dramatic frenzy.   As
late as 1775 Lessing, staying in Vienna on a visit, wrote
very discontentedly about the prevailing tragic style,
calling it " pompous and redundant."

As to comedy, the conditions were considerably better.
Stephanie, the younger, it is true, was a very monotonous
and coarse performer of old men, without grace or gentle-
manlike bearing, and without the power of expressing the
character of his impersonations, either by play or by
costume.   His prominent position at the theatre was due
to his knowledge of the world, his pleasant manners, and
his popularity as a dramatic author.   His military plays,
in particular, were popular all over Germany.   He had
been an officer himself, and as Lessing's military drama,
Minna von Barnhelm, had won such general favour,
Stephanie turned his personal experiences to account
by writing pieces of the same kind.   His *Recruiting
Officers* and *The Retired Officers* were on the boards
of all German stages.

But in the art of acting many others were his superiors,
such as the Jacquet family, among whom were the father,
a refined comic actor and *père noble*, and his two daughters,

Mad. Nouseul and Catty Jacquet, sincere and noble in their art, who at a somewhat later period introduced a more lofty tone into the drama and the higher tragedy ; the most excellent actor, Weidmann, who rendered low-comic parts with admirable truth to nature ; and the neat and pert, but somewhat indolent actor, Müller, who possessed some talent for painting, and who was a person of much account at the theatre, being afterwards entrusted with the duty of engaging new actors for the National Theatre.

II

Schröder with the v. Kurz Company—He undertakes the Leadership of the Hamburg Theatre—His Capacities as a Theatrical Manager—His first Period as a Leader.

JOSEPH VON KURZ, the principal champion of the old school, exceedingly popular as Bernardon, had been obliged to yield to the new taste. Von Kurz was a genuine Viennese, as light-hearted, dashing, and good-natured as his *Bernardoniades*, with nothing about him of the traditional clown, who off the stage suffers from the blackest melancholy, but a pleasant, easy-going *bon vivant*, unhampered by principles of any kind, and firmly convinced that the art of improvised comedy was infinitely superior to the stupid parrot-like repetition of other people's speeches. He was married to a beautiful, brilliant, black-haired, passionate Italian, the leading lady of his company, who reaped great and deserved applause when singing and dancing in the heterogeneous *répertoire* of the *commedia dell' arte*, but was less admired when she tried to accommodate herself to the modern taste and act regular tragic parts in her broken German.   It may, perhaps, have been some consolation to her that her husband was by no means more successful in his attempts in the serious line.

At the head of a merry and motley young company, consisting for the most part of South Germans and Italians, v. Kurz had gone into exile in the Rhineland, and was acting in the gay town of Mayence, when young Schröder entered upon his engagement with the company.

Schröder, who had been educated in supreme contempt of all jugglery and exaggerated courting of public favour, in a certain respect fitted badly into a company whose *répertoire* consisted essentially of pieces with such promising titles as the following :— *The Magic Drum of Orpheus, or Bernardon, the fortunate Possessor of Apollini's Plectrum, Comedy in three acts with Metamorphoses, Machines and Disguises; The Gnat Island or the Sparrow Magic, and Bernardon, the Mad Regens Chori, a Great Machine-Flying and Transformation-Comedy.*[1]

On the other hand he was admirably qualified to distinguish himself in the motley crew.   He proved at once to be a brilliant grotesque dancer; but what of his acting?   That was the great question.   Parts that were learned by heart counted for nothing with the chief.

---

[1] At the Theatrical Exhibition in Vienna, 1892, the Nurenberg town-library had exhibited forty-six play-bills of v. Kurz's company of 1766, immediately before it was joined by Schröder.   By far the majority of the announced plays belonged to the above-quoted category.   But here and there they are intermixed with some modern tragedies, such as *Miss Fanny*, by J. L. Brandes, and Kronegk's *Codrus*.

Was he able to improvise?—everything depended on that. Schröder's first appearance in improvised comedy was indeed anticipated with a certain suspense. With his usual self-sufficiency he had chosen one of the most famous and difficult Zanni-rôles, the valet in *Don Giovanni*.[1] And he at once struck the audience with surprise by reproducing from memory in his first monologue the speech of Molière's Sganarel in praise of snuff,[2] which was quite unknown to the v. Kurz company.

But later in the play the improvisation was genuine, and the words flowed from his tongue with a *verve* and ingenuity which took away the breath of his fellow-actors, especially of his master, Don Giovanni, young Bergopzoomer from Vienna, who had carefully studied and learnt his part by heart.

But in the wings stood the old expert *improvisatore* and clapped his hands with rapture, and when Schröder came out at last, followed by the joyous applause of the audience, he fell into the arms of his enthusiastic chief, who cried out emphatically, " *Mordio Sackerment !* That man is an actor! and beside him the others are mere ——! "

Though his stay with the v. Kurz company could have no improving or refining influence on Schröder, he would certainly have remained longer and felt more comfortable there than he did, if he had not, so to speak,

---

[1] In the v. Kurz company he was called Frontin ; at the Italian theatre in Paris his name was Harlequin and Trivelino ; in Molière, Sganarel ; in Mozart, Leporello. Comp. *Theatr. Art in Middle Ages and Ren.*, vol. ii p. 233 ff.

[2] Schröder knew it from a performance in Hamburg of the Italian Nicolini.

found too great favour, not only with the public, but still more with his associates.   He at once gained a warm admirer and friend in his comrade Bergopzoomer,[1] who was almost of his own age, and who was touching in his appreciation of his more gifted colleague.   This, of course, could only be pleasant and satisfactory to Schröder.

But the interest with which his northern beauty inspired Teresina v. Kurz, the beautiful, dark-eyed and passionate wife of his chief, brought him nothing but torments, especially as at the same time a young actress of the company, Johanna Richard, fell violently in love with him.   Exposed to this double fire, which was fanned into even fiercer flames by the burning jealousy of the Italian, Schröder, who was somewhat short spoken, and not particularly fond of women, felt anything but comfortable, and the quarrels and annoyances caused by this overwhelming and unrequited love were the reason why Schröder did not remain with v. Kurz for more than scarcely a year.

Johanna Richard, a young girl[2] whose love for Schröder was undoubtedly sincere, at any rate she had given it quite uncontrolled expression, afterwards married *par dépit* a ballet-master Sacco, who among other places had worked several years in Copenhagen.   The union did not turn out happy, but at a later period she obtained a very great position as actress in Vienna,

---

[1] Johann Baptist Bergopzoomer was born in 1742, and made his *début* in 1764 in Vienna, whither he returned afterwards, and obtained an important position at the Burgtheater.

[2] She was born in 1754, so was scarcely fourteen when she became acquainted with Schröder.

19

20

21

22

19—Johanne Sacco, *née* Richard (p. 148).
21—Charlotte Ackermann (p. 160).

20—Dorothea Ackermann (p. 158).
22—Christine Schröder, *née* Hart (p. 161).

where, to the close of the century, 1776 to 1793, she was the most shining and admired star of the Burgtheater.

Teresina v. Kurz probably consoled herself more easily. It is true that she was divorced from her husband in the following year, but this catastrophe was probably brought about by financial reasons. While Mme. Kurz continued the leadership of the company, v. Kurz shortly after their separation was recalled to the Burgtheater by the Italian adventurer, Giuseppe d' Afflisio, who was its manager at the time. However, the era of the *Bernardoniades* was evidently gone by in Vienna, and their originator was, so to speak, played out, though he started on new conquering expeditions.

Schröder, on the other hand, returned to his family circle in Hamburg, though by no means to a quiet domestic life, but to such work and such achievements as he had certainly never dreamt of while sowing the wild oats of his youth.

As was said above, the grand enterprise of the Hamburg National Theatre collapsed almost immediately after having been so pompously started, and old Ackermann, though thoroughly tired of the theatrical business, had had to resume the leadership of his company. But even during his lifetime most of the work was left to his wife and stepson, and the latter at once tightened the reins considerably, and in spite of his youth ruled the theatre with an energy that was considered reckless by many, even by his stepfather, and to which, of course, the actors were quite unaccustomed.

It was not, however, till after the death of Ackermann that the young chief fully realised what great heights might be attained, and came into possession of the power to work for his ends. "Good Ackermann," as he was generally called, the deserving, excellent actor and amiable, generous chief, closed his tired eyes on 13th November 1771, and a new era began, not only for the Hamburg theatre, but for German theatrical art in general.

The responsibility laid upon the shoulders of the young man seems to have produced a change in his character. In the body of the smart, overbearing and athletic sportsman the mind began to grow. If we examine the portraits dating from the successive periods of Schröder's life, this mental growth seems almost perceptible. After the superficial beauty of his smooth-faced early youth, where his face is like a *tabula rasa*, the soul shines out more and more, giving depth and expression to his eyes and, so to speak, remodelling his features, imparting firmness to his mouth, and calm reflective power to his forehead and the outlines of his face.

It seems that when he took matters into his own hands, with his mother as financial guarantee, his purpose was at once clearly settled. His life in Hamburg had gained him friends among literary men, and a warm and lively poetic sense, which he had hitherto lacked, had awakened in him. He felt that the important thing now was to bring literature and the theatre into close contact. He admired Lessing, and his first great achievement as independent manager was to produce Lessing's newly-published *Emilia Galotti* on the stage in the most perfect manner possible. Even dearer to his heart were the wild "stormy" geniuses, and his favourite among them was Lenz, the wildest of all, whose play *The Tutor*—which was considered impossible as a stage-play—it was his dream to have performed, and which he really did present on the boards. He was the first in Germany to act *Götz von Berlichingen* by the young Goethe, a year after its publication as a play in 1774, and what a revolution this meant as to mode of acting, costume and scenery, can only be fully realised by one who has a clear idea of the conventionality of theatrical art in those times. Even Ekhof played Canute the Great in Schlegel's *Canute* in a red velvet coat, full-bottomed wig, with a hooked cane hanging over his left arm. In *Götz* these remnants of a vanished French court-style had to be abandoned; powder, lace and dancing-master gestures would have been too incongruous with the gloomy, clinking armour and the curt language, so Götz with his iron hand tore the artificial wigs off the actors' heads.

But above all, it was the great English poet that haunted Schröder. Indeed, to all Germans who took an interest in art, the name of Shakespeare meant youth, originality and genius; but to the general public he was entirely unknown, and it was considered a great venture to produce him on the stage. Schröder hesitated for some years, but then he broke the ice and launched Shakespeare's plays one after the other, and the great stir made by these performances contributed more than anything else to the awakening of the German people to a sense of the ideal side of art.

Indeed, the 20th of September 1776, when Hamlet

made his first appearance on the German stage,[1] marks a turning point in German theatrical history, a much more important one than any performance of a national play had hitherto formed.   And it was a very fortunate hit of Schröder to choose *Hamlet* to introduce the Shakespearean era, for no other play and no other figure had so great a chance of attracting and fascinating a German audience as this brooding Danish prince, who satisfied its love of poetic dreaming and deep reflection ; and to the young generation of those times Hamlet in his gloomy atmosphere of despair and distraction stood as the ideal of a modern " stormer."

If Schröder had begun with *Othello* instead of *Hamlet*, and if he had allowed himself to be discouraged by the exceedingly sorry fate which befell this tragedy eight weeks after the performance of *Hamlet*, it is difficult to say whether Shakespeare would have been adopted so soon as a classic author on all German stages.   Certainly Schröder was not easily frightened ; he possessed a quality which is indeed rare and invaluable in a theatrical leader : courage.   After the fiasco of *Othello* he wrote very calmly to a friend : " The Moor of Venice has frightened the Hamburgers too much.   Now I have taken up Macbeth."

On the whole, it is marvellous to see what great things Schröder's love of Shakespeare enabled him to accomplish. In the course of four years—from 1776 to 1780, when his

---

[1] A few years earlier, it is true, an attempt had been made in Vienna, on 16th January 1793, with a performance of *Hamlet*, but it had turned out a failure and a burlesque, and therefore had remained without effect.   Curiously enough, some English comedians had acted *Hamlet* in Hamburg as early as 1625.

first period as a leader came to a close—he played, besides *Hamlet* and *Othello, The Merchant of Venice, As you like it, King Lear, Richard III., Macbeth, Henry IV., The Comedy of Errors, Much Ado about Nothing,* and *The Taming of the Shrew,* altogether eleven plays, every one of which was a revelation to the public that now crowded the Hamburg theatre, no longer as an indifferent and chance assembly who wanted to kill a few hours, but as an ardent, responsive audience, ablaze with intelligence and thought!

If we desire to form a just appreciation of the import-ance of these Shakespearean performances to the best men of the time, we may read, for instance, in *The Labyrinth*, by Baggesen,[1] of the author's delight at having had the opportunity of seeing *King Lear.* He writes : " Shortly before Klopstock came they had brought me the play-bill. Imagine my joy at reading *King Lear*! In my rapture I jumped up from my chair and upset the above-mentioned ink-stand. *King Lear*! the masterpiece of Melpomene, Shakespeare, and Schröder! *King Lear !* The Polar Star, the object and climax of all my theatrical desires! On my way hither I had settled with Cramer that I should beseech Schröder to act this play once during our stay here— and now—the very first day—a benevolent fate offered it unasked. Indeed that was more than could have been expected."[2]

Yet Schröder was by no means partial in his *répertoire*

---

[1] A Danish poet (1762 to 1826).

[2] Baggesen's *Labyrinth* appeared in 1792, but it was in 1789, during Schröder's second period of leadership, that Baggesen visited Hamburg.

during his first glorious leadership. Anything that seemed
to be of interest to his time was presented, such as the
pieces of the actor Brandes, popular at the time, but now
forgotten, Schmid's *Royal Favour*, a huge success, Goethe's
Clavigo, Cumberland's *West Indian*, etc.   Even ballets
and light musical pieces were kept up.   Sacco was engaged as ballet-master, so that Mme. Sacco, late
Johanna Richard, Schröder's former adorer, now again
came in contact with the much admired man—and
Schröder, as well as his sisters, and all in the company
who had the necessary qualifications, constantly appeared
as dancers.   It must have been surprising to see the
actor who one evening had awed you as the ghost in
Hamlet, or as Shylock, the next evening delighting the
pit by a grotesque dance.   Schröder himself did not give
up dancing till 1778, the year when he began acting
King Lear.   If he continued dancing so long, and compelled his sisters to do the same, it was not from a vain
desire to shine in all branches; on the contrary, he had
long been tired both of the ballet and of several of his
other parts, but from a business point of view he felt he
could not dispense with himself as the brilliant dancer
and popular low-comedian he knew himself to be, even
after his capacities as a tragic actor had manifested
themselves.   And the business side had to be kept in
view as well as the artistic one.   Not for the sake of his
personal profit, for Schröder had no share in the profits
—the enterprise was still his mother's—but for the sake
of honour the work had to be done.

     And, indeed, Schröder taught his people to work.
As yet the genuine art of acting in concert—the *ensemble*

—was an unknown thing on the German stage, except in the special *genre* of the old improvised comedy. Schröder was the first to understand how to impart *unity* to a performance. He always began by reading the new play to the actors, and as he possessed an admirable gift of characterising the different parts during the reading, he at once imperceptibly imparted his own conception of them to the actors. He had introduced this method when taking up the study of *Emilia Galotti* during the first year of his leadership, and kept it up ever after. In weaker, more mechanical plays, such as *Royal Favour*,[1] it was this masterly *ensemble* which produced the great effect upon the audience.

Strict order and punctuality prevailed in private at the rehearsals and performances, and on the stage the actors vied eagerly with each other in aspiring to perfection in their art; the public was enchanted and showed an unprecedented enthusiasm for the theatre. Among the spectators a select staff of *connoisseurs* came into existence, "a public in the public, a state within the state, a pit within the pit," as it was called by Schütze, a secretary of the Danish Chancellery at the time, who belonged to this little circle of amateurs. These experts usually sat in the front rows of the pit, and the general public silently yielded the place to this artistic Areopagus, although it was self-constituted, so that when one of them came late, the person who in the meantime had occupied his seat, willingly gave it up to its usual occupant. This

---

[1] A tragedy about the Earl of Essex, which the dexterous dramatic author, Prof. Schmid, had manufactured out of four English dramas about Essex (those of Banks, Brooke, Jones, and Ralph).

fixed circle consisted of scholars, lawyers, civil officers, and merchants, who on their travels had seen other theatres, all united by their common interest in dramatic art. Of course, this established clique, an institution hitherto quite unknown in the theatrical world, obtained a strong influence at the performances, they "applauded the good new plays or well acted scenes or finely delivered speeches ; they enforced quiet, order and silence, when voices among the audience, whether from the boxes or from the gallery, uttered unjust praise or malicious blame or committed other improprieties." [1]   Such an established clique, of course, had its dangers ; it may easily become tyrannical and partial ; but nowadays, when it exists nowhere in the world, and when all European theatres are filled with a chance public, who as a rule seek nothing but amusement, one may now and then feel inclined to sigh with regret for this little faithful, and always vigilant, flock that listened with strained attention, and on whom no word, no change of expression, no gesture was lost.

Those who witnessed the first period of Schröder's management assert that it was indisputably the most glorious period of Hamburg theatrical history, and anyone who compares it critically with other epochs in German theatrical life must come to the conclusion that neither Schröder himself during the later period of his career, nor any other leader of the same century, rose as high as Schröder did during these eight years.

[1] Schütze : *Hamburgische Theater-Geschichte*, p. 399.

III

Schröder's Company—Dorothea and Charlotte Ackermann—Schröder as
Actor—His King Lear—Other Parts.

THE company that was attached to Schröder during this
glorious period was—or rather, became—probably better
than any other which had yet been seen in a German
theatre.   Among the members of his own family was his
mother.   Though, when she was fifty-eight years old,
when her son took over the sole leadership and had long
been tired of acting, she undertook one of her best, though
also her last, new part, that of Lady Rusport in Cumberland's *West Indian*, the very first performance in the
new *régime*.   The same year she retired quietly, but
definitely, from the stage after her long and eventful
artistic career.

But now came the turn of her two daughters,
Schröder's stepsisters, to shine forth in all their power.
They differed very much in character and talent, as
well as in looks.   Dorothea, the elder of the two,
though only twenty years old,[1] could already look back
on a tolerably long, and by no means smiling career.
Having been forced on by her manager-parents in parts
that were far beyond her young capacities, she had, even
as a child, been very harshly treated by the public, and
especially by the critics ; so now, when public favour
smiled upon her, she was disillusioned, sick of the theatre.
She was one of the very rare instances of an actress unit-
ing great capacities for the stage with a genuine aversion

[1] She was born in Danzig on 12th February 1752.

to it.   The reverse is much more frequently seen.   If
her brother's violent energy and unbending will had not
urged her on—whipped up her talent, so to speak—she
would certainly have left the theatre even earlier than
she did.   Now, under his leadership, she became an
admirable actress, of whom we may say that she was
serviceable in all branches, and on the stage her dislike
of acting was not noticed.   She was tall and exceedingly
well proportioned, had a piquant, very expressive face,
which, however, was now and then a little marred by a
bitter line about the mouth.   Her voice was gentle and
sweet, but not strong, her training excellent, enabling her
to appear in ballets as well as comic operas, tragedies
and comedies.   She was most fascinating in the young,
roguish, female lovers of Marivaux and Goldoni, and her
Countess Orsina (in *Emilia Galotti*), Marie (in *Götz*),
Elizabeth (in *Royal Favour*), Ariadne (in the monodrama
of that name by Brandes) were admirably conceived, and
performed with the most delicate art.   Unfortunately for
the theatre and for the Hamburg public, whose high
admiration she had won, she retired from the stage at
the age of twenty-six in order to marry a Dr Unzer.

The theatrical career of her younger sister, the idolised
Charlotte, was even more brilliant and of still shorter
duration.   This most fascinating child, who, at the age
of only seventeen, held the position of the most wonder-
fully-gifted and admired actress in Germany, had, as a
matter of course, like all these children of the stage who
were born and bred in the companies, began working as
a small child.   She was born during a stay at Strasburg,
on 23rd August 1757, and as early as 1761, when only

four years old, she had acted in Karlsruhe the part of
the little girl Louison in Molière's *Malade imaginaire*.
Thenceforth she had scarcely been off the stage. She
was one of those rare and delicate plants which now and
then grow up in theatrical hot-beds, and in whom the
genius of art unfolds itself—we know not how or why—
unaccountably, but pure and wonderful, like the delicate
perfume of a rose.

She was small—smaller than her sister—and fair-
haired, light and slender, with large, dark-blue eyes. It
is difficult to form a distinct idea of her face, for the
portraits extant differ so much that we can scarcely
believe they are likenesses of the same person. The
descriptions, however—which are so enthusiastic that
even the smallpox marks that marred the faces of both
sisters are mentioned in terms of admiration—take for
granted that she was no regular beauty, but that she
exercised her spell by the brilliancy and pathos of her
expression. On the stage she was entirely guided by
inspiration, acting upon her unerring instinct, which
never needed reflection or training in the ordinary
sense of the words, as everything came, as it were, of
itself, and with a quickness and self-command that
belong only to the born genius.

Like her sister she played everything, but their
brother with his iron strength laid the capacities of his
sisters under heavy contribution. The general rule was
to study between twenty and thirty parts in a season, but
the choicest flowers of Charlotte's genius were probably
the grave and delicate female characters. Schröder
thought she was at her best as "die bange Rutland"

in *Royal Favour* and as Adelheid in *Götz*. But in all parts she was the idol of the Hamburgers, and when death carried her off before she had completed her eighteenth year, she became their Saint. Schröder, at the same time, was not very far from appearing a devil, because rumour accused him of having caused the death of the much-admired young actress, or rather of having by his severity driven her to suicide.

A whole romance was concocted round her sudden death, with a mysterious love affair, and so forth ; and there was great indignation against the Schröder family. The naked truth probably was that the Schröder-Ackermanns were a combative and nervous race, in whose home skirmishes were the order of the day. That a quarrel preceded the death of Charlotte, is a fact. Schröder flew into a rage over a ballet costume which his sister had put on, and which he considered indecent. He complained of her to the severe mother, who was as strict in her domestic as Schröder in his professional discipline, and Charlotte, on her return from the theatre, was treated with great coldness and severity. She was very sensitive, and for other reasons had been melancholy for some time ; and despair at this harsh treatment drove her out of her mind. Next day she was ill, and in spite of all the efforts of the doctors who had been called to her assistance, she died the following night. Whether she committed suicide can never be definitely ascertained, but much that has come to light since seems to point in that direction. At any rate her death hung like a dark cloud over the Schröder family, though none of them felt directly guilty or remorseful.

Schröder had found a good support and quiet help-mate in his young wife Christina, née Hart,[1] whom he married in 1773. A graceful little fair-haired dancer, Christina Hart had joined the Schröder company, while they were acting in Celle, trying to cheer up the sad heart of the unhappy Queen Caroline Mathilda.

By her gentleness and true German womanliness the young child of the stage at once charmed both Frau Ackermann and Schröder, who agreed in a very homely taste with regard to women ; and afterwards, when her husband placed her in the front rank of his company, it was by these very qualities that she pleased the less exacting portion of the public in a number of important parts, while the more fastidious spectators found her insignificant and without artistic individuality. In fact, in theatrical history she never became anything but Schröder's wife, and, no doubt, Baggesen (the con-temporary Danish poet mentioned above), hits the mark best in saying of her, after having visited the Schröders in their stylish home in Hamburg : " Her proper part, and perhaps her only one, is that of a wife, a mistress of the house, a hostess—off the stage."

The chief corner-stone of the company was, of course, Schröder himself, yet he was by no means an actor-manager in the usual sense of the word, least of all one of those prima-donna-like, vain theatrical leaders, whose abuse of their power nowadays leads to abominable artistic results. Though very self-conscious and self-

[1] Anna Christina Hart was born on Nov. 9th, 1755, in St Petersburg, of German parents. She was trained in Scolary's dancing school, and had been a member of the second-rate Wäser company.

asserting, he was quite free from the particular form of professional mania which makes its victim imagine that every leading part must needs be acted by himself or herself.   Schröder says : " The question with me is by no means to shine and to be in the front, but to *be* the character I represent and to fulfil my part adequately. I want to give to each *rôle* its due, neither more nor less."   And as these were not mere words in his mouth, he chose for himself a careful and gradual development, progressing from the somewhat one-sided, light comic art, which he had cultivated in his early youth, through greater, more complicated parts, to the greatest, most delicate reproduction of human character.   It may be mentioned, as an example, that when producing *Hamlet* on the stage for the first time, he did not take the part of the hero himself, though he afterwards proved quite capable of acting it, but gave it to the talented actor Brockmann, whose name thus became attached to one of the most important events in the theatrical history of the time, while Schröder cast himself for the smaller but difficult part of the ghost.   When *Emilia Galotti* came on the boards he took for himself the accessory character of Angelo, and it was only in deference to the remonstrances of his friends and colleagues that he afterwards undertook Marinelli, the great *rôle d'intrigant*, and not till still later, when he felt quite ripe for the part, that he played Odoardo with supreme tragic effect.

By this enforced gradual training Schröder, imperceptibly and without over-exertion of energy, reached his great, his, so to speak, almighty, mastery of his art.   And as a fully matured actor, he could say without presumption

23

24

23—Brockmann as Hamlet. A Hamlet Performance by the Döbbelin Company.
24—Schröder in his mature age (p. 164).
From a print by Chodowiecki (p. 162).

to his friend and later biographer Meyer : " It appears
to me that only he has reached the standard of true art
who conceives each character in such a way that nothing
alien enters into it, that it not merely suggests a type,
but distinguishes itself from kindred characters by
individual features, which the performer finds in his
own experiences, and by which he meets the desires of
the author.   This is what distinguishes the actor from
the good reader or reciter.   The latter may quite well
satisfy the spectator as long as he has not compared him
with the former.   But as soon as the actor appears, the
spectator must feel that the reciter only reminded him of
the person whom he now actually seems to see before his
eyes. *This point I think I have reached.   I believe that
I am capable of expressing everything that a poet true to
nature has intended to express by the words and actions of
his characters;* and I hope that by consulting no other
mirror than that of the truth, I shall be able to satisfy
the reasonable demands of a judge of human character." [1]

Schröder acted altogether seven hundred parts.   If we
enumerated them the majority of them would mean
nothing whatever to the modern reader ; so entirely
unknown are the plays which dominated the stage in
those times.   So short-lived is the immortality that falls
to the lot of the average dramatist !

Who, except the learned student, reads nowadays
Klinger or Lenz ?   Who knows the plays of Stephanie,
Brömel or Schröder himself ?   They are as completely
forgotten as those of Capus, Sudermann or Pinero will
be a hundred years hence.   Among the arduous works

[1] F. L. W. Meyer, *Fr. L. Schröder*, i. 337 f.

of a generation two or three plays may succeed in keeping above water and hold on to the steep and treacherous rocky shore of the stage ; all the remainder are mercilessly swept away by the ever rolling waves of oblivion.

But if out of this extremely heterogeneous gallery of about seven hundred figures we try to form a general idea, the first impression that strikes us is that of a universal mastery. To dramatic art the figure of Schröder stands in the same relation as one of the great masters of the Renaissance to the arts of painting and sculpture. Just like one of those splendid old geniuses, in whom the artist and the artisan had melted into a higher unity, he mastered everything that belonged to his profession : dancing, playing, singing, fencing, acrobatic feats, at the same time embracing all branches of acting, from the most utterly grotesque to the deepest tragical parts. It certainly was not like the amateur's dabbling a little in everything, but a real and thorough penetration into all the secrets of his profession.

As a master in his art Schröder in his own country became the typical expression of his time. For the eighteenth century marks a kind of renaissance in dramatic art ; it is the time of the great masters, just as our own time is that of specialists.

Nevertheless—in spite of his wonderful, gigantic powers—which allowed him in *Hamlet*, for instance, to play the ghost, Hamlet, the grave-digger and Laertes, all with equal perfection, there were some kinds of figures, some human passions, to which his physical and mental gifts naturally enabled him to give a deeper and particularly perfect expression.

The gentlest, most delicate and pathetic lyric notes were not in his line. The dominant features of his character were a will of steel, a clear intelligence, and a healthy naturalness, and these qualities came out in strong relief against the dark background of a choleric and passionate temperament. His tall, long frame, his large, expressive face, his voice, which had originally been a high tenor, and had been forced down by his own efforts to a deeper and more sombre pitch, distinguished him as the *man* on the stage, and all that art could make out of the mental and physical personality of a healthy, strong and passionate man became his achievment as an actor.

According to contemporary testimonies he rose highest in his King Lear; *his*, for it was not quite Shakespeare's. In the prose adaptation by Schröder himself, the first three scenes of the play were left out, and he showed Lear on his first appearance [1] as an old ruler in full possession of his powers, whose rugged energy was subsequently broken by the ever more furious collision with the hardheartedness of his children.

The modern actor in a civilised country can no longer indulge in such vagaries over Shakespeare; he must try to adapt himself as closely as possible to the intentions of the great poet; and therefore he must from the beginning show Lear with the stamp of senile madness, which Shakespeare has intentionally given him. Thereby the character becomes outwardly less grand, less gigantic, less commanding, but not less

---

[1] Act I. sc. iv. in Shakespeare. Lear: "Let me not stay a jot for dinner; go, get it ready," etc.

pathetic, and especially not less intelligible in the general poetic idea of the play.

However, as modified by Schröder, this marvellous character was most admirably suited to his artistic individuality, and also to the idea, which at that time prevailed in Germany, of Shakespeare as the violent, gigantic mind, the wild, unreflecting natural genius; and the character, as Schröder represented it, became an unsurpassed and immensely effective masterpiece, equally thrilling to the select few and to the general public.

Schröder's contemporaries in Germany have written much about his performance of Lear, all in the strongest, most enthusiastic terms—though, of course, he also had his adversaries, who exalted very inferior actors at his expense. Among Danish writers, too, he had found enthusiastic admirers. Thus Baggesen, in his *Labyrinth*, devotes a whole, very readable chapter to *Lear*, though it is rather a description of the effect produced on himself by Schröder's performance than a distinct statement of the artistic means by which the actor obtained his success. This is how he depicts the entrance of Schröder :—

"The way he entered, his mere presence, his face, his gait, gave me the thrill which nature in the embrace of art never fails to conjure up. And then his tone, his delivery, the movements of his head and arms, his facial play—the truth with which his voice, eyes, hands and feet rendered every speech! I never saw the like of it, nor shall I ever see it till I once again see—Schröder as King Lear. . . . I doubt if dramatic art ever showed, shows, or will show anything more perfect than Schröder's rendering of his part. Nature itself has bestowed on him a frame, face and voice so perfectly suitable to it, that if we were to form an ideal of Lear, it would be impossible to imagine him otherwise—and the art with which from beginning to end he turns to account this fitting frame, this appropriate face, this voice so happily suited to his parts, is the triumph of critical sense, theory and practice.   It is impossible for me to give examples, and to point out the places in which the correctest delivery, the most natural movements, and the most convincing gestures combined in the most refined harmony not only to reproduce, but to embellish the part— I should have to repeat it from beginning to end, and to write out all the speeches." [1]

After the performance a mutual friend accompanied Baggesen up to Schröder's tiring-room, as the poet wished to express his gratitude to the artist.   But though Schröder was now in complete *négligé*, Baggesen was still so overcome that he truly felt as if he had the genuine English King Lear before him, so he made a most reverential bow, and after a few minutes retired backward out of the room without having been able to pronounce a word.

Even on his fellow-actors in the play, Schröder sometimes produced the strongest impression.   When acting this part at a guest-performance in Vienna, he frightened the actress who performed Goneril so terribly with his curse [2] that she, who had previously acted this part

---

[1] Jens Baggesen, *Labyrinthen.*   Copenhagen, 1792, i. 155 and 160 f.
[2] In Act I. sc. iv.—
  " Hear, nature, hear ! dear goddess, hear !
  Suspend thy purpose, if thou didst intend
  To make this creature fruitful ! " etc.

repeatedly with Brockmann, now begged to be excused for ever after from exposing herself to the terror into which Schröder had put her.

Among other well-known parts created by Schröder, we may note the following of Shakespeare's : Macbeth, Shylock, Falstaff, Richard II., and Iago ; among Molière's his Miser was particularly celebrated, but even this play was considerably modified according to German taste ; besides this part he acted Arnolphe in *L'Ecole des Femmes*, Orgon in *Tartufe*, *Le Malade imaginaire*, etc. In Lessing's *Emilia Galotti* he played successively Marinelli, Angelo, and Odoardo ; in *Minna v. Barnhelm* Paul Werner was one of his best parts. Goethe and Schiller never obtained a prominent place in Schröder's theatre ; however, he played Carlos in *Clavigo*, no less than three of the numerous parts in *Götz v. Berlichingen* (Brother Martin, Lerse, and the Chairman of the Secret Board of Justice), as well as Philip II. in *Don Carlos*. But Wallenstein, which would have seemed the very thing for Schröder, and in which, moreover, Schiller very much wished to see him,[1] he never acted.

[1] In the Prologue of *Wallenstein* we read the following lines :—

"O ! möge dieses Raumes neue Würde
Die Würdigsten in unsere Mitte ziehn,
Und eine Hoffnung, die wir lang gehegt,
Sich uns in glänzender Erfüllung zeigen.
Ein grosses Muster weckt Nacheiferung
Und giebt dem Urteil höhere Gesetze."

("O, may the new worth of this hall draw the most worthy into our midst, and may a long-cherished hope be most gloriously fulfilled. A great model tempts to emulation and gives higher laws to judgment.")

This was an invitation on Schiller's part as amiable and delicate as direct, to come to Weimar and act *Wallenstein*, an invitation which Schröder never accepted, though it was repeated in the most flattering and pressing terms.

25

26

25—Schröder as Falstaff (p. 168).   **26**—Brockmann (p. 172).

Besides these he performed a large number of leading parts in modern plays, such as Bernau in *Misanthropy and Repentance*, Count Klingsberg in *The Ring* and in its sequel *The Unhappy Marriage from Delicacy*, two adaptations by Schröder of Farquhar's originals; O'Flaherty in Cumberland's *West-Indian*, etc.[1]

IV

Schröder resigns his Leadership in Hamburg and goes to Vienna—His Influence there — Return to Hamburg and Second Term of Leadership.

SCHRÖDER played all the most important parts of his great *répertoire* during his first eight years as manager in Hamburg, displaying a power of work which was simply marvellous. He acted up to thirty-nine new parts annually, and had on his hands the whole artistic and financial management, besides during the same period adapting, translating, and composing twenty-eight plays.

Nevertheless, it was by no means fatigue that caused him to lay down the sceptre which he had wielded with so much honour.

The reasons were manifold, above all the financial. The business management continued to be in the hands of his mother, and—as has been observed elsewhere— old Frau Ackermann was no spendthrift. Though during his management her son had about doubled the amount

[1] In Meyer's old Biography, ii. pp. 139-159, we find a tolerably complete list of Schröder's parts, in which, however, some mistakes have crept in, such as the statement that in 1782 Schröder played Imogen (!) in *Cymbeline*.

of the receipts, from an average of 32,607 Marks yearly to 63,883 Marks,[1] she continued to pay him the same ridiculous salary for his overwhelming work, which he had received long before on being re-engaged as an actor, viz. sixteen Thalers a week. Schröder might probably have been able to enforce better terms for himself, but he had the touchy pride that rather resigns than asks for what ought to be given of freewill.

This freewill, however, his mother did not possess, and being now thirty-five years old, he saw the positive necessity of entering upon a more lucrative way of life. Moreover, since the death of Charlotte Ackermann, the relations between Schröder and the Hamburgers had been somewhat strained, on his side in particular; in fact, he never forgot his grudge against them—somewhat unjustly, we think, considering their great admiration for him and the homage they paid him on several occasions. As late as 1789, when at the summit of favour and wealth as a theatrical leader in Hamburg, he spoke the following humorous but bitter words to Baggesen : " Of all imaginable positions in life there is only one more unpleasant than the actor's, and that is the theatrical manager's ; to be both in one person is almost too much for human patience—if the burden is not eased by an ample competency and encouraging honours."

It annoyed him also that there was discontent among his staff, though he ought to have known that there

---

[1] These averages I have calculated from the annual proceeds during Schröder's eight years of independent leadership, 1772-1780, as well as from Ackermann's eight years' term of management, which preceded the foundation of the National Theatre. The annual proceeds are found in Meyer, ii. p. 78 *seq.*

always is, in every staff and with every manager. Certainly by his energy and deep artistic insight Schröder had created the best company in Germany out of the Hamburg actors, but his theatrical experience was not yet great enough to tell him that gratitude for such benefits, if it comes at all, comes very late, and never from those who have enjoyed them.

In consequence of all these considerations Schröder had quietly made up his mind, and settled the business with his mother. The close of his first leadership came about in a somewhat dramatic way. One day, when the members of the company had gone to him in a body to present their grievances and their demands for the subsequent season, he forestalled them before any of them had had time to utter a word, by the following short announcement : " Ladies and Gentlemen, you are all dismissed from the 4th of March."

The consternation was great, not only among the actors, but quite as much among the public, when the news spread that Schröder no longer wished to continue his leadership, and everybody exclaimed, "Whatever is to become of our theatre ? "

But in spite of many attempts at mediation, Schröder remained inexorable. He calmly finished the season, and when his management closed, drew a sigh of relief and wrote in his diary : " *Sit nomen Domini benedictum.*" He even remained for some time under the new leader,[1] but then he started with his wife on a fresh tour, which

---

[1] A company of shareholders, the leaders of which were Etatsrath v. Voght, Postdirektor Bostel, and Agent Greve, had hired the theatre of Frau Ackermann for six years at an annual rent of 9300 Marks.

was to terminate in a very profitable engagement[1] for both at the Burgtheater in Vienna.

In the Austrian capital Schröder met several acquaintances. His old friend and pupil Brockmann had been acting for some years in the Burgtheater, where he reaped much success, and was considered a great actor; though away from Schröder's influence he had acquired a good deal of mannerism.[2] Schröder's former passionate admirer, Johanne Sacco, née Richard, was now the favourite idol of the Viennese, and had become a prominent actress in tragedy. Bergopzoomer had been his good friend and great admirer in the v. Kurz company. The older generation of leaders, the brothers Stephanie and Joh. Fr. Müller in particular, were not so well known to him, but even these men received the great actor with much kindness, though their apparent friendliness did not prevent them from weaving considerable intrigues against him.

To the artistic development of the Burgtheater Schröder's four years' stay became of supreme importance. Without taking any personal part in the stage-management, except by the power of his example, he changed the taste of the Viennese public and of those

---

[1] In Vienna Schröder received a much higher salary than any other of the Burgtheater actors, viz. 2550 Gulden ; his wife received 1450 ; this made a total of 4000 G., a considerable income for those times.

[2] Brockmann (Johann Franz Hieronymus) was troubled with no ballast either of character or culture, so he continually needed the support of a greater and stronger personality. Such support he found in Schröder, and with his excellent natural gifts he momentarily obtained great results ; but in the long run he lost his balance and the control of his talents, as well as that of his figure, which became too fat. Brockmann was born in Gratz, 1745, was originally a barber's apprentice, and after 1778 remained at the Burgtheater till his death in 1812.

among the actors who were at all susceptible to influence. The stilted, monotonous, or roaring tragic tone disappeared, and so did the exaggerated, farcical, tasteless style in comedy. So it is permissible to say that it was Schröder who, in spite of his distinctly North-German temperament, by his absolutely unaffected style, his delicate, never boisterous humour, and his sober sense, suited the Viennese particularly well, and laid the real artistic foundation of the Burgtheater, which afterwards was to win fame for its distinguished, always harmoniously controlled *ensemble*.

But to Schröder himself this sojourn brought no further artistic development. He was accustomed and probably born to be a ruler, an absolute ruler, and he had difficulty in submitting to the republican form of government which prevailed at the Burgtheater ; nor was it to his taste. After several collisions with the leaders—Stephanie the younger in particular—he withdrew into his own shell, and henceforth gave himself up exclusively to his work as an actor and an author.

It may be disputed whether or not Schröder had been right in breaking off so abruptly his first glorious career as a manager.

That he was a born theatrical leader, and therefore could not help returning to such a position, seemed to be a matter of course and a foregone conclusion. Schröder persevered in Vienna for only just four years.

The public, the aristocracy, and, last but not least, the Emperor Joseph, did all in their power to retain him. "You have tired of Hamburg twice," the Emperor said to him. "I tell you beforehand you will give it

up the third time.   Then you must go to no one but
me!"

But fate inexorably drove Schröder back to the town
on the Elbe, which attracted and repelled him like a
mistress, loved if not esteemed.   And, indeed, here his
presence was much needed.   During the few years its
proper lord and master had been absent, the theatre had
fallen into a sad state of dissolution.   Not financially, by
any means; a glance at the receipts shows that the
audiences had not been less numerous than in Schröder's
time.   But in art, discipline, and morals it had sunk so
low, that it was now generally despised instead of
being esteemed an honour to the town, as had been the
case four years previously.   It had constantly changed
hands; there had been five managements, each worse
than the one before.[1]   Now and again a manager had
been able to make some profits, but as to *répertoire*,
study of character, tone, taste and public conduct—all
had declined with terrible speed.

When Schröder came back and acted in Altona with
a newly-formed company, the difference was striking;
on one side order, firmness, precision, respect—every-

---

[1] The first triumvirate after Schröder's departure, composed of Voght,
Bostel, and Greve, quickly tired of the business and left the management to
Dreyer, the landlord of a restaurant, with the assistance of Brömel, a dramatic
author.   After a quarrel with one of the leading actors Dreyer closed the
theatre in the face of the public in the middle of a season, without any
notice or explanation.   It remained empty for about six months, after
which the always unsuccessful Seyler, whom we have mentioned before,
undertook it with very bad result   Subsequently it was managed with comparative financial success, but very much to the detriment of artistic taste,
by the actors Klos and Zuccarini.   Finally the latter was replaced by Joh.
Chr. Brandes, who by his complacent affability, his weakness and fickle-
ness, brought the theatre to the lowest depths of disgrace and decline.

thing, in short, that helps to produce a good theatrical *ensemble.* On the other, indolence and carelessness ; passive resignation on the part of the public, and in the actors a vainglorious exhibition of their own persons—an unmistakable sign of tasteless theatrical humbug, and the worst symptom of falling off in true dramatic art.

It must be said, however, that as soon as Schröder appeared, Klos and Brandes, the managers of the moment, declared themselves willing to yield their place to him. But he did not wish to act before the Hamburg public till he had properly trained his company according to his own principles.

After a year's arduous labour in Altona, Lübeck and Hanover, with the most enthusiastic support of the residents, Schröder began his second turn of leadership in Hamburg after Easter, 1786.[1]

He was now forty-two years of age ; his firmness, his unceasing energy, and his self-esteem had even increased. He did not want to cringe before a "highly-honoured public"—now less than ever ; he wanted to win it over, and, better still, to make it bow to him.

The "announcement" with which he introduced himself to the Hamburgers is very characteristic of him, and deserves to be read. It runs as follows :—

"Two years ago, when giving some performances as a visitor, I was fortunate enough to be so favourably received by the Hamburg public, that I resolved to come back here, though I was in secure enjoyment of many advantages where I was stationed. For many reasons, though desirous of doing so, I was unable to

---

[1] The seasons were reckoned from Easter to Easter.

present before now such a company as Hamburg is justified in expecting to see. I have spared neither trouble nor expense in giving it a training by which I hope to satisfy the public of this town.

" Now—patrons, friends, and fellow-citizens—it will depend on your support and approval whether I shall for life devote my work to you, or leave you, as regards this kind of amusement, to the care of others.

" I promise you order, the strictest morality, and as much display of scenery as the number of patrons of the theatre may permit. You will never be taxed by any kind of begging. Neither extensive programmes, nor prologues of any kind, perpetually repeating the same thing, will attempt to suborn your favour or your money.

" I promise you—not perfection (no theatre as yet can boast of that)—but a dramatic stage worthy of you, which the stranger can leave without occasion to blush, the morality of which will never come to occupy our law-courts. Help me to defray the expenses by frequent visits ; encourage the actors by forbearance and approval ; help to establish necessary order and good morals by suppressing the old custom, which is now banished from every proper theatre in Europe, of spending more time between the wings and in the tiring-room than in the pit.

" A good company supported by the Hamburgers must soon become an excellent one, and the joyful hope of attaining this end ought to encourage the public and the actors in mutual trust as regards the giving and the enjoyment of amusement."

This exhortation, or announcement, which many

people thought presumptuous and unbecoming, did not promise impossibilities and did not storm the skies; it had this advantage, that Schröder might afterwards say that he more than kept his promise. During the twelve years of his second rulership Schröder indeed raised his theatre to the position of the first stage in Germany; he created a firm and stable standard of good acting.

As an actor, no doubt he advanced more and more towards perfection; he deepened and fertilised his representation of human character, and never relaxed his demands on himself or on others. He became a rich man, and when his tall, distinguished figure in the blue cloth coat, with the nicely curled and powdered hair, and the gold-knobbed cane in his hand, emerged from the magnificent house on the Alster where he lived, and with dignified steps walked down to the theatre on the Gänsemarkt, it was as one of the most honoured citizens of Hamburg; he enjoyed consideration almost equal to that awarded to one of the great commercial magnates, and an immense gulf separated him from the master-comedians who but a few decades earlier had travelled to and from the town with their troupes.

Nevertheless—in spite of all the honour, wealth, and order—this second leadership of Schröder's was far inferior in general importance to his first period of management. What Schröder had effected with incredible toil and trouble for sixteen thalers a week was simply this: the marriage of dramatic and poetic art, the merging of them into a union so close as had never before existed in Germany. He made Shakespeare live

to the German public.   He forced the young generation
of poets to look to the theatre as their goal.

It can by no means be said that this union was
broken during his second reign, but the high ideals were
considerably lowered.   The young generation, who
ought now to have impressed their stamp on the theatre
were Schiller and Goethe, but the set who actually did
so were Iffland, Kotzebue, and Schröder himself.

Schröder saw perfectly well, and declared without
hesitation, that Schiller was the first dramatist of his
time ; and it was no fault of his that it did not come to
a match between the greatest actor and the greatest
dramatic author in Germany.   An advance on the part
of Schiller met at once with the warmest response from
Schröder, which was expressed in a letter as follows :
" My speedy answer must prove to you how welcome
your letter was to me.   I have no higher wish than to
ally myself with you—you, who alone can carry out my
ideas.   I do not possess the powers of doing it myself,
but my long and familiar knowledge of the practical side
of the stage might perhaps be of use to you.

" But a dramatic author must needs live near the
stage for which he works.   Are you free ?   Can you
exchange Dresden for Hamburg ?   And on what
conditions ? "

This warm, eager proposal for a union which would
have produced an exceptionally happy constellation, the
bearings of which were foreseen by Schröder, but not by
Schiller, was met with vague irresolution on the part of
the latter.

Perhaps it did no harm to Schiller that this plan

27

28

29

27—Schröder in his later age (p. 177).
28—Aug. Wilh. Iffland (p. 189).   29—David Beil (p. 191).

came to nothing—though, who knows what might have been the result of such collaboration? Nor was it, from a business point of view, detrimental to Schröder, since he turned to the authors who were at the time the most lucrative. But there can be no doubt that the glowing idealism of Schiller would have kept the fire of Schröder's youthful enthusiasm burning longer, and prevented his management and his art from becoming a little too respectable, too realistic, too practical.

Schröder's second leadership of the Hamburg theatre now became exemplary, in so far as all the demands of the time as to outward and inward technique were fully satisfied—there was no other stage in Germany of which that could be said—and in so far as he worked out and refined his art on the strictly realistic lines which he had adopted, and which sometimes in the fashionable Iffland-Kotzebue *répertoire* tended a shade too much towards homely happiness and prosperity.

However, after twelve years, and at the age of only fifty-four, Schröder again gave up his honourable position, and this time it was with the intention of leaving the theatre altogether. The last years had been very lucrative to him—the average proceeds had been about 150,000 marks against scarcely 64,000 marks during his first leadership—and if we are to believe his own assertions, his love of acting and of stage-management was not great, though while in action he devoted himself to both duties with untiring zeal.

This lack of love in the actor for his vocation is not so unaccountable or so rare as many, who are apt to consider it as a kind of affectation, are inclined to suppose ; and, strange to say, it need not be combined with any decline or slackening power in the artist.

Schröder was absolutely free from any kind of affectation, and his utterances about his art were unmistakably sincere.   I again refer to Baggesen, whose conversation with the great actor is very interesting, and has the advantage of being unknown to German biographers and historians of the theatre, so that the details of it have not yet been threshed out.

To the remark of Schröder referred to above about the position of the actor and the actor - manager, Baggesen objects : " But . . . the thrilling consciousness of one's own artistic value, the satisfaction that always follows vanquished difficulties, successful and masterly accomplished work, and finally, work in itself, *ipsa voluptas*, would not all this at least counterbalance the troubles and annoyances attached to it ? and is there any art in the world which repays industrious work more immediately than histrionic art ?

" My surprise turned to amazement when he assured me that, far from feeling pleasure in acting, he would quite as willingly do the work of a carpenter, a smith, or a teacher of the A B C, as act King Lear or any other of his favourite parts.

" ' So,' I repeated, ' you are not King Lear on the stage, while illuding others you are not under the illusion yourself ? '

" ' Do you think,' he replied, ' that I should succeed in making the spectators forget Schröder if for one moment I myself were Lear—or make them fancy they were seeing Lear, if for a moment I forgot Schröder ? '

" ' So you remain cold all the time you are acting ? '

" ' So cold that between the scenes and acts I play the part of manager as if I had done nothing but stand in the wings. My warmth is physical, not mental ; it is the heat of bodily exertion, not of enthusiasm.'

" Indeed," Baggesen adds, " I did not think there was so much resemblance between making verse and playing parts." [1]

With such feelings about the stage we cannot wonder that, as soon as he had attained financial independence, though still in his fullest vigour, Schröder followed his inclination, as he had hitherto followed his vocation, and retired from the theatrical career.

He had bought a property near Rellingen, in Holstein, a stately residence with three large halls and seventeen rooms. To this place he retired after the season of 1797-98, but he retained the ownership of the theatre and received rent for it. And that he was much more than a mere comedian, whose only importance is on the stage, or in connection with it, that his work had been that of a great artist, and that he continued to be a great man, he proved by his mode of living when far from the theatre. Reading his letters to his friends from the idyllic country seat in Holstein is just like conversing familiarly with a highly-gifted, universally-instructed man about the matters which interest ourselves, and we feel very far removed from the anecdotal style which frequently renders the writings and conversation of old actors so tedious.

Contemporary political events find in him a keen and

---

[1] Jens Baggesen : *Labyrinthen*, I. 171 ff.

eager observer;[1] nothing of importance in literature escapes his attention; himself an energetic free-mason of high rank, he sets himself to study and record the history of free-masonry in Hamburg. The practical management of his property occupies much of his time; in short, he appears a man to whom nothing human is alien.

Once more, after many years, the theatre tempted him to return to it. However—fortunately, we may say —it was not his acting propensities which were rekindled into a senile flame, it was only the ruler who felt it his duty to resume the management in order to put things once more on the old footing. But he had to retire after a year with burned fingers and with the humiliating consciousness that even the great and the wise may be outrun by time.

It was during the season of 1811-12, in his sixty-eighth year, that Schröder committed this last folly, from which, however, he escaped with the loss of some money, but without losing his humour or peace of mind.

He spent his last years in undisturbed peace, taking keen interest in politics, and living partly in Hamburg,

[1] As he lived on Danish territory, he naturally took an interest in Danish affairs, and he sometimes pronounced very clear judgments on events. This (in a letter of October 12th, 1807, to K. A. Böttiger) he wrote about the English attack in 1807 : " As I am convinced that Denmark would not have been allowed to keep its neutrality, I feel less inclined to blame the English for having taken the first step. Their act will also be much mitigated if they restore the fleet when peace is concluded. All my house can bear witness that when the papers spoke of a fleet which was being armed to go to the Sound, I declared that it was meant to proceed against Denmark. If the Crown Prince had done what even Holstein advised, that is, if immediately after the peace of Tilsit, he had withdrawn his troops, this thing would not have happened. But it is so fated, that not one of the potentates, except Bonaparte, is capable of showing common sense."

partly in Rellingen, where he died on September 3rd, 1816.

With Schröder, German dramatic art of the eighteenth century reached its purest and fullest development. The best of the typical qualities of the North-German national character were exemplified in him : honesty, strength, naturalness, and a warm heart. At the same time he was a little too self-sufficient, and now and then some-what off-hand and overbearing in manner. However, his superiority was very genuine and founded upon rich, deep and many-sided humanity.

It is not surprising, therefore, it is an honour for once perfectly well deserved, that his country-people should have called, and should continue to call, this man and the most commanding personality within the realm of dramatic art, a man who seemed created to stand as a monument of bronze in the free-town of Hamburg—"the great Schröder."

IFFLAND

I

THE little Court-Theatre in Gotha, where Ekhof quietly
went on cultivating the art he had created, was joined
during the last year of the great actor's life by three
young men, who in their enthusiasm for art, and also by
their education, were superior to the average level of the
Ducal company.

Their names were Beil, Beck, and Iffland. Beil was
the eldest[1] and was considered the most talented. He
had already been acting some years, when in 1777, as
a young man of twenty-three, he came to Gotha.
His lively, jovial face, full of humour and fun, his
plump, stout, middle-sized figure, his keen sense of
human absurdities, his facility in mimicking them,
naturally rendered him very popular in comic parts.

Beck was in many respects a perfect contrast to him.
The tall and slender youth—at the time of his appearance
on the Gotha stage he was only seventeen[2]—was a little
stiff and angular in the lovers' parts with which he was

---

[1] Johann David Beil was born 1754, in Chemnitz, and was the son of a
cloth-manufacturer.
[2] Heinrich Beck was born 1760 in Gotha.

entrusted ; but off the stage he was very amiable and refined.

The most remarkable of the three however, if not at first sight the most attractive, was Iffland. He was a year older than Beck, and, like him, had fled from the study of theology and followed his irresistible inclination for the theatre. But while Beck, who was a native of Gotha, had only had to apply to Ekhof to see his desire fulfilled, Iffland's path had led him through much more romantic vicissitudes. From his severe paternal home in Hanover, where his father was a highly-esteemed civil officer, without acquaintances or money, and pursued by his father's anger, he had wandered from town to town to find an appointment in the art which from his earliest childhood had exercised a wonderful fascination over him.

The plays which he had now and then seen in his native town, and the reading of Gœthe's *Werther* had filled his mind with a passionate, we may even say, a hysterical love of art. He now found himself in Gotha, at the goal of his ardent desires ; a youth unsettled in mind, longing for the home of his childhood, especially for his dearly loved sister Louise, who throughout his life remained the object of his deepest and purest attachment, yet more strongly determined than ever to prove to his family that he would be able to make his way as an actor.

And certainly, his chances were of the best. Between Schröder and Iffland there is a remarkable difference. While the former continued educating, developing, and deepening his character as a man and as an actor, so that in his mature age he was an entirely different person from what he had been in his youth ; Iffland's individuality remained the same from the beginning to the end of his life ; his tendencies, virtues, vices and characteristics remained unaltered till his death.   As a high and mighty Superintendent of the Berlin Royal Court Theatre, he was the enthusiastic, light-hearted, amiable, affectionate child he had always been ; and the love of money, the vanity and courtier-like snobbery that clung to him in his old age had characterised him even in his early youth.

As an actor, of course, he developed, but in a different manner from Schröder.   In the latter art progressed together with the human development, grew deeper and rose higher with it.   The art of Iffland formed itself into mere artistic perfection, to virtuosity supported by the peculiar temperament which was his natural gift.

No more illustrative example of the difference between the two actors can well be imagined than the way in which each describes his meeting with Ekhof.

Schröder's description has been quoted already.[1] We see him secretly admiring the master, yet keeping the sharpest eye on his human frailties, and prevented by youthful pique and pride, from wishing to bow down even before what he acknowledged as great.

Iffland, on the contrary, was always ready to bow both to genuine and to sham greatness.   Before Ekhof he simply revels in humility.   To form a just idea of his remarkably over-excited feelings, we must listen to his own words : " The following day I stood before him

[1] Comp. above, p. 97.

[Ekhof]. I finished half of my speech, but suddenly all memories from the past rose within me. Mellefont, Antioch, Richard, Linzeus, Codrus, Tellheim, Orosman,[1] all these characters rose up in my imagination and held their laurel-wreath over Ekhof's head. [!]

"The tears rose to my eyes—my heart adored the perfect actor—but I could not utter a word.

"He shook hands with me kindly, and I felt the thrill of consecration in all my limbs."[2]

Anyone who knows Iffland in youth knows him through life. But the character of the man was much too complex to be understood by merely dwelling on the enthusiastic sensitiveness, the strong and easily roused emotion, which strike us at first, especially in reading his autobiography. His sensitiveness was combined with great sensuality. He was very fond of a good table and a great admirer of the other sex. And these tendencies were combined with an excessive love of nature; it was his delight to roam about among woods and mountains, and he found it hard to live in a town; even from Berlin he sought refuge in the Thiergarten, where he bought a magnificent villa in order to escape from the dirty streets. On the whole he was very fond of pomp and display, fine clothes and banquets; and, being a very bad manager, he was constantly in debt, however large his income might be. On the other hand, he was a very active and industrious man. Writing, in particular, was a favourite occupation with him, and he had a very easy-flowing pen. Though

[1] A number of Ekhof's celebrated parts; as a boy Iffland had seen him play them in Hanover, when Ekhof acted there under the leadership of Seyler.

[2] A. W. Iffland: *Meine theatralische Laufbahn*, Leipzig, 1798.

his autobiography would give one the idea that he was constantly swimming in tears — for he cries on all occasions, from joy, grief, veneration, friendship, love, on birthdays, funerals, and at princely audiences—he was a gay, high-spirited man, fond of light, cheerful talk, and most amiable in society.

He was altogether very companionable, and generally disarmed the reproaches of his friends or enemies by at once most humbly acknowledging his faults. Moreover, he was the most grateful man under the sun. In his autobiography and letters it is remarkable to how many people he "owes everything"; the number of those to whom he owes gratitude is only exceeded by those to whom he owes money.

That at the age of nineteen he should begin running into debt in Gotha may have been natural enough, for his salary at the Ducal Court Theatre was only two *thalers* a week, besides three cords of firewood during the winter.[1]

No doubt, however, it was not merely for providing the necessaries of life that he incurred his first debts, since he received money from home to cover these expenses. Though he very soon became a popular actor, his private reputation—in spite of his amiability—was not very good. "*Ce misérable*," the Geheimerätin von Lichtenstein writes of him to his later chief, Dalberg, "*est bon acteur, mais très—mauvais citoyen.*"

Physically, Iffland had very good qualifications for the stage. His appearance was peculiar, but charac-

---

[1] A. W. Iffland's *Briefe au seine Schwester Louise und andere Verwandte* 1772-1814. Herausgegeben von Ludwig Geiger, Berlin, 1904.

teristic. His broad, square face, which lent itself admirably to making up, was dominated by a pair of large, brown, and most expressive eyes and a soft, very sensitive mouth. He had a long sharp nose and a pointed, protruding chin. He was of middle height, and somewhat stout. In later years he became very fat. His legs were not particularly well formed and rather crooked.

But—most important of all—his body was extremely expressive; his limbs, though wanting in beauty, obeyed him with an ease and grace that were of the highest value in light comic and emotional as well as in tragic parts. This mobility and expressiveness of face and body were his strong points, and helped him through difficulties in parts which otherwise did not seem very suitable for him. His voice, on the other hand, was his weak point; it lacked power and fulness, and consequently was apt to become shrill and screaming in very passionate parts, and rather monotonous in lengthy pathetic scenes.

At the outset, however, he limited himself to copying Ekhof, and this he did to such perfection, mimicking to the most minute details the peculiarities of the master, that Ekhof himself was sometimes seriously alarmed at it.—

The association of these three young men quickly developed into close and familiar comradeship, and in the case of Beck and Iffland into a lifelong friendship, while professional jealousy now and then disturbed the relations between Iffland and Beil.

All three were undergraduates, and a common en-

thusiasm for art drew them together. Theatrical performances did not take place every day in Gotha, so the
young actors had plenty of time for discussing, arguing,
criticising, and philosophising, and they made ample use
of their leisure. We know that ardent, purposeless, but
unselfish talk about the highest subjects, in which young
people like to indulge—those endless discussions all
through the night till dawn, regardless of sleep, hunger
and comfort—everything forgotten in the excitement of
arguing and debating. "That delightful, wonderful
time!" as Iffland says himself. "People did not understand us, but we were very happy—the happiest people
in the whole Duchy."

They frequently rose at night and began arguing
about their art, so loud as to make their neighbours
think they were murdering each other. There is a small
wood near Gotha, called the *Siebeleberwald*; this was
their refuge. Regardless of anything else, they marched
out of the town with their provisions, through the little
smiling villages up to the lonely wood on the rocky
slope, and camped close by the sparkling well, where
they could see the tiny, romantic Duchy spread out in the
valley below, the snug and dainty little town of Gotha
like a group of toy houses to the left, while the blue
Harz Mountains formed the background in a dreamy
distance.

Here they would remain for days, reading, talking,
sleeping, learning parts, reciting, in such remarkable
costumes that they frightened away the terrified passers-
by. Sometimes even their nights were spent there.
Then they would light a bundle of dry branches, and,

grouped round the crackling fire, listen to the midnight chimes from the creaking old clock in the tower of the neighbouring village church, thinking with a shudder of the ghost hour in *Hamlet*.

The country life of these three young men, with their ardent longings, their gushing display of feeling, became of importance to German dramatic art in so far as it introduced a new element of exuberant romantic sentiment (*Schwärmerei*) into it.

Both Ekhof and Schröder were entirely men of the eighteenth century. Clear-headed, conscious, with deep feeling, but without a vestige of hysterical sentimentality, they certainly struggled towards an ideal, but they preferred the shortest and straightest way to attain it. The course of their art is marked by the clearest light and the deepest shadows; for them there were no mysterious paths in the wood, with pale moonbeams effacing distinct outlines and troubling the mind with bewilderment or apprehension.

With Iffland the twilight of the soul, the mingled and complicated elements, found their place in dramatic art. This influence did not gain in strength, because Iffland was not great enough, or perhaps because he had still one foot in the bygone age. He is a connecting link, not the bringer of the new era. But the new element which he was incapable of imparting as a poet he momentarily introduced into dramatic art, and, though he did not in any way belong to the romantic school, his sensibility, his enthusiasm, his hysterically complicated feelings, led dramatic art a step further towards new forms.

II

Abolition of the Court Theatre in Gotha—The National Theatre in Mannheim and its Leader, von Dalberg—The Innovations of his Management—Schiller and the First Performance of *The Robbers*—Schiller
   as Dramatist and as Man of the Theatre—His Importance to the
   Mannheim Stage.

IN Gotha the three friends had no opportunity of carrying
their artistic dreams into action.   Ekhof died in 1878,
and the theatre, which was already in a feeble state and
continued to decline after the master's death, had become
a mere encumbrance to the Duke, especially as the
actors constantly tormented him with their quarrels and
intrigues.[1]   Consequently he gave up his Court Theatre
the next year.

Most of the members of the staff, however, im-
mediately received new offers from the so-called National
Theatre in Mannheim, which the majority of them gladly
accepted.[2]   Besides Beil, Beck, and Iffland, Joh. Michael
Boeck and his wife, and Frau Karoline Kummerfeld (*née*
Schulz) were the most important members of the company.
Boeck was much older than the three friends; born in
1743, he was six years their senior, but he was the
privileged performer of young heroes and lovers, while
Beil and Iffland, in spite of their youth, had hitherto

[1] *Ce sont leurs tracasseries qui est l'unique cause* (of the giving up of the
theatre), writes Sartory, the cashier of the theatre, to Mannheim.

[2] Iffland was the only one who made difficulties.   He would have preferred to join Schröder in Hamburg.   In his autobiography he throws a
poetic and ideal light on his objections ; however, the facts prove that, though
young, Iffland had a sharp enough eye for his own advantage, and that by
his somewhat underhand dealing he highly offended the distinguished
mediators Baron von Dalberg and Geheimerätin von Lichtenstein.   Cf.
W. Koffka, *Iffland und Dalberg*, Leipzig, 1865, p. 33 f.

acted scarcely anything but old men, and Beck had to
content himself with mere trifling parts.   Boeck, whose
peculiarities as an actor we have had occasion to mention
before,[1] had not changed for the better, either professionally or in his private character.   On the stage, however,
he continued to be very popular on account of his outwardly passionate bearing as hero, but his lack of intelligence and his greed for parts engendered bitter feelings
in his young colleagues, feelings which they could not
always control.

The Mannheim National Theatre, to which the
company trained by Ekhof was now to be transferred,
was quite new in its capacity of national—*i.e.* German—
stage.   It dated from Sept. 1st, 1778; having been
founded by the Elector Karl Theodor of the Bavarian
Palatinate as a gift to the Mannheimers, at the time
when the Elector went to reside in Munich.   So it was
no Court theatre, but enjoyed considerable independence
in its artistic management, while financially it was under
the control of the exceedingly petty and bureaucratic
Munich Court-office, which caused it many vexations,
and in the course of time became its ruin.

The principal superintendence of this National
Theatre was entrusted to Baron Wolfgang Heribert
von Dalberg, and it was this exceptionally fortunate
choice, in particular, which created the conditions of
progress for the new stage.   For von Dalberg was not
an aristocratic theatrical chief like most others.

In the first place, he was young;[2] in the second, he
was rich; and finally, most important of all, he took a

---

[1] See above, p. 106.   [2] He was born in 1749.

keen interest in dramatic art, and was a good judge of it, indeed he was himself a not unsuccessful playwright.

He had undertaken the post of theatrical superintendent from pure love of art, not from a desire to hold office, still less with a view to pecuniary profit. Though the remuneration had hitherto been pretty liberal, Dalberg persisted in serving quite gratuitously. And he devoted all his time and energy to making a success out of the young theatre.

At the beginning, however, he was unfortunate, though the external apparatus was in good order; a fine theatre, magnificent scenery, and a very rich and tasteful supply of dresses.[1] But being inexperienced, Dalberg had composed his staff of elements which contained the germs of dissension and dissolution.

For the post of stage-manager he had engaged our old acquaintance Seyler, and this amiable and now experienced director was accompanied by his imposing wife, *alias* Frau Hensel, who, like a thunder-cloud, always brought with her a fatal din. At the same time, by an unfortunate chance, Dalberg had also engaged the two Brandes, and Charlotte Brandes,[2] whose performance of tragic parts, especially of Ariadne in the monodrama of that name, had reaped success all over Germany, was

---

[1] T. C. Brandes, *Meine Lebensgeschichte*, ii. p. 272.

[2] Fate was always bringing the rival ladies together. The Brandes family, when driven away from Mannheim, went to Hamburg, where they fancied themselves safe from Frau Seyler. But when shortly afterwards the Seylers were dismissed by Dalberg on account of fresh scandals, they also went to Hamburg. Charlotte Brandes, on meeting her old enemy here again for the first time, exclaimed quite involuntarily : "O Lord, you here, too, Madam? Indeed I think that if I fled to hell from you I should find you there." *Cf.* Brandes' *Lebensgeschichte*, ii. 293.

the greatest eyesore and most dangerous rival of Frau Seyler.

This inevitably caused quarrels. The Brandes family soon left Mannheim, but as they had already become very popular there—not least so their fascinating daughter Minna—a bad feeling sprang up against the Seylers. The amiable good-natured husband of course became the scape-goat. He was annoyed and vexed in his function of rehearser, and one day, being particularly provoked by Mme. Toscani, a presumptuous actress whom, merely to irritate Frau Seyler, the public had spoiled, he lost his self-control and gave her a box on the ear. This put an end to his stay ; Dalberg at once dismissed him, and the man, cruelly tossed about by fate, but even more so by his wife, again started on new expeditions.[1]

Though at the moment all these quarrels and scandals had a depressing effect on the young staff, the removal of the Seylers was really most fortunate. It gave the impulse to an entirely new arrangement, which created such conditions for the little Mannheim stage as enabled it to become an original and fresh departure in German dramatic art.

After the dismissal of Seyler Dalberg engaged no new director, but introduced a republican constitution, to some extent after the pattern of the Emperor Joseph.[2] While himself undertaking the direct artistic and administrative superintendence, he was assisted partly by a

---

[1] Seyler, by the by, after the death of his wife, ended his days in peaceful leisure with his old friend Schröder at his country seat in Holstein.

[2] *Cf.* The Arrangement of the Vienna Burgtheater on p. 140.

so-called first *Ausschuss*, who was both producer and *régis-seur*, the latter of whom might be represented by another *régisseur* chosen by the staff; partly by another committee, a theatrical council, which assembled with the chief every fortnight, and with him discussed the future and the improvement of the theatre, proposed new plays and wrote criticisms on those that were presented to the committee. The chief gave his judgment, praise or censure, on the plays then running, and on the performance of each actor. The council presented their grievances and their proposals, and for the rest everybody, whether member of the committee or not, could appear before it and plead his own cause. Moreover, theatrical matters might be discussed quite in the abstract; the superintendent would propose dramaturgical questions, which the members of the committee answered by written papers. The questions were of the following kind:—"What is nature, and what are its true limits in theatrical representations?" "What is deportment on the stage, and by what means can it be acquired?"—"Can French tragedies please on the German stage, and how are they to be acted in order to win general favour?" And the answers by Iffland, Meyer, Renschüb, Beil, and Beck, though now and then a little *naïve* are, as a rule, surprisingly well conceived and well written. They are still to be found among the theatrical archives[1] in Mannheim, and may serve as an enduring

---

[1] They are printed in full in the appendix to W. Koffka's *Iffland und Dalberg*. Meyer remained first stage-manager till his death, which occurred as early as 1783. He was an able and reliable man, but without special gifts. After him Renschüb, a man of greater capacity, came to Mannheim in 1781 with his wife, *née* Sommer, Renschüb, whose proper name was

monument of the fact that actors, when allowed to express their opinions, can think and speak about their own affairs almost as well as outsiders, who, as a rule, undertake the task for them.

Under these favourable conditions, with an educated, cultivated, and interested leader, the Mannheim National Theatre made rapid headway and struck out a career of its own by its reasonable and humane constitution. Here we see the phenomenon of quite young men, our three friends from Gotha, in spite of their short experience, being allowed, merely on account of their ability and talent, not only to play comedy, but to have their share in the management and their say in the discussions about the plays and other theatrical matters. Truly, republicanism under autocratic rule, which may make an actor ponder in bewilderment over the blessings of modern democracy.

There was life and spirit in this young theatre; the highly distinguished superintendent and the young actors worked with equal zeal towards the common ideal. Plays were written or adapted. Iffland gained his first spurs as an author. Dalberg adapted Shakespeare's *Julius Cæsar*, which was staged with hitherto unknown antiquarian accuracy and picturesque splendour. The greatest event, however, during these first Mannheim's days, was neither Iffland's *début* as an author nor the

---

Büschner (which becomes Renschüb when read backwards), was no great actor, but an intelligent man and, as far as we can judge, an able producer. He held the management up to 1792, when he returned to his native town Frankfurt-on-the-Main. It was not till then that Iffland undertook the artistic leadership.

revivals of Shakespeare, not even the star performances of Schröder, though this great actor made the deepest impression both on the public and on his colleagues.   It was a young unknown man, named Schiller, whose remarkable play, *The Robbers*, Dalberg had discovered, who was destined to create the greatest theatrical events of those days.

Some (*i.e.* Schiller's biographers) have severely censured Dalberg on his relations with Schiller, but no doubt unjustly.   It was a great thing indeed that the Electoral General Theatrical Superintendent should be unprejudiced enough to allow the performance of such a revolutionary play as Schiller's first work, which was dedicated "*in tyrannos*"; how many chiefs of Royal and Imperial theatres would do as much in our days? We cannot find fault with Dalberg for not treating Schiller in those early days as the national saint who now in unapproachable sublimity poses as a monument by the side of Goethe.

It was possibly a mistake on Dalberg's part to enforce by his authority the setting of the action of the play as far back as the age of chivalry, to "the year when the Emperor Maximilian established the perpetual peace in Germany."[1]   In doing this, however, he was not prompted by any political fear.   What he dreaded was that the absurdities of the fantastic alliance of robbers and all the other improbabilities should appear too strange, and render the play too ludicrous if acted in modern costumes.   He carried his point, though, of course, the idea of the play was violated, and especially

[1] So we read in the first playbill, dated Sunday, Jan. 13, 1782.

the character of its language, which is anything but old German. But it is quite possible that he secured its success on the stage, and at the time this probably was of greater importance to Schiller.[1]

The performance necessarily became an event. The enthusiasm of the young poet and his wild declamations in the forest harmonised perfectly with the mood of the young actors. Unfortunately, none of the three friends was qualified for giving expression to the passionate revolt of Karl Moor. This character, which should properly have been represented by a young actor of Schiller's age, glowing with the same fire that burned in the author, had to be confided to Boeck, with his mechanical style. But to Iffland the part of Franz Moor opened new fields. This artificial, philosophising theatrical demon presented the best battlefield for the young actor. Schiller, who considered this character the most difficult in the play, was much pleased with Iffland's rendering of it. In fact, during his long stage career Franz Moor remained one of his finest parts.

The importance of the appearance of *The Robbers* on the Mannheim stage was essentially internal; its external success was not great. It was acted only five times during the season. But the effect of it was that Schiller tore himself away from his tyrannical sovereign, and fled to the young National Theatre in Mannheim as to a harbour of refuge, in order to devote himself entirely to the stage.

---

[1] Schiller, in fact, to a certain extent, shared Dalberg's opinion, whereas the actors' committee, consisting of Iffland, Beck, Beil, Kirchhöffer, and Meyer, were in favour of dispensing with the old German costumes. Even now-a-days a few German stages continue presenting *The Robbers* thus attired.

At first he had planned to become an actor himself. Fortunately, this idea was given up ; but throughout his life he was passionately fond of reciting and reading to others.   His speech, however, was marred by a strong Swabian accent, and he had a great tendency towards highly pathetic declamation, fostered by his education in the *Karlschule*, where the French tragic manner was taught as the model for beautiful recitation.   His deportment, moreover, was somewhat stiff and his neck a little bowed ; his movements also were anything but plastic.

Schiller, then, was not naturally qualified for being an actor, and on the whole not suited for practical theatrical work.   Dalberg at once appointed him author to the theatre, and the idea probably was to give him some share in the leadership.   He attended the meetings of the theatrical committee, but, as far as we can see, his presence there was of no consequence.

And there is not much reason to regret that he gained but slight influence on the stage management in Mannheim.   His taste in dramatic art was by no means refined.   Personally very quiet and modest, he was fond of the most grotesque theatrical effects.   During his later engagement as stage manager in Weimar, he persisted in requesting Lady Macbeth, after the murder scene in the second act, to besmear her hands with red paint, and in the fifth act of *Egmont* he decked out Alba in a large red hangman's mantle and made him pull his hat low down over his face.   He wanted the actors to hurl the final part of their long speeches towards the audience with violent pathos, and—as is shown by the stage directions in his plays—he desired the by-play to be over-demonstrative and exaggerated.   Otherwise he was the most obliging, amiable, and easily contented producer, and therefore quite unsuited to govern actors, to whose self-complacent volubility he became a too easy prey.[1]

During the years 1783-84 Schiller held the appointment of theatrical author in Mannheim, and during that time *Fiesco* and *Cabal and Love* were put on the stage, besides which he wrote *The Stage considered as a Moral Institution*, a treatise which became of great importance to contemporary views of dramatic art.   He also published his *Rhenish Thalia*.

Of his two dramas, *Fiesco* found no favour at all, though the cast was very good, and though, to please the public, Schiller had altered its conclusion to a peaceful one.   But the cry for liberty, the republican pathos, found no response in the snobbish little Rhenish town. Schiller himself writes : " The public did not understand *Fiesco*.   In this country republican liberty is a meaning-

[1] We know but one example of Schiller's flying into a rage during his work as stage manager.   Haide, an actor of the Weimar theatre, had the bad habit, when simulating violent emotion, of screaming at the top of his voice, besides gesticulating excessively with his hands and arms.   Goethe had desired Schiller to keep an eye upon him, and Schiller warned Haide several times without the slighest effect.   At last the actor entered upon a lengthy explanation of his personal and artistic reasons for these faults ; then Schiller suddenly lost his usual good temper, and exclaimed furiously in his droll Swabian dialect : " *Ei was ? mache Sie's wie ich's Ihne sage und wie's der Göthe habe will.   Und er hat Recht—es iseht a Graus, das ewige Vagire mit dene Händ und des Hinauspfeife bei der Recitation !*" ("Eh, what? Do as I tell you and as Goethe wants it.   And he's right—it's all nonsense, that everlasting waving of your hands and puffing and blowing as you speak your lines !"   The actors were dumfounded, for they had never before seen the good and gentle Schiller in such a state.   *Cf.* Eduard Genast, *Aus dem Tagelbuche eines alten Schauspielers*, i. 114 f.

less sound, an empty word—in the veins of the Palatines flows no Roman blood.   But in Berlin it was called for and acted fourteen times in the course of three weeks." [1]

Cabal and Love had a much better fate.   Indeed the subject, to begin with, was more congenial, but we cannot say whether the greater success of this play was due in part to the fact that the leading part was acted by Heinrich Beck, a young man of Schiller's own age, who thoroughly understood him and had become his friend ; whereas in the two former pieces the shallow routine of Boeck had been dominant.

On the whole the Mannheim theatre and Schiller had a fertilising influence on each other, but this influence was chiefly of a mental nature.   The Schiller performances were by no means such events as they became afterwards, when seen in the glorious light thrown over this poet by history.   Indeed, the contemporary plays of Iffland (*Crime from Ambition, The Wards, The Marksmen*) were much more successful and created a much greater sensation at the time.   Here, however, as everywhere, the quiet power was the stronger one in the long run, and Schiller's rich poetic vein like a refreshing stream poured down over the young actors and authors, and without their knowledge it made them flourish with an exuberance they would never have obtained without him.

Schiller himself conceived esteem and affection for the young theatre.   Comparison showed him how superior it was to the general average of stages.   After

[1] Letter from Schiller to Reinwald of May 5, 1784.

the performance of *Cabal and Love*[1] Schiller, with Iffland and Beil, went on a little starring expedition to Frankfurt, and from there he writes to Dalberg about his two companions, how they tower above the Frankfurt actors like Phidias's Jupiter above a carved ensign. "I never felt more thoroughly than here," he adds, "how far every other theatre is behind our own, and Grossmann [the manager of the Frankfurt stage] will have difficulty in keeping afloat in Frankfurt after the departure of our actors. Wherever we go people express the greatest esteem for the Mannheim theatre. The acting of Iffland and Beil has gained a high reputation among the Frankfurt public. A warm interest in the stage has sprung up. Indeed everybody says that Grossmann's actors have never played with such warmth as yesterday, which proves what great things good models and actors who play together are capable of achieving."

III

Iffland as Dramatic Author and as Actor—His Popularity in both branches —His Mannheim Period.

THE years that followed Schiller's retirement from the office of dramatic author were the best and most fruitful to the Mannheim National Theatre, and though Renschüb was the nominal leader, we may say that it was Iffland who impressed his stamp upon the theatre. He always speaks with great modesty of his authorship,

[1] Beck acted Ferdinand, and his charming young wife, Karoline, *née* Ziegler, was Louise ; Boeck had undertaken the President, while Iffland was Wurm and Beil Miller.

saying that his plays were only meant to be acted, not to be read. But though this modest appreciation was quite just, the public of the time, and some of the critics as well, thought quite differently.

The enthusiasm aroused by Iffland's plays was un-paralleled. Their simple, unsophisticated characters, evidently copied from real life ; the animated, frequently well-invented plot ; the noble sentiment which often reveals itself beneath a surface of drollery, and combined with quaint and very life-like characteristics ; the ardent rhetorical ecstasy that bursts out in effective scenes—all this was well adapted to make Iffland appear a great poet to the ordinary public ; indeed, nearly all his plays were greeted with enthusiasm.

Dramatic criticism also extolled him far above his merits. As an example we may quote from Schink's *Dramaturgische Monate*, a review of *Die Jäger* (*The Marksmen*), which—very transparently hinting at Schiller and the Sturm-und-Drang poets—proclaims the rising actor-author as a genuine poetic revelation. The critic says among other things : "*Die Jäger* is one of the best plays of the German theatre, and its author, Herr Iffland, is one of the few most highly gifted men in Germany who possesses a decided talent for this kind of poetry. In spite of all the noise of would-be geniuses, their croaking from all the swamps and pools of our German Parnassus, in spite of the roars and riots which surrounded him on all stages, instead of the bear-baiting and cock-fighting which our swaggering humbugs and eccentrics sold for dramatic art, Herr Iffland, unbiassed and unspoiled, in his *Crime and Ambition* and his

Marksmen, has started on the road of nature, pure and simple; he has given us human life without caricature, and passion without grimace and carnivalcoque monstrosities. By these fine contributions he has enriched our stage with a *genre* of art that . . . to the bulk of the public will always continue the most attractive." [1]

No wonder that Iffland prospered. He was attached to the beautiful Rhinelands by all the love of nature that was a sound and genuine element of his character. The fertile and romantic banks of the river charmed him even more than the Thuringian Forest, and it is the author's own enthusiasm that inspires the honest Warberger in *The Marksmen* when he sings:

> "*Am Rhein, am Rhein, da wachsen unsre Reben !*"
> ("On the Rhine, on the Rhine, there grows our vine !")

The public spoiled him; Royalties, to whom he offered the sweetest flattery in many a complimentary play, were most graciously inclined towards him, and presented him with many valuable gold snuff-boxes; even better still—since he did not take snuff, but was always in want of money—with many a welcome gratuity. His reputation, supported by the popularity of his plays, spread far and wide; he toured a great deal, and gave star-performances here and there with great success, even in Hamburg, the town of Schröder, though—as he was quite aware—he was unable to win the approval of the great master himself. He would have liked to ascribe this to jealousy; but, since it was Schröder who had invited him to appear on his own stage, and who wanted to attach him permanently to it, Iffland in his

---

[1] Joh. Fr. Schink: *Dramaturgische Monate*, Schwerin, 1790, i. 222 f.

innermost heart felt with a certain uneasiness that the man with the keen, cold, clear eye saw through all artifices, shams and illusive tricks, and sought for the kernel.

Iffland therefore never felt quite at ease in the presence of Schröder, and probably never acted his best when under the master's eye. This may to a certain extent account for Schröder's somewhat harsh judgment on Iffland as an actor, whose art he somewhat too sweepingly reduces to mere form and mannerism.

Iffland probably reached his highest point as actor during his star-representations in Weimar in 1796. Goethe's warm appreciation of his art rejoiced him and put him at his ease, and he acted fourteen of his best parts to general admiration, at the same time gaining for himself a literary monument which may be called unique.

Böttiger, a noted critic of the time, wrote quite a voluminous work[1] about these fourteen performances, in which he critically explains the minutest details in Iffland's acting; each movement of his fingers, each exclamation; the way he paints his face and wears his boots, and so forth. Such a work should be very useful to theatrical history, and would be so indeed, if its author had been a better observer and a keener critic. As it is, this vast work is a chaos of essential and un-essential matter, indiscriminate statements without discernment of what is due to chance or to design; faults turned to merits, physical advantages to ingenious points;

---

[1] Böttiger : *Entwickelung des Ifflandschen Spiels in vierzehn Darstellungen*, Leipzig, 1796.

it is nothing, in fact, but a shapeless panegyric which can give no true idea of its subject.

After reading the four hundred and odd pages of this book, one is left with the impression which had been previously received, but which this work produces in spite of its author, viz., that Iffland in his most vigorous days was a great virtuoso capable of representing a dramatic situation,[1] a death-scene, or some other horror with masterly realism, but that he had difficulty in sustaining a tragic character in its completeness from beginning to end. A Frenchman characterised his acting in the following words :—" *Point de nature, peu d'art, beaucoup d'artifice.*"

This, no doubt, hits the mark as to his tragic *répertoire.* Like all virtuosos, he was fond of leaving large portions of his parts quite in the shadow, so as to set off the effective moments in a glaring light. Another judge says of him :—" His dignity sometimes looks like stiffness, his resignation like insensibility, and when at last an outburst of passion pierces like a flash of lightning through the December sky of his acting, there is too much calculation in its precision and in every movement of his fingers, arms, and feet.[2]

---

[1] Marianne v. Eulenberg writes to Göthe, July 3rd, 1801 :—" Iffland's acting of Antonius [in Kotzebue's *Octavia*] has confirmed my previous opinion of him : his declamation was correct, he often drew the outlines right, and on many occasions rendered the details with delicacy. His death was appallingly true, so that a physician found it correct in all its symptoms ; the reality of the convulsions at the moment of death made the most disgusting impression on me, and I felt tempted to shout out the passage of the Propylai to him which opposes this kind of truth to nature."—*Schriften der Göthe—Gesellschaft* 17, 126 f.

[2] *Morgenblatt,* 1807, No. 234 ; quoted by Geiger : *Iffland-Briefe* ii. 253 f.

Iffland was evidently at his best in the mixed drama, in refined comic parts or in characters that required coolness and reserve, where he could, without particular effort, display natural dignity, graceful humour, or commanding gravity. But as time went on his taste inclined more and more towards grand tragic figures, such as Wallenstein and Lear, for which neither his appearance nor his voice was suited.[1]

Among Iffland's best parts in the mixed drama may be mentioned Count Wodmar in Gemmingen's *Deutscher Hausvater*, Army-Surgeon Rechtler in his own play *Sham Merits*, old *Kriegsrat* Dalner in *Loyalty to the Service* (also by himself), the Spanish recruiting officer, Lieutenant Wallen, in Schröder's *Still Waters Run Deep* (after Beaumont and Fletcher's *Rule a Wife and have a Wife*), and Geheimrat (Privy Councillor) Mantel in *Der Hausfreund* (by ——).

The period during which Iffland was working with ease and zeal as author and actor, from 1784-1795, was the heyday of the Mannheim theatre. In 1792 Iffland undertook the function of producer (on the first committee), when Renschüb had gone to Frankfurt as stage-manager. In this office, which would have seemed to be the very thing for the lively and sociable dramatist, his achievements were not quite what might have been expected, mostly on account of unfavourable outward circumstances. In the first place, two actors who had been among the chief pillars of the cast, died one shortly

---

[1] "Iffland appears with his crooked legs and his paunch, and all his efforts to produce a Wallenstein are vain," we read in a contemporary writer (G. F. D. v. Cölln : *Wien und Berlin in Parallele*, p. 95 f., quoted by Geiger—Iffl., Art. ii. 254).

30

31

30—Iffland as King Lear (p. 207).
31—Iffland as Mantel in *Der Hausfreund* (p. 208).

after the other.   These two were Boeck and Beil ; both
fell victims to intemperate habits—the latter being only
forty years old.   Boeck was replaced by an excellent
actor, Siegfried Gotthelf Koch (his real name was
Eckardt), and he, as well as his handsome daughter,
Betty (afterwards Frau Rose), became valuable supports
to the theatre.   Still, many of Boeck's tragic and Beil's
comic parts had to be undertaken by Iffland.   All this,
besides his functions as manager and author, overloaded
him with work.

Moreover, the great political events of the day, the
war with revolutionary France, threatened to reach
Mannheim.   The town had long been full of French
emigrants, who had even dominated the audience to an
alarming degree, and had introduced their boisterous
manners from the Théâtre Français, where they had
been in the habit of treating the performances as political
meetings, and had accustomed themselves to find allusions to the startling events of the day in every speech
of the play.[1]

But matters became much worse when Mannheim
was made the scene of action of the French and German

---

[1] Iffland himself, being a strong royalist, had shared in the demonstrations.   One evening when the opera *Richard Cœur de Lion* was being performed, in the last act of which a castle is stormed and Richard relieved by
Blondel, the emigrants were reminded of their unhappy King Louis XVI.,
who had just been imprisoned, and a violent tumult arose in the theatre.
The whole staff was summoned to the foot-lights by the noisy crew, who
jumped on the benches in the pit and burst out into frantic screams.   Then
Iffland stepped in front of the other actors, and said in French : " May the
King find a Blondel to save his life."   This allusion to current events, of
course, rendered Iffland very popular among the aristocratic *émigrés*, but
did not find equal favour with his fellow-actors, who justly thought that it
was no business of his—however sincere his sympathy might be—to interfere
with the internal affairs of the foreign nation.

armies, when it was bombarded and sacked, when, in spite of all, the generals demanded theatrical performances to cheer their officers and soldiers. The years 1794-95 were terrible. In the midst of war, in constant fear of bombardment, with all superfluous scenery stored in the shell-proof cellar beneath the theatre, costumes, library, and music packed up or removed, the plays continued until the shells flew over the heads of the actors, when they were returning home from the theatre at night. In 1796, when Dalberg was called to Munich, the whole authority was put into Iffland's hands under the most difficult conditions. His pliability and very obliging behaviour towards the officers, who dominated the town at the time, carried him safely through this troublesome period. But his indulgence to the military authorities was not appreciated by Dalberg on his return to Mannheim, and the relations between Iffland and his otherwise most liberal and urbane chief became less cordial than they had been before. The very existence of the theatre was threatened, as the Elector had become tired of maintaining it, and his officials annoyed Dalberg with petty and pedantic financial difficulties.

No wonder that Iffland, who was still a young man, felt inclined to seek another, safer and better appointment, even if by doing so he was bound to run counter to the gratitude which he certainly owed Dalberg, who had not only been a sympathising chief, but had personally given him the most unselfish financial assistance.

The Court Theatre in Berlin was the tempting goal. As early as 1794 the matter had been a subject of

32

34

33

32—Betty Koch as Iphigenia (p. 209).
34—Frau Unzelmann (Bethmann) as Maria Stuart (p. 218).
33—Fried. Ferd. Fleck. (p. 213).

negotiation,[1] but it was not till 1796 that Iffland accepted the appointment as leader of the Royal stage, thus entering into the first, most highly esteemed and most liberally remunerated post open to German theatrical functionaries.

IV

The Berlin Court Theatre—Fleck, an Actor of Genius—Iffland as *General Direktor* in Berlin—The Old and the New Era.

FREDERICK THE GREAT had taken no interest in the National Theatre; but even as Crown Prince his successor and nephew, Frederick William II., had shown an inclination to improve the conditions of dramatic art in Berlin. As soon as he became king he allowed the German company of actors to move into the fine theatre on the Gensdarmenmarkt, hitherto the stage of the French Court Company, granted it an annual subvention of 6000 Marks, and dubbed it the " National Theatre."

For several years Döbbelin had wielded its artistic sceptre. The metropolis had rubbed off some of his provincial manager characteristics, but on the whole he remained the same remarkable apostle of tastelessness as before. So King Frederick William soon found it necessary to provide him with some solid pillars of support, and for this purpose his choice fell on two men,

---

[1] As we see from the *Iffland Letters* recently published by Professor L. Geiger (ii. 53). In his autobiography Iffland puts a somewhat more ideal complexion on his rupture with Dalberg.

one of whom was the original, clever, and capricious writer, J. J. Engel, whose work, *Ideen zu einer Mimik*, and some felicitous plays, were supposed to qualify him for a leading theatrical position ; the other being Ramler, a morbid *savant* of the study, entirely lacking in practical knowledge of the stage.

The combination was not successful. Döbbelin soon retired from the new conditions, which did not suit him, and the practical stage-management was placed in the hands of Fleck, an original and very clever actor. This was certainly an improvement, but Engel did not possess sufficient practical knowledge of the theatre to maintain his independence as leader and the necessary authority to carry out his principles,[1] so he retired in 1794, and it was at this juncture that the first invitation came to Iffland.

At that time, as we said above, the negotiations led to no result, because Iffland was too deeply attached to his dear Rhinelands, and for a couple of years longer the management of the Berlin stage remained in the hands of Fleck and Ramler.

Joh. Friedr. Ferd. Fleck was a very gifted actor, indeed, he may be called the most distinguished of his generation ; and this was because his talent was entirely suited to the poetry of the time which he had to interpret. He was a born actor of the *Sturm-und-Drang*. He and Iffland were of the same age, but there was much more

---

[1] These principles, by the by, as far as art was concerned, were of a rather prosaic kind. He was a decided naturalist and hated verse, which he considered incompatible with scenic illusion ; this brought him into conflict with the new current of the time, the poetic enthusiasm of which he did not understand at all.

savagery and spite in his genius. His splendid natural
endowments alone—a middle-sized athletic frame, a
regular Apollo head, passionate, yet soft brown eyes,
a powerful voice of great compass, which was fine and
sonorous from the highest to the deepest tones—qualified him for the parts of the young heroes of Schiller,
such as Karl Moor, Don Carlos, Fiesco, and Ferdinand.
But more than that, he possessed the same fiery, hysterical,
artistic temperament which had created these characters,
who were strained to a pitch beyond ordinary human
nature. In these figures even Schröder's great, but
rational and realistic, mastership fell short. Schröder
was, without doubt, a greater and more distinguished
actor than Fleck, but the latter was the kind of wild
genius which the time required, both in his brilliant
qualities and in a good number of the defects and
oddities without which the ordinary public is disinclined
to believe in genius.

He was in the highest degree capricious and impulsive, and neither the audience nor his fellow-actors
ever knew what he might be going to do. Now revelling
in grotesque and tasteless absurdities, now rising to the
highest, most beautiful, and suggestive pathos, he was
the idol of the young romantic poets, and Ludwig Tieck
praises him in the most enthusiastic panegyric.

But the more sober connoisseurs tell us that he was
sometimes guilty of the most dreadful claptrap in the use
of his beautiful voice. For instance, when acting the
Governor in *Benjowsky*, he roared out, "May every
thunderbolt roll the curse of thy father into thy ears!"
and then in scarcely audible, melodious tones breathes

forth, "May each gently rustling wind whisper to thee the last sigh of thy dying father!"

Sometimes in his caprice he treated the audience with the most disdainful indifference by altogether omitting to act, only reciting his part as carelessly as if he were throwing bones to a dog. It was a saying among the Berlin public that they never knew whom they were going to see, the great or the little Fleck.[1]

An artistic nature such as Fleck's was not suited to the leading or controlling position of a *régisseur* or an instructor. For these posts Iffland was much better qualified. And in his way he certainly became an excellent leader of the Berlin Theatre, a position which he occupied from 1796 to his death in 1814.

In spite of his exuberant emotional temperament, his negligence and disorder in his own money matters, his easily influenced generosity where his personal affairs were concerned, his official duties were discharged with a firmness, order, and dignity which had a beneficial influence on the somewhat undisciplined staff. On the

---

[1] A characteristic anecdote is told about his incredibly negligent behaviour to the audience. One evening, in his specially famous part of Karl Moor, he was out of spirits because in the first scene he had not met with the expected applause. So he played with such marked *nonchalance* that the audience began to feel uneasy, and when, during a monologue, he went so far as to trifle with his gun, balancing it on his forefinger, people lost patience, stamped violently, and burst out into loud hisses. Fleck stopped, came down to the footlights, and looked out towards the spectators with his wonderful brilliant eyes. There was a dead silence, even the dust seemed to tremble in the hall, and every one held his breath under this glance. Then Fleck retired, completely altered his manner, and continued acting his part with such ardent enthusiasm and magic power, that not even his greatest admirers remembered ever having seen the like of it, and the audience, completely carried away, gave vent to its feelings in frantic applause.— Devrient, *Geschichte d. d. Schauspielkunst*, iii. 70.

whole, his principles were better than his practice. He was excellent as a teacher of the young, as he never based his lessons on his own sensational style of acting and of courting the public, but on the sound principles of Schröder.

A whole staff of young actors were trained under Iffland, and the Berlin Theatre now became, what it had never been before, a stage for real *ensemble* acting. It was the mixed drama in particular, the drama of Iffland and Schröder, in which the Berlin Theatre formed a veritable school. On account of its moral character this class of plays was also favoured by the King, Frederick William III.—who in 1797 had succeeded his father—and by his beautiful Queen, the adored Louise, but was in less favour with the public, especially the younger portion of it. The eighteenth century had passed; new times were dawning. The young generation was knocking violently at the door; what it required was not morals, noble civic virtues and ordinary human characters; it was poetry, strong and passionate, exalted feelings, mysterious depths, horrors, thrilling events, sublime pathos. To them plain nature, for which German dramatic art had struggled so hard and so honestly, was only a prejudice, a cloak concealing shallowness.

These were the cries that rose louder and louder against Iffland's school, that embittered the later years of his life and prevented him from enjoying undisturbed his great and highly-esteemed position. In 1810 he wrote to his sister: " A powerful poetical-political-natural-philosophical party, with all the masterful selfishness of such people, has recently arrayed itself against me in order to force upon me its works, its will and its methods.   It has influenced the press here and abroad in a more or less delicate or brutal way.   This has caused unavoidable vexation, for excitable blood and nerves are the soul of my vocation."[1]

Unfortunately Fleck died too early, in 1801, when scarcely forty-five years old, for he alone was able to keep the rising powers at bay.   Before his death he created his powerful character of Wallenstein in Schiller's trilogy of that name; but this caused his loss to be so much more severely felt.

Iffland, who undertook a large number of his parts in the so-called "ideal" *répertoire*—Wallenstein among others—had to replace Fleck's strong natural capacities with all kinds of stratagems, calculated plastic and mimic effects, which might indeed call forth the applause of an ordinary audience, who felt flattered and honoured by the attention and regard with which Iffland constantly met their capacities of appreciation, but which lowered his reputation as an actor in the eyes of the young generation of romantics.

After Fleck none among Iffland's staff was able to carry the banner of the high ideal except, perhaps, the beautiful, slender Mlle. Fleck, whose pathetic, maidenly tragedy fascinated the younger part of the audience.

Otherwise the company was trained rather in a rational and practical than in an ideal and sentimental spirit.   The Berlin Royal Theatre, for which Iffland

[1] Geiger : *A. W. Iffland-Briefe*, i. 222.

obtained a new building,[1] was both Opera and Play-house, and the staff was prepared to act in both *genres*. Thus the much-admired Frau Unzelmann—afterwards Frau Bethmann—was *prima donna* in the drama as well as in the opera ; she played Lady Macbeth and Phædra, or warbled her songs in the French light operas, as the case might be.   Even Fleck undertook parts in operas.

Iffland's real contribution to the artistic development of the theatre belongs to his Mannheim period.   His long leadership in Berlin certainly did not lack outward appreciation ; his King and Queen were always most graciously inclined towards him, which was of great value to one who continued to be a staunch and ardent royalist (no less so than any of the figures in his court-festival plays) ;[2] as the first actor in Germany he was

---

[1] The new Royal Playhouse opened on 1st January 1801.   It was burned down in 1817 ; its site was the same as that of the present theatre, which was built in 1819-21.

[2] Iffland himself gives a characteristic example of his royalty-worship in a letter of 30th December 1809, in which he relates how, after a somewhat long absence of the King, during which he (Iffland) had shown courage in opposing the Napoleonic rule, his Majesty summoned him to the Royal box in the theatre. He writes to his sister as follows : " I do not know if Gottfried [his brother] has written to you what the King said to me after summoning me to his box. He rose and met me with these words : ' I have always thought you a great artist and an honest man ; during my absence you have in every way shown yourself as a true patriot.   This evening you have given me a fresh proof of it which touches my heart ; I could not deny myself the pleasure of telling you so in person.' ' Will your Majesty favour me with a pleasure for which I have been longing three years [!], that of kissing your hand ?'   He held out his hand with indescribable kindness and dignity, and I could not let it go.   The Queen said some most gracious words to me, which I was too much agitated to hear.   I kissed her hand. ' So long have I been anticipating this hour, and now that it has come, I am unable to say any-thing to your Majesty.'   Then I just caught a glimpse of her father in tears, and after that, I really do not know how, with dimmed eyes and trembling knees, I managed to go downstairs and back to my room."—Geiger : *Iffland-Briefe*, i. 221.

made a Knight of the Red Eagle; he had the title of
"General Director" conferred on him, received a large
salary, and was sought after by the best circles, as he
was unsurpassed as an amiable companion in society;
he lived in grand style in his magnificent villa in the
Thiergarten; the public spoiled him with its applause.
But time—time, that hurries on with inexorable speed—
had outstripped him.   He felt it himself, and tried to
soothe his ambition by more and more frequent star-
performances in different places, where his ever-increasing
virtuosity procured him a noisy but ephemeral fame.
Thus he became the prototype in Germany of the
travelling stars, who may easily be imagined dripping
with perspiration, bowing to the audience with a fatigued
smile, smothered in laurels, whereas ever less notice is
paid to their art which has worn itself out like the pins
on the cylinder of a grammophone.

Iffland wore himself out also by eternal feasting,
which was interrupted only by fatiguing administrative
work.   While Schröder to the day of his death stood
firmly moulded like a statue, Iffland gradually dissolved
into the looser substance of his nature, vanity, snobbery,
displays of virtuosity; his only solid qualities being a
never-changing kindliness and amiability and an enthusiastic and touching love for his old home represented
by his beloved sister Louise.   In the year 1800, when
at the summit of his fame, honoured to a rare degree
both as actor and author, he pays the warmest homage
to the small citizen's wife in Hanover, in words which,
in spite of their effusiveness, are beautiful in their tender
feeling: " In truth, you, my beloved, my dear, faithful,

never-to-be-forgotten sister, to this day you are my
first love, and you shall be my last thought. Any good
that is in me comes from you. Whatever I may accomplish for the benefit of others is due to you." And
two days before his death, on 20th September 1814, in
the last letter he wrote in his life, he dictated as follows :
"My love for you is the spirit of my life, and my life
is warmed and nourished by this flame."

With Iffland the dramatic art of the eighteenth
century died in Germany. But before his death he had
opened the door to the new era. One of his last acts as
manager was to attach Ludwig Devrient, the greatest
dramatic genius of the romantic period, to his stage, and
by doing so he himself gave admittance to the new
generation, who had struggled so hard against him
during the last years of his life.

ADRIENNE LECOUVREUR

I

AT the beginning of the eighteenth century the conditions of dramatic art in France were just as settled and centralised as they were desultory and confused in Germany at the same period.

Theatrical performances were certainly to be seen all over France, but the dramatic achievements in the larger or smaller provincial towns do not count; they have no history. All the lesser lights were eclipsed by the radiance of Paris; and here again theatrical art was entirely centred in the Théâtre Français.

This state of things was not the consequence of natural development, it was due to Royal authority, to the will of the great Louis. Since 1680[1] French acting had been allowed nowhere but in the theatre of the "King's Great Actors." Nay, during the last years of the King, when he lived under the influence of his bigoted mistress and the priests, even the hitherto highly appreciated Italians were banished,[2] and the great capital had only two dramatic resorts, the Royal Academy of Music, *i.e.* the Opera, and the Comédie Française.

---

[1] *Molière and His Times*, vol. iv. pp. 258-60.

[2] In 1697, comp. Italian Commedia dell' Arte (*Hist. of Theatr. Art*, vol. ii. p. 317 f.).

Thrifty and persevering managers, it is true, tried to
keep up the custom of acting popular plays at the fairs,
and, in spite of all prohibitions and persecutions, they
succeeded at last in evading the law by all kinds of
cunning tricks in preserving this amusement, nay in
creating new varieties of these entertainments.[1] But
though several writers, even of the better sort,[2] contributed plays to be acted by the merry and irreverent
comedians of the fairs, their art remained outside the
pale of æsthetic laws and jurisdiction, being a queer and
exciting combination of acrobatic feats, conjuring tricks,
and odd caricature of true dramatic art.

The bestowal on the Théâtre Français of the monopoly of the right to represent the legitimate drama did
not tend to benefit that theatre.   The strenuous life
which had animated it in the time of Molière had relaxed
into calm security and too contented self-complacency in
authors and actors, even, we may say, in the public.

Dramatic literature flowed on in the grooves that had
been originated by the great names of the preceding
century, without fresh ideas or new forms.   Tragedy
was in the worse plight, and it is certainly a trying task
to read works by La Grange-Chancel, the Abbé Telle-
grin, Fontenelle, La Mothe, and others, among the
epigoni of Racine.   It was absolutely impossible for
dramatic art to derive fresh substance from these formal,

---

[1] Thus the *Opéra comique* developed out of the old musical plays performed at the fairs, some of which parodied the style of the serious operas,
whence the title, comic operas.

[2] Above all Lesage, who, having had many difficulties at the Théâtre
Français with his best comedy, *Turcaret*, turned to the actors of the fairs,
for whom he wrote many an amusing play.

florid declamations. We must content ourselves with
admiring those who had patience enough to learn these
endless alexandrines by heart, and could make others
listen to them.

Comedy, indeed, fared a good deal better. Though
no comic author rose to the level of Molière, because
none aimed with such intense power as he at the foibles
of mankind and of his time, there were, about the year
1700, a good number of able writers who composed
amusing plays which not only dominated the comic stage
all over Europe, but among which many may still be
read, and even acted, with pleasure. In France, Regnard,
the great traveller and experienced man of the world, is
considered as a semi-classic, and his best comedy, *The
Gambler*, is indeed considered a model of an easy and
natural character-play in the taste of the time. Voltaire
said, "He who cannot appreciate Regnard is not
worthy to admire Molière." The wit of Lesage is more
heavy and coarse, but not less natural, and with his
Turcaret he introduced a new type on the stage, the
man of money, the upstart, the financier, who in actual
life held such an important position at a time when the
State was making violent efforts to procure money at any
cost, and whom, at the beginning of the century, people
were only too pleased to see ridiculed on the stage.

Somewhat inferior to Regnard were Dufresny, a
schemer and an eccentric, and d'Ancourt, both of them
popular and fertile playwrights, whose easy style and
purposeless comic humour pleased the public of the
Regency, who wanted nothing but amusement. Among
the plays of Dufresny, *Baguette de Vulcain, Attendez-*

moi sous l'orme, Lot supposé, and *Double Veuvage,* and
among those of Dancourt, *Chevalier à la mode, Fête de
village,* and other rustic plays, in which this author ex-
celled, were found in the *répertoires* of all European
stages. Writers of a somewhat later generation were
Néricault, Destouches, and Marivaux, both genuine
eighteenth century men, in whom both philosophy and
the influence of English morals appear in the bud.
Destouches, the refined diplomat, the trusted ambassador
of the Regent to the Court of St James, had in London
become acquainted with English literature, and borrowed
material from it in his own way for his lightly-moralising
character-plays, among which *Le Glorieux* became the
most popular. Marivaux philosophised ingeniously and
elaborately over the tender feelings, and invented complicated plots for the display of his elegant characters.

However, none of these authors, who wrote a fluent
and comprehensive style, broke new ground. We very
seldom meet with a new character, a fresh type from
life, like the coarse, ridiculously vain financier. This
abundance of new plays contained no poetic wealth, only
well-cultivated productive ability. The same situations,
the same characters, though somewhat modified by time,
recur over and over again, and dramatic art, which found
no creative genius to regenerate it, naturally became
stereotyped in accepted forms and departments to a
degree unknown before. Its different branches were
more sharply divided than ever before, and stress had to
be laid, and was laid, more on artistic and elaborate
diction than on fresh and vivid delineations of human
character.

Just as an opera-singer has his special branch allotted to him according to the compass and quality of his voice, so the actor was limited almost exclusively to one domain of art.   Each actor had his speciality beyond which he did not go ; he was engaged for a certain *emploi*, as it was called, which he had the sole right to occupy and the obligation to master.

Male parts in tragedy were *kings*, *tyrants*, and *lovers*, besides the so-called *seconds rôles*—parts of second rank—confidants, etc. ; the female parts were *princesses*, *mothers*, *lovers*, and *seconds rôles*.

Comedy had its *financiers* and *manteaux*, *i.e.* old comic parts ; after *Turcaret* the financier became a standing type ; *manteaux* were such parts as Harpagon, Orgon or Géronte ; besides these there were *lovers*, *valets*, and *peasants*.   The female divisions were *duègnes*, *i.e.* comic old women like Mme. Pernelle, Frosine, etc., *les grandes coquettes* (Elmire, Célimène), *amoureuses*, and *soubrettes* (maid servants).

Besides those mentioned there were all the small parts, which were filled by the *utilités*, or, as they were called in theatrical slang, the *bouche-trous* (stop-gaps).

It was not the custom as yet to engage actors for tragedy or comedy separately.   The tragic lover also played the young men in comedy, and was the *jeune premier* of the company.   The princess in tragedy was at the same time the *grande coquette* in comedy.   As a peculiarity it may be noticed that kings and peasants were generally included in the same division.

The foremost representative of a *genre* was called *chef d'emploi*, but each chief had his *double* (under-study), whose duty it was at any time to step in and undertake the part of the chief. Sometimes a part was even given to a third actor, thus, according to a technical term, being doubled both *en second* and *en troisième*.

An actor or actress was engaged for his or her special *emploi* by *les Premiers Gentilshommes de la Chambre*, who also issued regulations for the financial or disciplinary leadership of the theatre. After its alliance with the government, the conditions of the theatre, on the whole, were less free than before. However, the old republican forms dating from the time of Molière, were still maintained in the discharge of daily business, the artistic management and the distribution of the proceeds.

There was no single leader, but all the shareholders assembled once a week,[1] on Monday at 10 A.M., and discussed the affairs of the theatre, heard new plays read, accepted or refused them, distributed the parts, and so forth. The male shareholders discharged the daily business by turns, each for a week, and the actor who served as *régisseur* was called *semainier*.[2]

If the dramatic art of this period was restrained within the narrow limits of recitatives and dialogue, it was due in a great measure to the external conditions of the stage.

The theatre in which the Comédie Française acted at the beginning of and throughout the eighteenth

[1] In order to secure the presence of all the members, each of the assistants—according to a custom which still exists in France—received a counter, which was redeemed with ten francs. Afterwards, on seeing that most of the *sociétaires* attended the meetings very punctually, the value of the counter was lowered.

[2] It was this arrangement which the Emperor Joseph introduced at the *Burgtheater* in Vienna. Comp. above, p. 141, note.

century, had been built in 1689, when under a futile
pretext of the Sorbonne[1] the company was driven from
the Guénégaud theatre, and, after incredible vexations
caused by the clergy, had found new ground in the old
tennis court, " The Star," which was situated in the Rue
des Fossés, Saint-Germain-des-Près.[2]

The playhouse was quite a new building, and, though
not large, had been comparatively very expensive.[3]   As
a stage, however, it was unpractical, or suitable only
for the kind of comedy which was in fashion at the time.
It was long and narrow, like a corridor ; and the pit had
no seats.   There were three tiers, where the conditions
both for seeing and hearing were but moderate on account
of the oblong form, and—worst of all—half of the stage
was occupied by spectators, which left only a narrowly
confined space for the actors to move in, and which absolutely prevented every decorative and especially every
picturesque effect.[4]

The part of the stage which was left free from
spectators did not measure more than fifteen feet across

[1] It was asserted in the Faculty of Divinity that the close neighbourhood
of the theatre would have a disturbing influence on the college (" of the Four
Nations ") which was to be established in the vicinity.

[2] The front wall and some traces of the stage still exist in the Rue de
l'Ancienne Comédie, No. 14.   Even after the purchase of the ground the
clergy continued their obstinate struggle against the existence of the theatre.
An attempt was made to buy the ground surreptitiously, and in order to
make the seller break his word, his son-in-law, a shopkeeper, was threatened
that, " if he did not side with the clergy, God would curse his business, and he
would be ruined, but if he broke his promise to us [the actors (it is La
Grange who tells this story in his *Registre*)], he might even now consider
himself as blessed."   The honest shopkeeper, however, renounced the
ecclesiastical bliss and remained true to his word.

[3] It cost the actors all in all 198,233 liv., 16s. 6d.

[4] The reader will find a plan of the interior of this theatre in *Molière and
his Time*, p. 102, and details about spectators on the stage, p. 100 f.

35—"French Actors," after Watteau. The two central figures are Quinault Dufresne and his wife ; the figure farthest to the right is Paul Poisson (p. 227).

at the front and eleven feet at the back, and to this small space the actors were confined, closely surrounded by spectators except at the back. The space behind the gilt balustrade on the stage was crammed with *petits-maîtres*; to the left—seen from the pit—the so-called Queen's box was suspended so as to project in front of the stage, to the right the King's box,[1] and in the orchestra, close up to the stage, were rows of seats for spectators.

It is clear that under those conditions the methods used nowadays for scenery, make-up and costumes were unavailable. Make-up, especially, was limited to the absolutely indispensable, and did not go much beyond ordinary face-painting, such as was also used in private life ; and the costumes were quite conventional, resembling as far as possible contemporary court-dress.

In the seventeenth century some feeble and clumsy efforts had been made to create a kind of historical costume. These attempts were now totally abandoned, and were replaced partly by purely contemporary dresses, partly by the fantastic conventional finery of a masquerade.

In tragedy, and in all plays of whatever kind and period, the actresses generally appeared in contemporary court dress, with large *paniers,* with diamonds and feathers in their hair, and their dress loaded with fringe, lace, and bright ribbons.

The actors had adopted a hero-costume, which had

---

[1] Royalties were very seldom seen in the public playhouse ; they commanded the actors to play in the Court Theatre. The Royal boxes, therefore, were generally let to other spectators. When the Royalties now and then went to the public performances, those who occupied their seats had to leave them. The right hand side of the theatre was called the King's, the left hand side the Queen's, after these boxes.

to be worn in all parts.   They wore large Louis XIV. wigs, even after they had gone out of fashion, three-cornered hats with large bunches of feathers, elaborately worked gilt armours, wide silk sleeves, and a fine cambric shirt with lace cuffs.   Below the armour was a small round wicker-work frame, a *tonnelet*, to which was attached a short skirt with gilt fringe reaching down to the knees. Above the skirt was a broad sword-belt, also fringed, with a small ornamental dagger.   The hands were covered by gilt-fringed gloves, the legs by silk stockings and a kind of embroidered half-boots, trimmed with gold, and with high red heels.

On the stage heroes and heroines almost invariably held something in their hand, a fan, a magic wand, or some other object, and it was considered a daring innovation when Mlle. Maupin, the eccentric singer, when playing Medea in the opera of that name, attempted to omit this.

In contemporary comedy, of course, fashionable dress was adopted ; in antique plays, which were still in great favour, the characters appeared in the traditional costumes of the preceding century, but the lover appeared in the dress of the time.

The demand for rich and magnificent costumes on the stage was excessive, and no less great was the ambition of the performers to surpass each other in splendour.   Such costumes were enormously expensive ; an ordinary court dress might easily be worth 3000-4000 francs, and the dress of an actress, without particular extravagance, about 10,000 francs.   It frequently happened, however, that exquisite and distinguished courtiers, who only wore their clothes half-a-score of times, made a present of them to actors, thus enabling them to appear according to their assumed rank, nor were the actresses always obliged to defray all their expenses for dress out of their salary.

Nevertheless, in all this magnificent display, which appears ludicrous to modern eyes because it was used on all occasions, there was the thoroughly consistent and refined style frequently met with in depraved periods, which saved it from the vulgarity of a new comer. But, of course, this brilliant frame of gold, silk, feathers, lace and powder, patches and expensive gloves, was not the proper setting for strong, original, popular art, nor the proper vehicle for pure and fine poetry. A gaudy hot-house plant, which could not thrive in the open air, pompous and bizarre—such was the dramatic art cultivated within the walls of the Théâtre Français : show and declamation in tragedy ; raillery and grotesque jokes in comedy ; minute care in the elaboration of outward forms, but no outlook beyond established ideas, no desire for fresh subjects.

The Comédie Française was no meeting-place for the people,[1] it was a *rendezvous* for the old world of fashion. There was a stock pit of literary and learned

---

[1] For one thing, it was too expensive for them. The majority and the most expensive of the seats, *i.e.* the boxes in the first storey ; the balcony, *i.e.* the boxes above the stage ; the seats on the stage ; the orchestra and the amphitheatre, *i.e.* the raked seats behind the standing pit, cost 4 fr. ; the second tier, 2 fr. ; the third tier, 2½ fr. ; and finally, the pit, which, like the third tier, was unnumbered, 1 fr. As in those times money was worth about four times its present value, so that the cheapest places came to more than three shillings, it is clear that the Théâtre Français was not calculated for the pleasure of petty-folks.

men, officers and *beaux-esprits*, who formed the nucleus
of *connoisseurs*, encircled by a row of boxes filled with
fashionable ladies attended by their cavaliers, a stage
audience of smart and *blasé* young courtiers and dandies.
All these people knew each other as well as the actors.
They came night after night and amused themselves at
the play in a very different way from that in which we
seek enjoyment in the theatre nowadays.

There were no fine spectacles, no picturesque effects
of light, nor was there what may be properly called
dramatic suspense ; most of the things acted were known
by heart ; even the new plays were so much like the old
ones, so regularly cut after the old pattern, that the plot
could never cause surprise or suspense.

Everything depended on the treatment, declamation, diction, gesture, facial play. People wanted to hear
whether Mlle. Duclos would deliver such and such a
speech better to-night than last time, whether Beaubourg
would make them cry, whether Mlle. Desmares surpassed
Mlle. Beauval as such or such a *soubrette*, whether
Poisson equalled his father as Crispin. It all seemed
like a large party where the guests were entertained with
serious or diverting recitations, and where the audience
leisurely weighed and censured the different contributions.

This to a certain extent altered the position of the
actors. They came even socially into much closer contact with their elegant public. They no longer stood
apart as a distant, strange caste, who might indeed
sometimes be allowed to appear among other people,
but who could never count as anything but a sort of
remarkable gipsy-folk.

36

37

36—*Tragédienne* in costume (p. 228).   37—Mlle. Duclos (p. 235).

II

WHEN on the death of Louis XIV. France drew a breath of relief after the oppressive bigotry which had weighed on it for so many years, the strict social restraint was at once somewhat relaxed ; and without really being considered in a new light, or with a humane and democratic recognition of their being created like other mortals, these well-dressed, amusing, voluble people, whose wit was as sharp as anybody's, and who had acquired all the good manners of society, were accepted in the fashionable world.   There they moved like fish in the water; the actresses received duchesses in their drawing-rooms,[1] and in everyday life nobody noticed the deep gulf which was constantly kept open by the aristocracy between themselves and the world of artists.

The company who occupied the boards of the Théâtre Français at the death of the old King, were fully representative of their time.   There was no genius with high aspirations, with a firm purpose, placing art above everything else, with fresh visions, or bringing hidden treasures to the light.   All its members possessed a perfect delivery, for the pit had no mercy on offences against language, and was quite capable of hissing even one of its favourites, if the miserable sinner had committed a *pataquès*, *i.e.* pronounced a t for an s, or *vice*

[1] More intimate ties also were formed between the nobility and actors or actresses.   It happened very frequently that a fashionable *amoureux* of the stage became the accepted lover of some lady of high rank, and that actresses had their *liasons* in the highest circles.   The memoirs of the time unveil innumerable gallantries of this kind.

versâ, at the end of a word when the following word begins with a vowel.[1]

A few veterans of the classical period still remained at the Théâtre Français : the respectable old Guérin, second husband of Mme. Molière, who even at the age of eighty played his *manteau* parts in the comedy, and his confidants in tragedy to the unqualified satisfaction of the audience, and Pierre Lenoir la Thorillière,[2] a most excellent comic actor, in fact Molière's successor in all parts of the Scapin type, an admirable performer of all the cunning valets in contemporary comedy, Hector in *The Gambler*, Champagne in *La Mère Coquette*, Carlin in *L'Etourdi*, etc.   A smile on his bright, open face, a wink of his beautiful kindly eyes, was enough to charm the spectators.   While in his earlier days he had been apt to exaggerate, in his mature age he became a model of graceful comic art according to the school of Molière.   By this time he was somewhat advanced in age—he was born in 1656—but he was as popular as ever on account of his amiable humour, which won pardon for his too great inclination for the bottle.   He continued on the boards up to his seventy-fifth year, when he died, universally missed as the last disciple of the great master-comedian.

Another offshoot of an old family of actors was Paul

---

[1] This happened among others to the very popular Mlle. Contat, who was even hissed twice in the same play, Dancourt's *Chevalier à la mode*, once on account of false pronunciation and once for a slip of memory.

[2] P. L. la Thorillière was the second and the best of three generations of actors of that name.   His father, formerly a cavalry officer, belonged to the company of Molière, where he was a trusted man, but as an actor he was inferior to his son.   The last of the three, Anne Maurice Thorillière, was a mediocre copy of his excellent father.

Poisson, who entered completely into his father's [1] famous *genre*, in which he became almost as popular and amusing.

But if the comic school adhered faithfully to the teaching of Molière, the tragic style had found performers whose art must have made him writhe with pain in his tomb.

When Baron, the cleverest pupil of Molière, the lover and hero born, retired from the stage for the first time, in 1691, his parts were allotted to a provincial actor, Beaubourg,[2] who was chosen out of a number of different aspirants at a kind of competition, partly because he was the son-in-law of an excellent comic actress, Mme. Beauval, partly because his rivals for the *sociétaire*-ship were even worse than he.

Beaubourg succeeded after an amazingly short time in pulling down all that Baron had built up in the tragic style. The noble, dignified simplicity, the natural expressive delivery, the restrained easy movements, the thoughtful delicacy with which he rendered the gradations of sentiment,—for all these qualities that had been admired in Baron Beaubourg substituted their opposites. Being of very limited intellect, he constantly put deep meaning into irrelevant things, and accentuated them excessively, while passing lightly and hastily over the essential idea. He was not good-looking, and lacked natural dignity, and, to make up for these defects, he puffed himself up to sham distinction, and to violent, absurd gesticulation. His voice was badly trained, and

---

[1] Raimond Poisson, the great Crispin. *Molière and his Times*, p. 127 ff.

[2] Pierre Trochon de Beaubourg was born about 1662. So he was nearly thirty years old when he made his *début* at the Théâtre Français. He retired in 1718, and died in 1725.

his delivery not sufficiently cultivated, so he chose to roar out his feelings in a frantic, ear-splitting fashion.

It was this last expedient which imposed on the public and made him fancy that he was a great actor. Strong physical efforts frequently delude the performer and make him think that he really feels the passion he interprets, and this illusion also imparts itself to the spectator and makes him feel as if he heard and saw grand things. So, if carried out energetically, the boisterous manner will never quite miss its effect. And certainly Beaubourg did not lack persistent energy. He would roar out a speech which was meant to be delivered with absolute calm and coolness, with such mad fury that the audience could not help bursting into applause, quite forgetting the absurdity of it.

No wonder, therefore, that Beaubourg even formed a school by his antiquated tricks. Mlle. Champmeslé, who in spite of all her defects possessed a distinct tragic temperament, had died in 1698, but she left two pupils, one of whom, her niece, Mlle. Desmares,[1] minutely copied her artificial chanting declamation in tragedy (in comedy she was the most fascinating, frolicsome *soubrette*), while the other, Mlle. Duclos,[2] exaggerated it to extremes, and

[1] Christine Antoinette Charlotte Desmares was born in Copenhagen, in 1682, while her father, Nicolas Desmares, and her mother, Anne d'Eunebaut, were engaged at the French court-company in that town. Her *début* was in one of her aunt's tragic parts (Iphigenia in *Orestes and Pylades*, by La Grange-Chancel). She retired in 1721, and died in 1753.

[2] Marie Anne de Châteauneuf, called Duclos, was born in 1670. At first she was engaged at the Opera, but subsequently in 1693 became an actress at the Théâtre Français. She continued acting till the age of sixty-three though by that time her style had gone quite out of fashion. She married in 1725, at the age of fifty-five, a very young actor, who ill-treated her and became the scourge of her life.

perverted it after the fashion of Beaubourg into ridiculous bombast, which for a time won her many admirers.

Beaubourg and Mlle. Duclos together represented the exaggerated school, which by provincial troupes and foreign court-companies propagated the French tragic manner. We have become acquainted with outrunners of this school through the efforts among others of Karolina Neuber and Döbbelin.

The only actor at the Théâtre Français, who at this time maintained a sound and genuine tragic style, was Ponteuil, but his stout, fat figure did not suit him for the *jeune premier*, so he remained throughout in the second rank.

A strong and dominating position at the theatre was occupied by the Quinault family, which numbered no less than six members, a father and five children, besides sisters-in-law and other relatives. Family rule is always detrimental to a theatre; in this case it was particularly so, as this family dominated more by their number than by prominent abilities. The most important of them were the two brothers Jean-Baptiste Quinault[1] and Quinault-Dufresne. The former was a tolerably able actor in the light-comic *genre*, but he was especially serviceable to the company by his talent for music, as he was the composer of most of the little musical pieces which at the time were fashionable as after-plays.

Quinault-Dufresne was a very fine young man—he was born in 1693—who at the age of nineteen made his *début* as Orestes in Crébillon's *Électre*, and was at once appointed the *double* of Beaubourg. He formed a pleasant

[1] The father seems to have been in a low position. He retired in 1717.

contrast to this tragedian, in so far as he had no taste at all for furious acting. Where Beaubourg roared Dufresne cooed, and his gentle, pleasant voice melted the hearts of the elegant ladies in the boxes. When Beaubourg retired in 1718, Quinault-Dufresne, though very young, undertook all his parts, and became a lover and hero quite to the average taste of the Regency : impudent, depraved, heartless, but with excellent manners, a superficial ready wit, and a caressing amiability that won him great favour with the other sex.

From Baron, whom, as it seems, he wished to resemble, he had inherited, not the genius, but the absurd self-adoration, which in one who had nothing to justify it became mere affectation and parody, and tempted him to treat the audience with the arrogant insolence that was successful in the case of Baron, but turned out a miserable failure with Quinault-Dufresne. Thus one evening, when he spoke so low that nobody could hear him, and voices from the audience cried, "*plus haut !*" he contemptuously descended to the footlights and said in a commanding tone, "*Et vous plus bas !*" But this arrogance was not well received, and the following evening he had to make an apology for his impudence.

The examples of his tragic style which have been preserved are abominable in their studied affectation. In the first act of Corneille's *Cinna*, where the hero has a long speech to Emilie about the horrors of the proscription, Dufresne held his hat or helmet, to which was attached a large red plume of feathers, behind his back, and when he came to the lines,

38—Scene of *Le Glorieux*. The central figure is Quinault Dufresne ; the lady by his side, Mlle. Gaussin (p. 236).

" Ici le fils baigné dans le sang de son père
Et sa tête à la main demandant son salaire,"

he suddenly held out his hat and shook the feathers, as if it were his father's head with the bloody curls.

As Pyrrhus in Racine's *Andromaque* he used even a worse trick.   In the speech—Act II. sc. v.—where Pyrrhus repeats the words of Andromaque to her son Astyanax, he pronounced the following lines in the soft, velvety tones of a female treble :

" C'est Hector" (*disait-elle en l'embrassant toujours*),
" Voilà ses yeux, sa bouche et déjà son audace !
C'est lui même, c'est toi, cher époux, que j'embrasse "—

then suddenly changing into a deep male voice :

" Et quelle est sa pensée ?   Attend-elle en ce jour
Que je lui laisse un fils pour nourrir son amour ?
Non, non, je l'ai juré, ma vengeance est certaine," etc.[1]

No doubt, in comedy Quinault-Dufresne was much better than in tragic heroes.   Many of the vain young dandies were the very characters suited to him ; some of them, such as Jufière, the leading part in *Le Glorieux*, the most successful play of Destouches, were written on purpose for him and modelled on him.[2]

Mlle. Clairon hits the mark when she says of

[1] These examples are preserved by one of the many compilations of the eighteenth century : *Anecdotes dramatiques* of 1775, articles *Cinna* and *Andromaque*, vol. i. pp. 75 and 205.

[2] From mere carelessness Quinault-Dufresne kept this play lying on the tester of his bed for three years without reading it.   So great was the power of the actor, that Destouches dared not till then urge him to open the dusty MS. and read it.

him in her Memoirs : "More dazzling than deep, refined, but never terrible, without system or artistic principles, lacking all the great features that characterise genius, Dufresne owed his successes exclusively to the extreme beauty of his person and his voice, and there can be no doubt that in those times the public did not demand so much as it does nowadays."

In 1727 Quinault-Dufresne married Mlle. de Seine, an actress of talent, but of delicate health, who remained only for a short time at the theatre, and whom he tormented in every way.   They were soon divorced, after he had spent her dowry and sold her jewels and clothes.[1]

Of the three sisters Quinault the two elder did not obtain great importance ; one of them, who became Mme. de Nesle, possessed talent, but died very young ; the other, who had no gift for the stage, left it very soon.   With respect to her the remarkable fact may be mentioned that after acting for about nine years she received her annual pension for seventy years, probably through the influence of her powerful family.

The youngest sister, Jeanne Françoise, became a very spirited *soubrette*—she doubled Mlle. Desmares in this character — but she became more widely known after her departure from the stage, when her home became one of the best known literary resorts, among whose central figures d'Alembert occupied a prominent position beside the fine and stately hostess.

On the whole the kinship among the families at the

_____
[1] See the documents of the divorce suit in Campardon : *Les Comédiens du Roi*, pp. 240-43.

39

ADRIENNE LE COUVREUR
Actrice du Théatre François
Née à Fimes en 1690. Morte à Paris le 20 Mars 1730.

40

39—Mlle. de Seine (p. 238).　　　　　40—Adrienne Le Couvreur (p. 240).

Théâtre Français was very close. Besides the La Thorillières, the Poissons, the Desmares, and the Quinaults, we meet with the families of Dangeville —who were afterwards to put forth so fine a flower as the fascinating Marie Anne Dangeville—and Dancourt, among whom the husband, Florent Carton Dancourt, has already been mentioned as a very popular and fertile playwright.[1]

These families again were intermixed by marriage, the Dangevilles with the Desmares, the d'Ancourts with the La Thorillières, and so on : it is quite a puzzle to find out the relationship among these old actor families.

III

Adrienne Lecouvreur—Her Special Position as Actress—Her Person— Her Mystic Death.

IN the solid and practical institution for family-main-tenance which the house of Molière had become, on this stage of gay luxury, petty quarrels, professional inflation, indolent geniality, abundant artifice, cham-pagne-bubbling, humour in comedy and over-powdered, stunted art in tragedy, we see the sudden apparition of a delicate, poetic figure. Among all the self-complacent, smiling or affectedly tearful faces our eyes at last dis-cover the grave and characteristic features of Adrienne Lecouvreur.

It was on 27th March 1717, that Mlle. Lecouvreur

---

[1] He was also an able and popular actor in the comic line, but very bad in tragedy. The Misanthrope is mentioned as one of his best parts. Born in 1661, he now belonged to the older generation, and was a fat, merry and witty *viveur*, who, like the brothers Quinault, was a favourite in the light-living refined society.

was seen for the first time on the stage of the Comédie Française as Électre in Crébillon's tragedy of that name, and as the artful Angélique in Molière's *George Dandin.*

But by that time she was already a developed actress and a woman who had passed through many emotional experiences. Adrienne Lecouvreur was of humble extraction ; her father was a poor village hatter, Robert Couvreur, who, fortunately for art, in 1702 had followed his inclination to settle in Paris, when his little daughter was ten years old.[1]

How it was that, educated under miserable conditions and without the slightest contact with any kind of art, she conceived a desire and acquired abilities to interpret the over-refined poetry of the old French dramatists, is one of the ever recurring enigmas which meet us in our researches into the ways of genius. So much is certain, that we see her at thirteen years of age a member of one of the amateur troupes then so frequent, astonishing her hearers by reciting Corneille's verses, and as Pauline in *Polyeucte* in a peculiar way, unlike the usual declamation.

Adrienne had an aunt who was a laundress, and who was employed by a Mr Legrand, *sociétaire* of the Comédie Française. This man was a bad actor, but a clever and original character. He had formerly acted abroad with French companies and owed his appointment at the Théâtre Français to the patronage of the Dauphin, the son of Louis XIV. He served as *double* to Ponteuil in the king and peasant line, but had to suffer much from the noisy discontent of the pit, though

[1] She was born on 5th April 1692.

he knew how to disarm the malcontents by his cool, ready wit and unsparing self-criticism.[1] He was an ugly man, stout and square-built, with a broad, comic face and a strong, sonorous voice. He employed his intelligence and wit in writing a number of light comic plays, which are forgotten now, but several of them were very popular at the time in the Théâtre Français, at the Opera and on the Italian stage.

This original, who was as good a teacher as he was a bad actor, took charge of little Adrienne, whom the laundress had recommended to his patronage, and there can scarcely be any doubt that his lively, intelligent instruction was most effective in promoting the development of the child, who as yet only knew that she loved her art.

At the age of sixteen Legrand made her rehearse before a colleague of his, the widow Fonpré, who was to

---

[1] When the actors were ordered to play at Court, it was of course the best of them who had to obey the call, and the Parisians had to content themselves with the *doubles*, which was far from pleasing them. Thus one evening Racine's famous *Mithridate* was acted by a choice collection of mediocrities. The pit was in a rage and kept hooting and hissing the unfortunate actors in the first act so furiously that they did not dare to reappear, and suggested that the performance should be cancelled and the money returned to the playgoers. This arrangement, however, did not suit Legrand, who had not yet been on the boards, and he said : "No, no, my dear friends ! We have a considerable sum in the cash box ; I will go and speak to them ; leave it to me." So he ordered the curtain up, stepped on towards the foot-lights, bowed humbly to the audience, and said in a sad and modest tone : "Gentlemen,"—it was customary to address the pit, which contained only men,—" Mlle. Duclos, Mssrs. Beaubourg and Ponteuil are obliged to play at Court. We are exceedingly sorry not to possess their talent, thus being unable to replace them. However, if the theatre were not to be closed to-day, we had no choice but to play *Mithridate*. We admit that it is performed by very bad actors—you have not even seen the worst, for I will not conceal the fact that I myself am going to play Mithridate." At this unexpected self-depreciation the impressionable pit burst out laughing, and the performance was allowed to go on in peace.

undertake the leadership of the theatre in Lille.   The able and commanding manageress was pleased with the clever novice and engaged her at once.   And in Lille, the Flemish fortress, which just at that time was subject to the horrors of the War of the Spanish Succession, Adrienne Lecouvreur made her *début* in 1708, the same year in which the town was taken by the Duke of Marlborough and Prince Eugène.

The young girl gained immediate success and was whirled away into a tumultuous life of art and love. But Adrienne took both more seriously than was the custom with her colleagues.   She soon experienced the disappointments of love, but she never learned to treat it *en bagatelle*, with the airy superiority of her century. And she gave herself up to her art with the same unfashionable gravity.   War and troubled political conditions were very far from impeding theatrical affairs.[1] Possibly the French officers were even more skilled as playgoers than as warriors, and Adrienne Lecouvreur gained her first laurels from these appreciative spectators, who favoured her original talents and fresh beauty with all the enthusiasm of exiled Parisians.   Ere long she became the acknowledged leading lady in the provinces.

For nine years she travelled about in the country and finally occupied the position of leading actress in Strasburg, which possessed one of the finest provincial theatres.   It was managed for a number of years by Jean Quinault, the father of the large Quinault family of

---

[1] Voltaire in his *Siècle de Louis XIV.* tells us how during the siege of Lille a bomb fell close to the theatre without the performance being broken off.

the Théâtre Français. Had not serious trouble, caused by an unfortunate love affair, driven her away, it may be doubted whether she would ever have gone to Paris. The son of a high civil officer, Count de Klinglin, had offered her marriage and had become her lover, but at the moment when she was to give birth to his child, he forsook her and married a lady of his own rank. In despair at his faithlessness, and too proud to continue her relations with him, she left Strasburg and went to Paris, where she presented herself to make her *début*, and was at once accepted. This event, which created the greatest expectations and made people say that she began as the greatest actresses used to finish, became a turning-point in the history of the Comédie Française, in so far as her independent art opened the eyes of the public to the empty mannerism of the old school.

She had only worked thirteen years in Paris when a mysterious and miserable death carried her off; years full of opposition and intrigues, especially from the Quinault family, but also of great victories of intellectual life, appreciation and sympathy from the best men and women of the time, advantages which she could never have obtained in the provinces, where she had trained herself in solitude.

The new element which Adrienne Lecouvreur infused into dramatic art was just what it had lacked for many years, what may be expressed in one word—soul. Contemporaries, in their wonder at the inexplicable power of her acting, use many circumlocutions to illustrate the fact that it was by giving up her whole personality to her art that she reaped her success in it.

Her voice was rather feeble and had no large compass, but she knew how to give an infinite variety to her comparatively few tones, to put animation into them which struck the hearers as something quite new. Nor was her person tall, but she was slender and had a very good figure, not exuberant, as was usually the case with *tragédiennes*. Her face was delicate and characteristic, with a gently curved nose, large expressive eyes, and a small, full mouth—a genuine eighteenth-century type.

Her facial play was very carefully worked out, and her art has been compared with that of a miniature painter. A contemporary gives the following graphic description of it :—

"She never appeared on the stage without seeming to be penetrated by her part. Her eyes told you what she was going to say—her fear, her anxiety, were pictured in her face. . . . The spectator yielded himself up to all her emotions, he was as deeply stirred, as overcome, as she. He feared, wailed, trembled with her, nay his tears dropped before hers. This is not surprising at all, for you saw nothing in her which did not seem real and genuine. It was her heart more than her voice which spoke to you." [1]

All testimonies agree about the technique of her delivery. It impressed people as being perfectly new and surprisingly independent, because for some twenty years they had been unaccustomed to an art of speech founded on nature. In fact, "nature" is the word we

---

[1] *Seconde lettre du souffleurs de la Comédie*, which is ascribed to Du Mas d'Aigueberre ; quoted by Georges Monval, *Lettres de Adrienne Lecouvreur*, p. 71.

meet with everywhere in connection with Adrienne Lecouvreur. Yet her delivery was the fruit of elaborate art, according to the school of Baron, with many delicate shades, transitions, and pauses. But there was true art in this imitation of reality ; it impressed you like nature itself, compared with the monotonous chanting or roaring delivery. The natural genius of Adrienne Lecouvreur was not of the kind which blindly follows the impulse of the moment. Her naturalness was method, and had been acquired with full consciousness. In an interesting letter to the Marquis de la Chalotais she writes : " You say that you wish me to teach you the art of declamation, of which you are in need. But have you forgotten that I do not declaim ? The simplicity of my acting is its one feeble merit ; but this simplicity which chance has rendered so fortunate to me must, I think, be unavoidable in a man like yourself. First of all, one must have as much *esprit* as you possess, and then leave all the rest to dear nature ; to over-exert it is to spoil it. Grace, nobility, and simplicity of expression, special force only in argument and in real facts, all this you can show in word and deed better than anybody else." [1]

Though she recommends the marquis to leave everything to dear nature—perhaps only because she knows how difficult it is to teach people not to recite in a rhetorical, but in a natural way—she herself did not obey this presumably too simple rule, but worked out her naturalness to a high degree of perfection, supported by the example and personal teaching of Baron. It may have been her talent, the style of which entirely suited his taste—that tempted

[1] *Lettres de Adrienne Lecouvreur* lettre xlviii.

the great actor in his sixty-seventh year to return to the scene of his former triumphs and continue acting for several years with his clever pupil.[1]

Of these two great geniuses Baron was probably the greater and the more versatile, because, for one thing, he mastered comic characters as completely as tragic,[2] whereas the noble dignity and deep feeling of Adrienne could not easily adapt itself to the comic *genre*. Her parts in comedy were performed with spirit, elegance, and delicacy, and some of them, which did not require too much hilarity, she acted most charmingly ; but she lacked the genuine comic spirit, and her adversaries said that in her comic parts she was always too much of a queen.[3] Racine was her principal author and her idol ; nearly all his leading female characters, such as Iphigénie, Phèdre, Andromaque, etc., belonged to her *répertoire*. But besides these she acted in the plays of all the contemporary tragic authors, and she helped to introduce young Voltaire's first dramatic attempts (*Artemire, Œdipe, Marianne, l'Indiscret*) to the stage. He was an enthusiastic admirer of her talent, and wrote the memorial address which was spoken in the Théâtre Français after her death.[4]

[1] Baron's characteristics as an actor are treated in *Molière and his Times*, pp. 237 f.

[2] In his seventy-third year he took up an entirely new branch, performing for the first time, Arnolphe, in *L'Ecole des Femmes*, together with his young pupil Mlle. Angélique.

[3] See, *e.g.*, the opinion of Collé in his *Journal historique*, edit. Bonhomme, p. 140.

[4] In which he says, among other things : ". . . this incomparable actress, who almost invented the art of speaking to the heart, and of showing feeling and truth where formerly had been shown little but artificiality and declamation."

Among her comic parts those that suited her best were probably Célimène in *Le Misanthrope* and Elmire in *Tartufe*, as well as *L'Andrienne* by Baron. She frequently played in Marivaux's *Surprises de l'Amour* (though in this play the author was not satisfied with her) and in *Roi de Cocagne* by her old teacher Legrand.

But the play in which she acted most frequently of all was *Inès de Castro*, an abominable fashionable tragedy by La Mothe Houdard.

At the Théâtre Français, without pushing or intriguing at all, Mlle. Lecouvreur soon acquired an absolutely leading position, which could not be shaken, either by the united efforts of the Quinault family or by the older leading ladies, Duclos and Desmares. The sympathetic Mlle. Desmares retired a few years after the *début* of Adrienne, whereas Mlle. Duclos, though twenty-two years older than her more fortunate rival, without the slightest encouragement from the public, continued to play even three years after the death of Adrienne.

This death, it is true, occurred while the great actress was in the prime of life, at the height of her fame, and the climax of her art.

Externally, the position of Mlle. Lecouvreur was extremely brilliant. Her house, as that of a highly-honoured theatrical queen, became a meeting-place of the most distinguished society. "It is an established fashion to have dinner or supper with me, because some duchesses have shown me this honour," she writes in a letter of 5th May 1728. Her apartments were fur-

nished with great taste and luxury.[1]   The most intellectual men and women of the time were received by her;
she herself wrote charming verses and clever letters.
And though this all-absorbing society life was not really
to her taste—"I spend three-quarters of my time in
doing what I do not care for," she writes in mentioning
it — she might well be excused if this familiar intercourse with distinguished men and women made her—
the once poor child of an artisan—think that she was
now accepted, if not as an equal, at least as a person
who possessed rights and claims to justice, no less than
those who surrounded her.   Time was to teach her and
others that people in her condition had not the right to
live, nor even to die, like *les honnêtes gens*.

Adrienne Lecouvreur had a lover.   This was no
remarkable thing for an actress at that time, no more
than for a lady of rank, unless in so far as it was the rule
to have more than one.

The favourite suitor of Adrienne was Count Maurice
of Saxony, one of the many natural sons of the Elector,
Frederick Augustus.[2]   This fashionable and athletic
warrior, however, was also desired by others, not least
by one of the highest ladies in France, the young and
beautiful Duchesse de Bouillon, *née* Princess of Lorraine,
a type of the depraved women of the Regency, whose
cold-blooded passion formed a remarkable contrast to
her youth and fresh beauty.   She had already conferred

---

[1] This is seen from the inventory made after her death.   Her plate
alone was valued at 7848 fr. 15 sous.

[2] Afterwards King of Poland.   Maurice's mother was the beautiful
Aurora Königsmark, his Swedish mistress who gave birth to this son in
Goslar, in 1696.

marked distinction on the theatre, as at least three of its male attractions are mentioned as having been her lovers.[1]

In the struggle between these two women—the great aristocratic lady and the celebrated actress—for the man, who to the former was only *un instrument de plaisir*, while to the latter he was the object of a deep and self-sacrificing love,[2] it was Adrienne who had to succumb.

The dark and hideous byways of this sad story have never been, and probably never will be, quite cleared up. It is a fact that in the summer of 1729 Adrienne was warned against the Duchesse de Bouillon by a little hunch-backed Abbé, who was a miniature painter. He asserted that the Duchess, whose portrait he had painted, wanted to poison Adrienne. He presented the venomous pastilles which were destined for the purpose. They were examined by himself, the Count of Saxony, and Adrienne, and produced sickness in all three in consequence. The affair seemed clear enough, but when the police had been informed of the matter, it was not the profligate Duchess against whom they proceeded, but the poor little Abbé. He was thrown into prison. Seeing that his only means of escape was to retract, he revoked his accusation, and took his punishment. The

[1] The handsome conceited Quinault-Dufresne, Tribou, the opera-singer, and Grandval, the charming *jeune premier*, who made his *début* in 1729. At this time the Duchess was only twenty-two years old.

[2] Unfortunately Adrienne's letters to Maurice de Saxe are lost, but there can be no doubt of her genuine love for him through several years. As a small proof it may be mentioned that while Maurice was trying to win the Duchy of Courland in 1725, and was in want of money, she sold ornaments, diamonds, and plate to the value of 40,000 livres, and sent the money to her hero.

affair was now settled in a simple and easy way. But only for a time ; for in spite of all efforts to hush it up, the story became known among the scandal-mongering Parisian public, and its dramatic second act was placed on the stage itself.

Adrienne Lecouvreur, seeing that it would be impossible for her, the actress, to obtain justice against the criminal Duchess, took her little vengeance in her own domain. On 18th October she acted *Phèdre*. The Duchesse de Bouillon was in her box, as beautiful, brilliant, and calm as ever.

But when Adrienne as Phèdre came to the celebrated lines in which she says to Oenone, her confidante :

Je sais mes perfidies,
Oenone, et ne suis point de ces femmes hardies.
Qui, goûtant dans le crime une tranquille paix,
Ont su se faire un front qui ne rougit pas,[1]

she suddenly turned towards her dangerous enemy and hurled the words into her face.

The audience, who knew and understood the human drama which was blazing up behind the old verses, burst into frantic applause, while the Duchess had difficulty in concealing her fury.

Five months later, on 20th March 1730, Adrienne Lecouvreur died from a sudden and violent gastric attack, which the physicians declared to be an internal hæmorrhage.

It was not the custom in those times to shed tears over the tragedies of real life, and it did not even create

---

[1] Act III. scene 3.

much indignation that the great actress should be denied not only burial with religious rites, but burial of any sort—whether for the reason that she had refused to repent of her disgraceful profession, or because the powerful hand of her rival persecuted her even after her death—so that the body of the noblest, most refined French actress was wrapped up like a parcel, laid on a hired cart, driven away at midnight without attendance, and laid in the ground, nobody knows where.

Two days later, it is true, on the 22nd of March, a meeting was held by the *sociétaires* of the Théâtre Français, at which Voltaire was also present. The actors, of course, were indignant at the contempt with which their colleague had been treated, and Voltaire encouraged them to declare that they would stop acting unless it were guaranteed that they, who were appointed by the King, and were entitled to receive a pension from him, should be treated like his other subjects, who did not stand under his special patronage. This the actors enthusiastically promised to do, and then continued to act without thinking further of the matter.

But Adrienne Lecouvreur had no grave on which an admirer of her noble art might have laid a memorial wreath.

THE SCHOOL OF VOLTAIRE

I

Voltaire as Dramatist—English Influence—Shakespeare and Voltaire—
Voltaire's Relations to the Actors and their Art—Voltaire as Stage-
Manager.

In 1726 Voltaire was exiled from France. He went to
England and lived there till 1729. These three years
in the country of Shakespeare, Newton, Locke, and of
personal liberty, worked a perfect change in him, and
became of the greatest consequence, not only to himself,
but to the whole intellectual development in France. It
was the theatre, in particular, which drew advantage from
it, the institution which in the eyes of Voltaire was " the
noblest and most useful thing invented by the human
mind to form and polish morals and manners."

A few months after his return from London,[1] and
after having seen, to his great indignation, that the
body of the greatest French actress had been flung into
the ground like the carcase of an animal, he received
news from England that the remains of Mrs Oldfield
had been most pompously buried in Westminster Abbey.
The different way of thinking of the two nations at once
put Voltaire, the fanatical hater of all fanaticism, into a
glowing heat, which he tried to impart to the phlegmatic

[1] In most biographies of Voltaire and Adrienne Lecouvreur we read that
Voltaire returned from the splendid funeral of Mrs Oldfield and became a
witness of the disgraceful treatment of Adrienne Lecouvreur. But the death
of Mrs Oldfield occurred on 23rd October 1730, seven months after that of
Mlle. Lecouvreur.

actors. In London he had seen large, well-built theatres, the stages of which had long been purged of that enemy of illusion, the presence of self-assertive spectators. Here again was an object for his propensities as agitator.

And finally, the drama itself. In his early youth Voltaire had blindly yielded to the tragic recipe of the seventeenth century, and had constructed some declamatory tragedies, which were neither better nor worse than the rest of these "epigonic" productions, and among which a few had really won some favour.[1]

Now he had seen so many strange things on the English stage, so much that went directly against the holy rules of the time of Louis XIV., but was nevertheless effective on the boards — this old Briton, in particular, of whom the English were so proud, this Shakespeare, with his *Hamlet*, his *Julius Cæsar*, and his *Othello*. It was ludicrous, chaotic, inartistic, in the highest degree ; and being so, it could not but offend the sense of propriety and good manners of every Frenchman. Still, there was something in it that might be used. The crude mixture, like that seen in real life, of things comic and tragic, the many shifting scenes, the complicated action, which showed the saddest ignorance of the Aristotelian unities, all this would be impossible in France ; but a little of these varied subjects, of the life and passion that animated them, would, no doubt, freshen up the French Melpomene, whose graces had certainly somewhat faded.

And all the stirring truths that might be expressed within these new forms ! What a means of touching

---

[1] Especially his *Œdipe*, written at the age of twenty-three.

the people all these novelties would afford! Though it would be impossible constantly to change the scene as Shakespeare did, at least a new one might be presented for every act ; it would be a venture, an offence against the unity of place, but it would be novel and diverting.   The idea of representing the Roman Forum with Brutus and Antonius talking to the assembly, with Cæsar's bloody body, and the people mad with rage, is grotesque, but would not be without effect, even on a polished French audience.   The motive of Othello's jealousy is excellent, but it is absurd to allow the hero to be an elderly Moor, scarred and roughened by many years' warfare and toil, unacquainted with the intricate aberrations of love ; convert him into an amiable young Turk, and his glowing jealousy would please the French ladies, even though it would be deprived of its deeply human motive.

There can be no question whatever of kinship between Voltaire and Shakespeare.   With his quick, keen eye, the French author discovers a vein of ore in a huge mountain ; he gets a little silver out of it, and at once works it out into good current coin ; but he has not the remotest idea of the size of the mountain, or of its rich and hidden mines.

However, the contact with Shakespeare, and, on the whole, with English dramatic culture, offered a rich harvest to Voltaire.   He was no poet born, but a fighting genius in agitative.   The multitude of pieces which he wrote after his return from England are nearly all forgotten ; they are no longer acted, even in France, and are read only by the historians of literature or of the

41

42

43

41—Voltaire (p. 253).

42—Mlle. Dumesnil (p. 265).   43—Mlle. Clairon (p. 274).

theatre; but on their appearance, some of them at any rate, such as *Brutus, The Death of Cæsar, Zaïre, The Orphan of China,* and others, were admired as poetic revelations all over the civilised world, and Voltaire became king of the theatre as he was already king of literature.

And, indeed, this remarkable man possessed very special capacities for conquering the theatre, capacities, however, which, just as in his conquest of literature, were independent of the intrinsic value of his works. There were fire and spirit in his plays, and also a certain kind of sentiment, or perhaps rather sentimentality; but the poetic expression is feeble and shallow—it is sacrificed to rapid action and calculated for brilliant acting.

But in his capacity for placing himself and his work in relief, for animating the actors, for making the public anticipate the performances of his plays with as much suspense as if they were events of universal importance; in short, of surrounding himself and his ideas with a halo of gossip, publicity and sensation, he was the unequalled master of his time, nay, perhaps the real inventor of the dramatic and literary *réclame* in the grand style, the tricks of which even the skilled manufacturers of fame in our own day would not be ashamed to learn.

In proportion to the clamour which even to this day surrounds the name of Voltaire, the theatrical inquirer will find surprisingly little at this period which is really new or genuine, more great names than great art, and more external than internal reforms.

A passionate love of acting attached Voltaire to the theatre. Though never appearing on a public stage, he

frequently played in private theatricals.   In his house in
Paris he built a little stage for himself; afterwards he
acted in his own tragedies at the Court of Frederick the
Great, and at Ferney, his palace in Switzerland, he had
a private theatre where many plays were acted, in which
he joined with his usual passionate zeal.   Early in the
morning he would put on his costume and walk round
the garden, astonishing his gardeners with his long white
beard when he was going to act "le bonhomme Lusignan"
in *Zaïre*, or in Arabian, Greek, or archiepiscopal attire.

Like most authors, he liked, or at least he could not
throw off, a very pathetic, old-fashioned rhetorical style.
He admired the simple, natural acting of Adrienne
Lecouvreur, but it was not in his power either to imitate
it or to teach others to adopt it.

At the Comédie Française he had no official function,
and on the whole he spent most of his time away from
Paris.   Nevertheless, his influence there was enormous;
or rather it became so by degrees as the public and he
himself fixed his position as number one among dramatic
authors.

All his plays—during the first decade after his return
from England he wrote no less than twenty—were not
equally successful.   But Voltaire found out a method of
securing applause which was quite new at the time, but
which nowadays is only too common.   He bought a
large number of tickets for the first performance and
distributed them among his friends and acquaintances,
with the secret or openly avowed understanding that
they were to applaud heartily.   This distribution of
tickets was more and more regularly organised, and thus

Voltaire became the real founder of the *claque*, which in France has attained an unparalleled degree of shamelessness.

His stratagems, one of which was to make his supporters summon "the author" to the footlights—a hitherto unknown proceeding—were soon found out, and his detractors did not miss this opportunity of unmasking him. Thus Collé tells us in his diary that on the first night of *Semiramis* Voltaire had bought the whole pit; but the play was so dull that a number of the claqueurs yawned aloud while applauding, which amused everybody in the theatre except Voltaire.[1]

Though apparently his position at the Théâtre Français did not differ from that of any other author, his power—judiciously built up of flattery, good advice and general helpfulness—was unlimited and unequalled. He assembled the actors in his home and read to them the play he wanted them to act at the time, perhaps quite a different one from that which he had previously announced. To reject a play of Voltaire was entirely out of the question. He instructed the actors, invited them to his palace, and made them alter their way of acting. He encouraged them when they were injured by court people, and supported them against old prejudices and class-pride.

We have already seen how, on the death of Adrienne Lecouvreur, he tried to revive the relaxed sense of honour of the *sociétaires*. A well-known theatrical scandal caused several of the best actors and actresses

---

[1] Ch. Collé: *Journal et Mémoires*, edited by Hon. Bonhomme, Paris, 1868, p. 1 f.

of the Théâtre Français to be imprisoned because they had refused to act with a rascally colleague, whose re-engagement had been enforced by a courtier, who was interested in his handsome daughter.   On this occasion Voltaire wrote to Mlle. Clairon : " I have spent my life in fighting for your cause, and I am almost the only one who has had the courage to do so.   If the actors who have talent had firmness enough to declare that they would cease serving an ungrateful public as long as they were denied the right which is their due, the public would soon be forced to repair such cruel injustice "—the injustice which he elsewhere qualifies as "a too absurd contradiction ; to be imprisoned in the Fort l'Evêque when they do not act, and to be excommunicated when they do."   And when Mlle. Clairon— alone—actually followed his wise encouragement to strike, and left the theatre never to return, because no reparation was offered her for the wrong she had suffered, she was censured by all for her pride, and Voltaire defended her in these glowing words : " I cannot blame an actress who prefers giving up her art to practising it with shame.   Among the thousand absurdities which during the last fifty years have exasperated me, I think the most monstrous is to call those persons dishonourable who obey the order of the King to recite beautiful verses.   Pitiable nation, whose existence in Europe at present depends on the fine arts, and who tries to defame them." [1]

All human injustice strongly affected Voltaire—to this his whole life bears sufficient testimony—and he

[1] Letter to the Comtesse d'Argental, of 18th April 1768.

certainly did more than most people to shake the deeply-rooted prejudice in France against actors as a class. Neither did he spare other prejudices, whether technical or artistic, but continued to strike at them with persistent and relentless blows.

Thus year after year he never tired of attacking the absurd French custom of allowing spectators on the stage, and he did all in his power to get it abolished. At first both the public and the actors opposed him, the former because they found it amusing to be in such close contact with the leaders of the stage, the latter because it was very lucrative to sell the expensive and much-coveted seats. After many years' struggle, however, only the financial difficulty remained—the expense of rebuilding the theatre ; and this difficulty was solved at last by the Comte de Lauraguais, a liberal adherent of the ideas of Voltaire, who offered the necessary sum as a gift.[1]   In the year 1759, therefore, Voltaire had the joy of seeing the Théâtre Français purged of another of its worst absurdities, and the satisfaction of finding his long struggle appreciated on all sides.

As a teacher, or rather as an inspirer, Voltaire had a most animating influence on the actors.   As far as can be concluded from the scanty information extant about his work as stage director, he had no fixed system or established artistic principles, but worked rather as a

---

[1] The reconstruction cost 60,000 fr., and the theatre remained closed for three weeks before opening on 23rd April 1759 in its new shape.   " At first there was a fear that the stage would appear empty when the actors occupied it alone," we read in the *Mercure de France* on this occasion, " but this fear rapidly vanished on seeing a comedy, the whole action of which lay in the liveliness of the dialogue.   Mlle. Dangeville and M. Préville in the little piece, *The Legacy* [by Marivaux], sufficed to fill the stage."

strong, stimulating power, which, as long as rehearsal was going on, never tolerated dulness or indolence, scarcely even natural repose.

When the little man, as lean as a skeleton, rushed about in his zeal, frequently in most eccentric attire, correcting, complimenting, or scoffing at the actors, with quick, biting words, while his small, sly monkey eyes shot flashes of lightning, the usually most self-satisfied *sociétaires* spun round like tops under the blows of his whip, and no peace fell on the stage till the goal was attained.

It is related that once during the rehearsals of his *Mérope*[1] he had toiled so long with Mlle. Dumesnil, trying to make her put more vigour and fire into her violent speech to Polyphonte in the fourth act, that she at last burst out a little impatiently, "Really, one ought to have *le diable au corps* to strike the note you want." "Just so, Mademoiselle," Voltaire replied, "*le diable au corps* in all art, if you want to attain perfection."

After the death of Mlle. Lecouvreur and Baron, tragedy was neglected; it was seldom acted, and its style had fallen off into a dull exactness of delivery.

It became one of Voltaire's tasks, besides writing a new kind of tragedy, to inspire the mode of acting with new fire and *verve*,[2] to give it *le diable au corps*, and in order

---

[1] The first performance of *Mérope* took place in 1743.

[2] It may be noted, as an example of his successful efforts with *Mérope*, that Mlle. Dumesnil, who on the whole gained a great triumph with this part, for the first time ventured to run on the stage. In tragedy the gait had always been measured and regular, as in a ballet, but here the actress was seen running across the stage when hurrying to the assistance of her son Egiste. This created a great sensation.—*Anecdotes dramatiques*, i. 548 f.

to produce this result he used all the means nature had given him : a sharp tongue, an unsurpassed quickness of perception, and a subtle knowledge of human nature.

Since the days of Molière the actors had not been accustomed to an absolute artistic director.   The older members had helped the younger ones, the more intelligent their inferiors, but always in a prudent and courteous way.   Now, through the occasional leadership of Voltaire, they became acquainted with a master who, regardless of ceremony, railed, sneered, was rude or ironical, but always aimed at a definite point, and was never afraid of making an exhibition of himself by personally showing how he wanted the parts to be acted.

Lekain, his most famous pupil, in his memoirs gives us several examples of Voltaire's mode of instruction, one of which seems particularly characteristic.   In his own theatre Voltaire was rehearsing *Mahomet*, with Lekain in the title *rôle*, and a very young and charming, but too bashful and reticent lady as Talmire.   Voltaire had been listening patiently to the extremely modest way in which the amiable young girl uttered the furious curses which she had to fling out against her tyrant ; at last he interrupted her and said gently : " My dear young lady, try to realise that Mahomet is an impostor, a rascal, a fellow by whose order your brother has been assassinated, who has just poisoned your father, and who now, to crown his good works, insists on possessing you.   If all these little tricks please you to a certain extent, well, then you are right in treating him as you do.   But if you hate them, look here how to show it. . . ."   And

Voltaire began his curse, while the young novice stood blushing and trembling, wondering what it meant to have *le diable au corps.*

II

The Two Great Tragic Actresses, Dumesnil and Clairon—Their Art and their Life.

AT first the company with which Voltaire had to work was but feeble.   Among the Quinault family and their adherents who dominated the theatre there were several capable, easy, and pleasant actors, but none of distinction, still less of genius.   The self-complacent ladies' idol, Quinault-Dufresne, was treated with great prudence and diplomacy[1] by Voltaire as long as the author had not yet obtained a firm footing at the Théâtre Français, nor is it probable that he would ever have been able to develop those qualities in Dufresne which he appreciated in dramatic art.

A certain Sarrasin, whom Adrienne Lecouvreur had discovered, and in whom she interested herself,[2] no doubt

[1] Concerning the ingenuity with which Voltaire contrived to attain his ends we possess an amusing little anecdote.   Voltaire had a mania for constantly correcting his plays, which greatly annoyed the actors, not least Quinault-Dufresne.   So, in rehearsing one of his plays, the actor took great care to keep aloof from his energetic author, who could never find an opportunity of telling him the numerous alterations he wanted to make in his part.   But Voltaire did not give in.   One day he knew that Dufresne was going to have a large dinner-party, so he sent him a splendid pie, surrounded by partridges.   The gift was most gratefully accepted, but on close examination the actor discovered that each partridge had in its beak a small rolled-up paper, on which were written Voltaire's corrections of his part. The actor could not resist this amiable persistency, and learned the alterations.

[2] Comp. her letter to Piron, in which she prefers his art to that of Quinault-Dufresne.

possessed a fine and genuine talent; he had created, among others, some of Voltaire's leading *rôles*, such as Brutus, Cæsar, and Lusignan in *Zaïre*. But Sarrasin's gentle, level, somewhat vague mode of acting showed to best advantage in the emotional mixed dramas [1] of Chaussée and Mme. de Graffigny, and was not so well suited to the fiery energy of Voltaire, with its tendency to strong effects.

It was not till the middle of the century that the new actors of talent appeared who were suited to the ideas of the great agitator, and who were to raise his works to honour and dignity, at the same time casting radiant glory on the French stage. Dumesnil and Clairon are the names of the two great actresses, each in her way a genius, who throughout the century represented the two opposite conceptions of dramatic art.

Contrasts in everything: natural gifts, appearance, character, inclinations, vices, virtues, views of art, they continued rivals for many years, yet even to this day it is difficult to decide which won the palm of victory. The one relied upon her exuberant temperament, stimulated it with wine, and yielded to her impulses in life as in art; the other shrewdly calculated all her chances, on the stage as in the world, and made the utmost use of her capacities in art as in love; the one was warm-hearted and careless, the other passionate, yet cold.

Marie Françoise Marchand, who adopted the stage-name of Mlle. Dumesnil, was born in Paris, of a bourgeois

---

[1] Among other parts, he played that of Dorimond in Mme. de Graffigny's *Cénie*, the President in La Chaussée's *The Governess*, the title part in *Maximien* by the same author, Ariste in *Ecole des Amis*, and Argant in *Ecole des Mères*.

family, on 2nd January 1713.[1] We know scarcely anything about her youth, except that she became a provincial actress at an early age—the ordinary beginning of a stage career in France in those times—acted for some years in Strasburg and Compiègne among other places, until at the age of twenty-four, on 6th August 1737, seven years after the death of Adrienne Lecouvreur, she was allowed to appear for the first time in Paris at the Théâtre Français, as Klytemnestra in Racine's *Iphigenia in Aulis.*

Tragedy was not fashionable at the time, and the actors did not treat it with respect. A few years previously, in order to fill the theatre and create a facile sensation, the same classical tragedy in which the young actress now made her *début*, had been parodied by making the two actors of grotesque comedy, La Thorillière and Poisson, represent Agamemnon and Achilles respectively. True, the incredibly tasteless experiment was most emphatically rejected by the audience. Still the actors continued to neglect the serious *genre*, and had to submit to a severe admonition to uphold tragedy.

Meanwhile the *début* of Mlle. Dumesnil created a sensation ; her peculiar temperament pleased the audience, and she was engaged at once,[2] which was

---

[1] Most biographers have a different year and date of birth, but the certificate of baptism published by Campardon (*Coms. des Rois*, p. 101) excludes every doubt. By the bye, the life of Mlle. Dumesnil has been very little treated, compared with that of her rival. The uninteresting booklet which was published by Coste d'Arnobat, under the title of *Les Mémoires de Mlle. Dumesnil*, is only a reply to the attacks of Mlle. Clairon in her Memoirs, and does not contain special information about her life.

[2] She was appointed to the "princess" line as *double* of Mlle. Balicourt, an actress of no great importance, and a member of the Quinault family,

unusual. It has proved impossible to find information about her on her first appearance, for, as far as I have been able to ascertain, no accounts exist of her *début* or the first years of her theatrical career. But she must very soon have arrested the attention of Voltaire, for as early as 1740 she played the title *rôle* of his (entirely unsuccessful) tragedy *Zulime*. And we may be allowed to suppose that the exciting influence of Voltaire was decisive for her talent. At any rate, in 1743 she obtained her first great signal success in his *Mérope*.

We have already described how he worked with her in this play, urging her on to the utmost violence, which subsequently became a characteristic feature of her acting. The result was a great success for him, but he modestly refused accepting the honour for it, saying, " It is not I who have created this piece, it is Mlle. Dumesnil."

And to the now mature actress of thirty it meant the full display of her rich abilities, and the final acceptance of the name of Dumesnil as that of the great tragic actress whom the theatre had long been wanting.

It has already been observed that in her art Mlle. Dumesnil relied chiefly on her temperament, which under the influence of Voltaire had been strained to its utmost tension. Her temper was naturally violent, and she succeeded best in strong, untamed characters. Her figure was tall and slender to begin with ; afterwards

---

whom she soon superseded, and who retired from the stage a year after her *début* ; also as third *soubrette*, doubling the two excellent comic actresses, Mlles. Quinault and Dangeville. As a *soubrette*, however, Mlle. Dumesnil never gained distinction, and she played parts of this kind only a very few times.

she became stout, but was never imposing, because
she lacked firmness of bearing, her deportment as well
as her dress were careless, her face did not possess the
nobility which in those times was particularly appreciated, but its features were very flexible; her voice was
coarse and strong, but not pleasant; in fact, she lacked
nearly all the qualities which were admired in her time :
noble movement, elegance in speech, refinement in dress,
but she made up for all these defects by the wonderfully free and powerful flight of her art, by her enthusiasm which carried away everybody, and which now
in its untrammeled passion, now in its intense and warm
feeling, laid a stronger hold on the heart than any other
contemporary histrionic art.

But her capacities were very uneven. She would
leave large portions of her part almost untouched, or go
through them with superficial carelessness, and then
suddenly rise to marvellous summits which made her
spectators quite giddy. An admirer compared her art
to an ode of Pindar : " higher than the clouds," and
added that, like Corneille, she flew too high to be able
to maintain herself at the same level.[1]

Another more sober observer, Ch. Collé, the keen,
sometimes too keen critic of contemporary dramatic art,
says of her : " Mlle. Dumesnil . . . in her acting is
always good only in the violent parts of her characters,
and I confess that in these passages she has more depth
and warmth of feeling than Mlle. Lecouvreur. She
rises higher than this famous actress. But how different

---

[1] Lemazurier (*Galerie des acteurs du Théâtre Français*, ii. 197) quotes
these words without naming his authority.

in all the rest! Her play is good only where she has to show passion and fury. Otherwise no dignity, no nobility ; love is badly rendered, pride only moderately well ; she is often rhetorical. Face without nobility, forced deportment, unpleasant voice. But where she *is* good she is unsurpassed ; she makes you forget all her faults and all her ungracefulness." [1]

Thus Mlle. Dumesnil swung between extremes, almost ludicrously careless where she considered her part irrelevant or dull, and absolutely sublime where the situation or the feeling roused her interest, always uneven, not unfrequently indifferent to an irritating degree, but momentarily stirring your innermost heart more deeply than anybody else.

Several instances are given of the effect which she produced on the spectators in her grand moments. Once, seized by involuntary horror, the whole pit drew back several steps, leaving an empty space in front, while Dumesnil as Cleopatra [2] hurled forth her wild curses. And in the same play, an old officer, who was seated on the stage, on hearing the speech,

Je maudirais les Dieux s'ils me rendaient le jour,

suddenly took illusion for reality, and in his rage slapped the actress violently on her back and furiously burst out : " Go to hell, you d——d jade ! " However, when the curtain had dropped Mlle. Dumesnil thanked him for his blow ; it was, she said, the best compliment he could pay to her acting.

[1] Ch. Collé : *Journal et Mémoires*, ed. Bonhomme, i. 141.
[2] In Corneille's *Rodogune*.

A nature such as hers required constant excitement. During her first years at the Théâtre Français Voltaire had been the stimulator of the impulsive actress ; afterwards, when the great author but very rarely incited the actors by his personal presence, she stimulated herself with wine. "Mlle. Dumesnil drinks like a groom," says Bachaumont in his Memoirs.[1] "While she acts her lackey constantly stands between the wings with the bottle to wet her whistle." Even if this is an exaggeration, all testimonies agree in stating that the great actress, whose everyday life was uneventful, kindled her enthusiasm at the treacherous flame of wine, in order to produce the visions which were to render her acting grand and overwhelming. Her vice probably did not shorten her life—at any rate she lived to the age of ninety—but there can scarcely be any doubt that it gradually blunted her powers, reduced her physical and mental elasticity, and increased her natural carelessness.

In one field, however, her art was more even, less desultory, than in the great tragic parts, and yet she rose very high in it ; this was the mixed tragedy, the emotional drama, the so-called *comédie larmoyante*, which, under English influence and that of the pieces of La Chaussée and the moral tales of Marmontel, had become the fashion in France. Parts such as Orphise in Mme. de Graffigny's *Cénie*, Mme. Vanderk in Sedaine's *Philosophe sans le savoir*, Mme. Fonrose in Desfontaine's *Bergère des Alpes*, and the Governess in La Chaussée's play of that name show, if not the zenith of her art, at least the best acting produced in

[1] *Mémoires secrets de la republique des lettres*, 1808, i. 3.

this new *genre* by a French actress.   Nobody equalled
her in expressing warm, rich, motherly feeling; and
at the same time she possessed a simple, natural
humour which was admirably suited to these popular
pieces.

In private life she was much simpler, and more
even-tempered than we should have supposed from her
capricious, impulsive acting.   Voltaire called her "good
Mlle. Dumesnil."   And indeed, she was remarkably free
from the spirit of intrigue, the nervous craving for being
number one, which frequently renders intercourse with
distinguished actresses so difficult.   Self-advertisement
and greed for parts were far from her mind, nor did she
care in the least to be a literary or social centre, or to
display the extravagant splendour of a courtesan.   The
opposite extreme was more to her taste.   In her modest
home she cooked her own food and knitted her own
stockings.   At the rehearsals in the theatre she appeared
in a loose, comfortable, anything but becoming lapelled
bodice, while her sisters in art were fond of parading in
all the stiff, tight, fashionable finery of the time, and she
never succeeded in obtaining, nor even coveted, a leading position among her colleagues.   With no bitter feeling she yielded the leadership to her younger rival,
Mlle. Clairon.

Six years after Mlle. Dumesnil, though she was ten
years younger, this second great star made her first appearance on the chief stage of France, on 19th September
1743.   She arrived with a name rather notorious
than famous, escorted by a whole regiment of rich and
distinguished lovers, by whose influence she obtained her

début, and who started her on her career, to the great indignation of the *sociétaires*, none of whom gave her any assistance, except the good-natured unconcerned Mlle. Dumesnil.

The young actress of twenty had already a tolerably long career behind her. The illegitimate child of a sergeant and a loose-lived sempstress,[1] she took her origin in the lowest depths of society; she was early tossed about by fate, and saw much evil, and little that was good. The mother, whose life was condemned even by her daughter, left the small provincial town which was her home, and went to Paris with her child, and here little Claire spent many bitter, unhappy hours in the small room, while her mother was roving about. On one of these days of confinement the child of eleven had climbed up on a chair to look at the passers-by in the street. Her eyes fell on the house opposite where the windows were open. In the room she saw a charming woman moving in beautiful attitudes to the tones of a violin. Other fine people were looking on.

It was, as she heard afterwards, the fascinating actress, Mlle. Dangeville taking her dancing lesson.

And after the dancing all the other people, who were her relations, clapped their hands, and her mother went up to her and kissed her.[2]

This peep into a strange world of beauty, grace, and

---

[1] Her father's name was Lérys, and her mother's Marie Claire Scanapiecq, a young girl of the working classes from the northern boundaries of France, living in the town of Condé, where she gave birth to her child on 25th January 1723.

[2] *Mémoires d'Hyppolite Clairon*, 1798, i. 259 f.

tenderness, which the little girl imbibed with all her senses, left a deep impression on Claire; nay, it brought about a complete change in her.

From that day she delighted in being locked up, so that she might see the beautiful lady dance. And she tried to imitate her, and to practice all her movements and steps. Thus the child led her own little life, and the sense for beauty and art was awakened in her.

And when, one day in a fit of good humour, her mother had allowed her to go to the play with a friend, and on her return the child remembered several hundred lines by heart, and was able to mimic all the actors, and, moreover, showed that she possessed a good singing voice, her mother's practical sense became aware that something might be made out of these talents. She took the little prodigy to M. de Hesse, an actor of the Italian theatre, and he was pleased with her at once. She had lessons in writing, dancing, and music, and thus equipped, the girl of scarcely thirteen made her first appearance at the Comédie Italienne, on 8th January 1736.

However, she did not succeed in finding a firm footing there, but went into the provinces and travelled about for six years, gathering a certain *réclame* about her stage-name Clairon, and still more about her pet name Frétillon, which was given her on account of her in-

---

[1] Mlle. Clairon, and after her Goncourt in his biography of the actress, call him Deshais, but his real name was de Hesse. He was Dutch by birth, played Zanni parts, and afterwards became ballet-master at the Italian Theatre in Paris. His wife was the daughter of the famous Harlequin Thomassin.

numerable love-adventures, and which she had difficulty in shaking off even at her most eminent period.[1]

It was, in fact, much more in her character as a coveted mistress than as an actress that she at last came to Paris in 1743, at the age of twenty, and found employment at the Opera as a singer of quite secondary parts, after having made her *début* as Venus in the opera *Hésione*,[2] and it was on account of the same character that, when tired of the Opera, she sought, and by the influence of her powerful patrons obtained her *début* at the Théâtre Français.

But the astonishment was immense, when she, the little third-rate singer and provincial *soubrette*, had the boldness to choose for her *début* Phèdre—the sublime classical masterpiece of the great Racine, the tombstone of all great *tragédiennes*.

Her boldness, which her subsequent colleagues called impudence, had its reward. The *début* was successful. *Le Mercure de France*, the leading paper of the time, substantiated the success, and small pamphlets corroborated it. One of them gives a minute description of her person and appearance, which shows how great a

---

[1] A libellous pamphlet, *Histoire de Mlle. Cronel* [an anagram of Clairon, which was frequently written Cleron], *dite Frétillon*, treats of her vagabond life during these years. The little book is exceedingly mean and coarse, and probably for the most part a fiction, but it may be, and probably is, to a certain extent founded on fact, for Mlle. Clairon was by nature a courtesan, and continued to be so ; too many absolutely indisputable statements testify to erotic inclinations and actions which are no less discreditable than the stories in the libel. The authorship of the *Histoire de Frétillon* has been attributed to a certain Gaillard, a colleague of Mlle. Clairon's ; this, however, seems to me incredible, chiefly because the few scenes in the book which are laid in the theatre are treated without professional knowledge or local colour.

[2] By Danchet, music by Campra.

sensation attended her first steps on the French stage. It says : " Mademoiselle Clairon is twenty-two or twenty-three years old. [This is a mistake; she was only a little over twenty.] Her complexion is very fair, and her head is well poised on her neck. Her eyes are very large, full of fire and voluptuousness. Her mouth is adorned with beautiful teeth ; her bust is well formed and heaves naturally. Her figure is lissom and easy in its movements, and her bearing very graceful. A modest and pleasing expression speaks in her favour. She is no perfect beauty, yet you cannot be captivating without resembling her. She sparkles with intelligence, her speech is gentle and fascinating. Being a musician and an actress full of enthusiasm and very docile, she is fit for everything, and without effort can make of herself what she wants to be."

The anonymous author of the little pamphlet, from which we have quoted the above passage, had an uncommonly keen perception of the young girl, whose first serious theatrical attempts interested him. The difference between Mlle. Dumesnil and Mlle. Clairon was just that—that while the former became what she was destined to be and allowed herself to be unresistingly carried away by the powers which nature had implanted in her, Mlle. Clairon became what she was because she willed it so. It may be contested whether she was the greatest actress of her time ; many perhaps prefer the richer inner life of Mlle. Dumesnil. But there can be no doubt that Mlle. Clairon was the more perfectible; one who by strength of will reached every goal she had set before herself, and thereby obtained relative perfection.

274 HISTORY OF THEATRICAL ART

Her older colleague, Mlle. Gaussin,[1] whom she supplanted in tragedy, and who lacked this will-power, said
of her at the beginning of her career: "*Allez, allez!
Mlle. Clairon sera une grande actrice, mais elle ne fera
jamais pleurer.*"

No doubt she was right. But though Clairon did
not possess the depth and warmth of feeling which makes
the heart throb and the tears flow, there are other chords
for dramatic art to play upon, even in tragedy. Tenderness, motherly love, and grief were not in her line, but
erotic passion, proud anger, despair, horror, coldness,
were feelings to which her nature adapted itself easily.
And by her intelligence, energy, and assiduity, her
mastery of acting attained a perfection unequalled by
any contemporary actress.

As a proof of her complete control of her artistic
capacities, an eyewitness[2] describes it in the following
way: "Once Mlle. Clairon sat down in an easy chair,
and without saying a word, without making a single
gesture, she depicted, with her face alone, hatred,
rage, indignation, indifference, sadness, pain, love, pity,

[1] Mlle Gaussin (1711-1767) was much admired for a time in love parts,
especially in tragedy. Her fame dates in particular from her acting in
Zaïre, which Voltaire studied with her in 1732, and in which she gained his
full admiration. But Clairon superseded her, not only in the good parts, but
also in the opinion of Voltaire. However, she remained popular in comedy
and in the mixed drama, where among other parts she acted as the first
Cénie in the fashionable play of Mlle. de Graffigny. Her appearance was
charming, her expression gentle and roguish, very different from the
energetic profile of Mlle. Clairon. But her morals were almost as light as
those of her more fortunate rival, though in a different way, rather in consequence of a mild, yielding disposition than of violent passion. When being
blamed for having so many lovers, she replied, shrugging her shoulders:
Que voulez-vous! Cela leur fait tant de plaisir, et cela me coûte si peu."

[2] *Hérault de Séchelles* in *La décade philosophique*, n. 80, p. 82 f.

naturalness, cheerfulness, joy, etc. She pictured not only passions in general, but also the shades and differences which characterise them, such, as for instance, all nuances of terror, anxiety, fear, excitement, uneasiness, apprehension, horror, etc."

The minute technical calculation and the preparation of all details became a principle in the art of Mlle. Clairon, whereas that of Mlle. Dumesnil was founded on spontaneity and absolute trust in the impulses and inspiration of nature. And to these principles the two great actresses adhered firmly throughout their whole career.

A much younger colleague of theirs, the afterwards very popular comic actor, Dugazon, has preserved a conversation between the two rival actresses, which throws a clear and amusing light on their different conceptions of their art.[1]

In the little theatre Boule-Rouge, used for rehearsing plays, where Talma prepared himself for his glorious career, the two aged[2] actresses met after many years, both taking an interest in seeing the first attempts of the young tragic actor. Mlle. Clairon appeared as usual in a ceremonious attire, an extravagant court-dress and flying feathers, while Mlle. Dumesnil wore a comfortable gown, and carried her lap-dog with her. A discussion took place between Talma, his teacher Dugazon, the poet Chénier, and the two old *tragédiennes*, in which the ladies finally took the lead.

---

[1] It is reproduced in Regnault-Warin's *Mémoires historiques et critique sur F. J. Talma*, Paris, 1827, pp. 240-252.

[2] The scene took place in 1787. At that time Mlle. Dumesnil was 74 Mlle. Clairon 64.

Talma had said something which called forth the approval of Mlle. Dumesnil, and she exclaimed: "Bravo, young man!" She holds out her hand, which he kisses respectfully: "Of course, one must neither play, nor even represent. You are not to *play* Achilles, but to *create* him. You must not *represent* Montagu [*i.e.* Romeo], you must *be* him.

MLLE. CLARION (with dignity and emphasis).—My dear, you labour under a great delusion. In theatrical art all is conventional, all is fiction. The poet obeys his own rules, so does the actor. Would they be obliged to do so if those rules were in the order of nature? When the gentleman there (pointing to Chénier[1]) makes Charles IX. speak, he is neither that king, who did not always talk in verse, though he sometimes wrote poetry, nor is he himself, as he does not think like a feeble monarch, nor like a murderous despot. What is he then? A talented writer whose pliable imagination constructs events that have never taken place, and uses a language which is spoken by nobody. I may say almost the same of an actor. What am I when I act the part of the Queen of Carthage or the mother of Iphigenia? I am neither Klytemnestra nor Dido. I wear their dress in order to delude the senses, and I have the figure and face of a woman, which completes the illusion. But you must remember that what I want to produce is an illusion, and I do produce it, and that, however successful I may be in attaining my end, it can never be anything

---

[1] Marie Joseph Chénier, the fertile dramatist of the time of the Revolution, who at this period was working at his tragedy *Charles IX.*, which was to create the first signal success both for himself and for Talma.

but play.   Don't you hear them exclaim in the midst of their admiration, applause and enthusiasm : "What splendid acting!"   So it is Mlle. Clairon, Mlle. Dumesnil, or M. Larive whom they applaud, not Dido or Klytemnestra.   These princesses do not care for the bravos, but Racine and M. de Pompignan[1] want them. And as for Mlle. Clairon, there was a time when she valued them highly, in the days when they were not wasted on mediocrity.

MLLE. DUMESNIL.—It could not be better expressed, my dear friend, but it might be better done.   To show intelligence is not all; everything depends on *doing* the right thing.   I have a hundred times disproved what you said just now, though without having heard it. You know how——

MLLE. CLAIRON.—Yes, you acted from nature.   But there was much art in your naturalness.

MLLE. DUMESNIL.—Not the least.   I was full of my part, I felt it, I yielded myself up to it.

MLLE. CLAIRON.—I have never understood how one could do without calculation.   I should have been quite out of it if I had yielded myself up.

CHÉNIER.—It seems to me, ladies, that you are both right, because each of you was in harmony with her character, her soul and her gifts.

DUGAZON.—It is just like the authors who write poetics for their own works; when you have learned their rules you are not certain if they are right, but you are quite sure of the talent of their authors.   The talent of Mlle. Dumesnil and Mlle. Clairon has never been

[1] Author of the tragedy *Dido*.

disputed, and it is not the question of the present discussion.   Nor is it our object to know whether dramatic art exists, as that is unquestionable, but whether in this art fiction or reality is to dominate.

MLLE. CLAIRON.—Fiction.

MLLE. DUMESNIL.—Reality. . . .

As soon as her successful *début* and patronage had procured for Mlle. Clairon a firm establishment at the Théâtre Français, she underwent a complete change, an intentional change, which she carried out with indomitable energy and female sagacity.   She no longer wanted to be the merry little *fille du régiment*, who had been the delight of garrison towns, nor the smart opera-singer with the magnificent attendance of titled lovers.   Now she was to become the first *tragédienne* of the Comédie Française, and for this purpose her manners were entirely altered.   Not with respect to the number of her lovers ; on the contrary.   But otherwise a complete change was displayed in her bearing, ways, and habits.   First of all in her name.   The little Claire Lérys or Scanapiecque, as she was called after either her equally obscure father or mother, became a pompous Claire Hippolyte de la Tude Clairon.   She acquired knowledge, studied history, improved her handwriting and her language, and even in everyday life adopted a queenly air and a grand demeanour, which certainly made her comrades laugh, but which nevertheless procured her the respect she coveted.   At the same time this sublimity of speech and gesture became an artistic principle with her, as in her opinion it was the only means which could make her feel quite at home in the grand tragic parts

44—Mlle. Clairon as Medea (p. 278).

that henceforth became, so to speak, the only field of her acting.

Her pompous manners never left her, and became second nature.   We read that once the Princess of Galitzin paid her a visit, and found her suffering and reclining in an easy chair.   The Princess very sympathetically asked where her complaint was, but Mlle. Clairon pretended not to hear.   The Princess insisted on knowing, and at last the *tragédienne* answered impatiently : " *Au cul, princesse.*"   And she is said to have uttered these in themselves not very sublime words with such dignity that the Princess felt quite struck.

Her influence at the theatre increased with extraordinary rapidity.   She soon became the favourite actress of Voltaire.   They kept up a regular correspondence, the form of which was always highly flattering to the actress. She repeatedly visited Voltaire at his country seat, and on these occasions he took great care to nurse her delicate health.

The other writers for the theatre treated her as a queen, and with some of them her relations were very intimate.   Marmontel, in particular, was her lover for a long time, and remained her friend for life.

Marmontel, the dexterous diluter of the thoughts of great or noted philosophers and of the artistic forms of distinguished poets, the invariably pleasant, healthy, self-satisfied *homme de lettres*, who was at home in all branches of literature, but eminent in none, was probably the author who next to Voltaire had the strongest influence on the art of Mlle. Clairon.

More natural than Voltaire, and with sounder views

of genuineness in dramatic art, Marmontel during their love episode constantly tried to influence his pompous lady towards a simpler, less bombastic style, urging her to infuse greater variety and feasibility, less furious violence, into her speech.[1] But he could never carry his point with the self-conscious actress. By degrees, as their love-relations cooled, the words of her wise friend took root in her mind, and after a journey to Bordeaux, where she gave star-performances in 1752, and where a very small stage had forced her to abandon extravagant means of effect, she returned to Paris with a much simpler, finer, and more natural technique than before, and now, to the joy of Marmontel and others, she attained a noble perfection, a plastic simplicity in her movements, a rich variety in her expression of feeling, which she had never before displayed, in spite of all her brilliant declamation à la Voltaire, but which henceforth, when she saw her way clear before her, never left her. Her pompousness and somewhat too sublime grandiloquence could not be shaken off; it had been too thoroughly assimilated into her nature ;[2] but in spite of this weakness for a show of sublimity, which, after all, agreed well with the French taste of the century, that liked to see noble sentiments expressed by noble attitudes, she was and remained the most perfect, most typical representative of the dramatic art of her time.

[1] See the detailed description by Marmontel of their quarrel about art in Jullien's *Histoire du Costume au Théâtre*, p. 94 ff.

[2] Edmond de Goncourt is absolutely wrong when, in his otherwise excellent biography of Mlle. Clairon, he thinks that she was the first to break with the inflated, chanting declamation. Readers of the present book must have understood that both Baron and Adrienne le Couvreur advanced much further than Mlle. Clairon in natural and vivid delivery.

46

45

46—Lekain (p. 285).

45—Mlle. Clairon visits Voltaire (p. 279).

III

Lekain the Most Distinguished Pupil of Voltaire—His Partial Renovation of Tragic Art.

THANKS to Mlle. Dumesnil and Mlle. Clairon, the serious play was once more restored to honour and dignity. That it became fashionable was due, in particular, to the latter and to a male ally, who in the middle of the century entered the ranks of the champions of tragedy. His name was Lekain.[1]

The *début* of this young man at the Théâtre Français on 14th September 1750—as Titus in Voltaire's tragedy of *Brutus*—roused a veritable storm of disagreement. He had enthusiastic and persistent admirers, especially among the young spectators in the pit, and furious, bitter opponents, among whom were not a few of his future colleagues.

At that time the Théâtre Français was but badly provided with actors, though their number was large enough.[2]

The serious branch, in particular, was poorly supplied. After Quinault-Dufresne, who had retired in

[1] The name is very variously written ; but, without apparently sufficient reason, the above form has been generally accepted. His grandfather called himself Kaïn ; Kaïn's children added the article, and Lekain's brothers and sisters changed K into C and dropped the article again. The tréma was abandoned in ordinary pronunciation, but the actor continued to sign himself H— L. Caïn. See the written complaint reproduced in Campardon. —*Les Comédiens du Roi*, p. 212.

[2] There were seventeen actors to nine actresses. In 1750 the members of the company were : The actors Grandval, Sarrazin, Armand, Poisson, La Noue, La Thorillière, Rozelly, Le Grand jun., Paulin, Deschamps, Dubreuil, Dubois, Dangeville, Bonneval, Ribou, Drouin, Baron jun. ; the actresses, Dumesnil, Gaussin, Clairon, Dangeville, La Mothe, Grandval, Gautier, Lavoye, Beauménars.

1741, the leading tragic parts were in the hands of Grandval,[1] a graceful and amiable interpreter of *petits-maîtres* and light lovers as long as he kept to secondary parts, but incapable of adequately representing the tragic heroes who had now fallen to his share.   At the *début* of Lekain, it is true, he was not more than forty years old, but he was somewhat stout, and the effort of passionate acting fatigued him too much and rendered his performance unnatural.   Flushed, and with a furious expression, he always over-exerted his natural powers, which were decidedly suited for comedy and the mixed drama. Moreover, he had the shortcoming—to French ears unpardonable in a tragedian—of speaking in a thick voice and not rolling his r's.

Besides Sarrazin, whose strong and weak points have been mentioned before, and who, no doubt, was the only actor of the preceding period possessed of genuine though limited talent, the tragic parts were represented quite mechanically by La Noue, who was tolerably intelligent, but as ugly as a monkey and entirely without inspiration.   He was so cold that Voltaire suggested that he should be trellised and exposed to strong southern sunlight, in order that he might be properly matured ; and by Paulin, who played the tyrants in the boisterous style, and who, as Collé says, never spoke to the princesses without holding his clenched fists up to their noses.

Among such a choice collection of mediocre elements

[1] Charles François Racot de Grandval, b. in Paris, 1710 ; made his *début* in 1729 under the name of Duval ; retired in 1762, and died in 1784 in the house of Mlle. Dumesnil.   He was also the author of a number of light comedies.

it might be thought that a young and talented actor would have had no great difficulty in making his way. Yet it cost Lekain exceedingly great efforts, though he was both young and very gifted. This may partly have been due to the fact that his *début* was forced upon the company, and that the intention to push him was too evident ; for though it was no less a person than Voltaire himself who supported the young man, the *sociétaires*, who preferred to have their own way, as well as certain sections of the public, did not relish being urged to admire what they had had no share in discovering.

Lekain's acquaintance with Voltaire dated from one of the private comedies in which the young artisan's son,[1] who at an early age was a fanatical admirer of dramatic art, had taken part. Voltaire had been invited to be present as guest of honour, and with his usual eagerness had asked for the name of the lover. On hearing that the young man, though as yet only playing as an amateur, intended to become an actor, he invited him to call upon him the next day.

In his otherwise very brief Memoirs, Lekain describes minutely this meeting which was so momentous to him. In particular, he gives a most vivid picture of Voltaire and his half-assumed, half-spontaneous sensibility and effusive helpfulness. We hear that he had his heart in his mouth when going up to the great man, and that he was too much overcome with emotion to say or do anything ; but Voltaire helped him out of his dilemma by taking him in his arms, " thanking God for having

---

[1] Henri Louis Lekain was the son of a goldsmith, and was born in Paris on 31st March 1729.

created a being who had touched him by reciting some tolerably bad verses."[1]   Thereupon he examined him about everything—his position, his father, his education, his plans for the future—all the while pouring out and drinking about ten cups of chocolate mixed with coffee.

Voltaire learned that the young man was fairly independent, as he possessed a small capital which yielded about 750 fr. in annual interest, but that it was his highest and most ardent desire to become an actor in the Royal company.   The poet exclaimed : " My dear friend, don't think of it !   Take my advice ; play comedy for your own pleasure, but never become a professional actor.   It is the finest, rarest, most difficult of talents, but it is degraded by barbarians and anathematized by hypocrites.   The day will come when France will respect your art, but then there is no longer a Baron, a Lecouvreur, a Dangeville.   If you will give up your intention, I will lend you 10,000 fr. to establish yourself, and you may return the loan at your own convenience.   Now, good-bye, my friend ; come again at the end of the week ; think the matter well over, and give me a definite answer."

Confused, touched, but firm in his purpose, young Lekain bowed, stammered some words of gratitude and was about to retire, when Voltaire called him back and asked him to recite something.   Lekain began a speech out of Piron's tragedy *Gustave*,[2] when Voltaire, furious and

---

[1] The play in which Lekain had acted was *Le Mauvais Riche*, a versified comedy in five acts by d'Arnaud.

[2] Voltaire did not like Piron, who in his merry parodies of the fairs had mocked him in sarcasm almost as biting as his own.   For the Théâtre

with a thundering voice, stopped him : " No, not Piron !
I don't like bad verses.   Recite something of Racine."

The young man was nervous ; he searched in his
memory and found *Athalie*, which he at once recited
from the beginning.   Voltaire now became enthusiastic :
" O Lord ! the beautiful verses !   And the marvellous
thing is that the whole piece is written throughout with
the same ardour, the same purity from the first scene to
the last.   Splendid poetry indeed ! . . . Good-bye, my
child !" he added, embracing Lekain, " I prophesy for
you a voice that will go to the heart, and that you will
some day win the enthusiasm of Paris.   But, whatever
you do, never go on a public stage."

However, Voltaire's admonitions were of course as
fruitless as such warnings usually are.   And on seeing
that the young man was perfectly serious in his passionate
love of dramatic art, the poet—wonderful to relate—not
only took him into his house in order to give him steady
instruction, but even built a little theatre at the top of
his house, where young Lekain was allowed to act with
the nieces and acquaintances of Voltaire.

As Voltaire never stopped half-way when he had
made up his mind to do a thing, he even procured for his
protégé and pupil the coveted *début* at the theatre, though
he had great difficulty in getting him placed there.

The fact was that the young man's appearance did
not speak in his favour.   Middle-sized, with a bad
figure, bandy legs, a flat, red, pimpled face, hollow
cheeks, a broad thick-lipped mouth and a small snub

Français he wrote, besides *Gustave* (où Gustave Vasa), the comedy *La
Métromanie*. Both these plays held their ground for a long time on the stage.

nose, he naturally did not show to advantage, especially
in the French conventional costume which was customary
for heroes in the drama.   His only physical attraction
was his large, expressive brown eyes, which reflected the
light of his ardent soul.

No wonder, therefore, that the elegant *sociétaires*
shrank from accepting this little plebeian artisan.   Mlle.
Clairon, in particular, could not bear this ugly specimen
of a man.   But Voltaire championed his cause in the
most effective way ; part of the public may also have
been struck by his inborn fire, which had been further
nourished by Voltaire ; others were stirred up to furious
opposition ; in short, the young man was pushed in
the most emphatic Voltairean way.   While the young
generation looked upon Lekain as a genius, and applauded him fanatically whenever he appeared, Collé,
otherwise so keen-sighted, but a reactionary critic, wrote
of one of his *débuts* : " He is a little rascal, who will
never attain distinction nor even mediocrity ; he is absolutely devoid of sentiment, he has a little, but very little
intelligence, his voice cracks and becomes rough as soon
as he has recited twenty lines ; his face, moreover, is so
ugly that La Noue looks almost an Adonis beside him." [1]

The struggle over the acceptance or nonacceptance
of Lekain at the Théâtre Français lasted for fifteen
months.   The waves rose high, especially within the
walls of the playhouse, whence Mlle. Clairon, whom the
young actor had been imprudent enough to offend by
his rudeness, used all her influence to have him expelled,
while Voltaire stirred up all his powerful friends to

[1] Collé's *Journal*, November 1750, ed. Bonhomme, i. 244.

procure a permanent engagement for him. At this period such theatrical questions were treated in France with as many ceremonies and a seriousness as great or greater than the most important affairs of state, and in this case it was King Louis XV. himself, who in general took no great interest in questions of art, who had to decide the matter.

The struggle was carried to further extremes, when shortly after the *début* of Lekain another young man, Bellecourt, was allowed to try his luck in the same branch. He was insignificant as an actor, especially as a tragedian, but good-looking and amiable, and would have had less difficulty in being generally accepted. But Lekain, who had rehearsed all his parts under the instruction of Voltaire, especially, of course, in the author's own pieces, was allotted, through the powerful influence of his teacher, all the *rôles* for which he was suited ; and especially as Orosmane in *Zaïre*, he excited such enthusiasm that the King wished to see him. *Zaïre* was acted at Fontainebleau with Lekain as Orosmane. Meanwhile many intrigues were going on among the most distinguished section of the public ; for Mme. de Pompadour and the Maréchal de Richelieu were the patrons of Bellecourt, while the Duc d'Aumont and others sided with Lekain.

However, the young actor's first appearance at court turned out a complete success. The ladies, who on his entrance had whispered quite audibly, " How ugly he is ! " afterwards forgot his appearance, which their tears even prevented them from seeing ; and when after the performance the Lord Chamberlain came to the King to hear his Majesty's opinion, the brief answer was : "He has made me cry, I who scarcely ever shed tears. I accept him!"

Thus the affair was settled, and the Théâtre Français had acquired another great actor.

The opposition with which his colleagues had met him soon vanished, as his eminent skill compelled them to respect him. Formed in the school of Voltaire, and full of admiration for this idol of his time, who just now stood at the zenith of his fame, Lekain became the Voltaire actor *par excellence.* He was the masculine counterpart of Mlle. Clairon, and these two disciples[1] gained a universal and strepitous fame for the effective plays of the ingenious old author.

The art of Lekain was heavier, more robust, and violent than that of Mlle. Clairon ; perhaps also deeper and more affecting. But in the main it was of the same kind : minutely calculating, technically perfect, with very little room for simple naturalness or immediate inspiration. He was a tenacious worker; he developed his voice, which by nature was neither full nor fine, did his best to reform the costumes, in opposition to most of his colleagues, struggled with all his might to have the spectators expelled from the stage, was very skilful in getting up plays and an excellent teacher—a man, in short, who had mastered all the branches of his *métier,* and who cultivated it with passionate zeal. But the

---

[1] The quarrel between them was made up, but they were never in sympathy with one another. Lekain made fun of Mlle. Clairon's grand and stilted manner, which he could mimic with a comic humour that unfortunately never had opportunities of being displayed on the stage, and she thought him crafty and not improving in appearance as years went on.

historian who, to the best of his ability, studies the art of Lekain, and tries to penetrate to his individual characteristics as an actor, cannot help seeing in him rather a virtuoso than a profound, great, and genuine master.

This most probably was due to the fact that he was confined to a very limited *répertoire*, in which his parts always aimed at the same kind of effect. We can easily imagine that if it had fallen to the fortunate lot of Lekain to act Shakespeare, his art would have grown with his tasks; his passionate violence, his affecting voice, his eloquent facial play, his well-developed technical perfection only seem to have been waiting for the great poet to display themselves to their full power. As it was, his abilities had to content themselves with Voltaire and his inferior contemporaries, and without knowing their great prototypes he threw himself with glowing ardour into these feeble reflections of great masterpieces. Thus it was that he attained only great virtuosity, not the highest art.

But it must be admitted that this virtuosity was developed to the highest degree of perfection in his particular line, besides embracing the whole compass of tragic art, which at that time, however, was very limited. Nobody could raise his voice to such a pitch, so heart-rending, so terrifying; nobody could—or dared to—fill up immense pauses with such fascinating and eloquent facial play and gesture. In Voltaire's *Semiramis*, in which he had undertaken the part of Ninias after Grandval, who soon acknowledged his own inferiority, he was celebrated for his silence—it could not be called a pause—which lasted for some minutes, during which,

pale, bloody, trembling, with wild, flowing hair, he leaped
from the grave of Ninus, while slowly, very slowly,
hollow groans rose from his breast, and at last gave vent
to words.

There was a comparative naturalism, a nascent sense
of reality, in the acting of Lekain, which infused a certain
amount of new life into the otherwise conventional French
dramatic art, that had become stagnant in accepted forms.
And he introduced the same partial innovation in the
costumes.   To modern eyes this latter reform of Lekain's
seems irrelevant ; his costumes look different from, but
no less absurd, than those of his predecessors ; perhaps
even his acting, if we could see and hear it, would appear
as affected, as conventional and unreal, as we imagine
that of Beaubourg or Quinault-Dufresne.   But if we look
a little more closely at a portrait in costume, such as that
of Genghis Khan — in Voltaire's *Orphan of China*—
we understand that Lekain's attempts at reform meant
something at the time.   The skirt, the three-cornered
plumed hat, the gilt fringes, the full-bottomed wig, the
white gloves, the stage dagger—all this had disappeared.
And what replaced it was, to be sure, not the full truth
to nature or historic reality—Lekain's Genghis Khan,
with his flying ostrich feathers and dapper Cupid's bow,
does not much resemble a real Tartar chief—nay, after
all, it may be called an absurdity of another kind ; but
this other kind was freer, less restrained, better qualified
to stir the imagination.

Thus also we must imagine the acting of Lekain.
He swept aside the over-stiff, affected and pedantic
style, and substituted for it, not full, true naturalness,

47

48

49

50

but a new convention, which excited the mind by its strangeness.

There can scarcely be any doubt that Lekain himself, as well as his admirers, considered his art unique, very different from any other. He was fond of isolating himself from his colleagues and raising himself above them. It was he who first introduced star performances, and organised them into a system. He constantly went off alone to the provinces or abroad[1] to show off his new art, while his colleagues in Paris found fault with him for sacrificing his health on these starring tours, so that he frequently had to put himself on the sick-list, thus neglecting his duty at home. His health, indeed, was delicate, and his life was not long, but it seemed as if his active mind made use even of his illness to render his art more perfect. Talma, at any rate—who saw Lekain when a child and quite a young man—asserts[2] that during the last years of his life, after a long and severe illness, Lekain reached the summit of his art. The audience, he explains, was prepared to show forbearance with a man weakened by illness, but on the contrary, he seemed to be quite a new being, purged of the less pure and genuine elements which might formerly have clung to his art. "No screams, no exertion of the lungs, none

[1] He also acted in Berlin at the French Court Theatre of Frederick the Great, and the Prussian King wrote about him to Voltaire in the following terms :—" Lekain has acted the parts of Œdipe, Mahomet, and Orosmane [all by Voltaire]. We have heard him twice as Œdipe. This actor is very efficient ; he has a fine voice, he bears himself with dignity and has a noble gesticulation, and it is impossible to accentuate the facial play more than he does. But shall I tell you quite openly the impression he made on me? I wish he were a little less exaggerated ; thus, I think, he would be perfect."

[2] Talma, *Quelques réflexions sur Lekain et sur l'art théâtral*, in Regnault Warin's *Mémoires hist. sur F. J. Talma*, p. 545.

of these commonplace outbursts of pain or fits of weeping, which debase the character and draw it downward. His voice, which was at the same time broken and sonorous, had acquired peculiar accents and vibrations that echoed in all hearts ; the tears which sometimes moistened it were manly and sincere. His full, deep, pathetic, profoundly affecting style of acting, purified of all boisterous effects that leave no lasting memory, continued to haunt the spectators in their very sleep."

It is said that Lekain possessed an irresistible talent for burlesque—he was capable, for instance, of mimicking the high and mighty leading lady affectation of Mlle. Clairon in the most ludicrous way—but he could never be persuaded to exercise this talent on the stage. In the list of characters represented by him we do not find a single comic one, scarcely now and then a character, in the mixed drama, such as young d'Esparville in Sedaine's very popular *Le Philosophe sans le savoir*. For the rest, all his parts belong to the heavy ordnance of contemporary or older tragedy.

Lekain did not care for parts outside this *répertoire*, and it was therefore no privation to him to leave the regeneration of comedy to other hands.

IV

Comedians—Préville and the New Elements in his Art—Molé—The Palmy Days of the Théâtre Français—The Apotheosis of Voltaire.

It has already been mentioned that comic literature had passed through a development from the classic satirical character-plays through the perfectly shallow and light comedy of the Regency and the first years of the reign of Louis XV. to a more sentimental, half serious, and sometimes quite emotional *genre*. This new style of composition required new interpreters. The classical period had been anything but sentimental in its comic works; sentimentality was entirely unknown on the old comic stage, and when France had shaken off the torpor of bigotry, which had reigned during the last years of Louis XIV., there was a desire to laugh at everything. The old generations of comic actors, La Thorillière and Poisson, had had an easy task with their readily laughing public, and might offer them the coarsest jests.

But now these old families were dying out. The last Poisson, François Arnould, succumbed in 1753; he was amusing, but an impudent drunkard. The last La Thorillière, Anne Maurice, went on rather longer—he died in 1759—but he had never been anything but a coarse, grimacing copy of his excellent father.

It is true that in Armand[1] the theatre possessed an admirable performer of the rascally, depraved, sharp and witty valets; he had few equals in delivering a joke or singing an amusing couplet. But this character was now on the wane. The latest *genre* of comedy did not require this conventional figure; he was changed, first into the more realistic eighteenth century type, the polished, well-trained lackey, the faithful helper and banker of his master, to-morrow perhaps his superior;

[1] His real name was François Armand Huguet. He was born in 1699, made his *début* at the Théâtre Français in 1725, retired, and died in 1765. His line was the so-called *grande livrée*, which he undertook after the second La Thorillière.

and later into the pathetic, trusted domestic servant, who with tearful eyes and upward glances, but with unalterable fidelity, sees his master tread the ways that lead to destruction.

The old impudent comic actors could not adapt themselves to the new roundabout fashions.   All they wanted was to make people laugh ; now they were also expected to make them cry, nay, to make them smile through tears.   They were not capable of jokes of that kind ; the only thing left them was to drain their bottle and retire.

Fortunately new men appeared on the horizon.   The female staff was well provided already.   Besides Mlle. Gaussin, who, as has been mentioned before, acted both the gay and the serious love-parts with grace and delicacy, there was the very popular actress, Mlle. Dangeville, a niece of Mlle. Desmares, whom she fully equalled in popularity on account of her fascinating freshness, ready wit, and humorous performance of the smart and witty *soubrette* in modern comedy.   At the time of which we are speaking neither of these two actresses was in the bloom of her first youth,[1] but they knew how to progress with their time, and they were typical representatives of the eighteenth century refined style of comedy.

There was a man, however, whose task it became to infuse new life into it.   On 25th August 1753, the last Poisson died, and the young man who made his *début* in the same character at once made his mark, and very

---

[1] Marie Anne Botot Dangeville was born in 1714, left the theatre in 1763, but did not die till 1796, when she was eighty-two years of age.

soon far surpassed his predecessor. He was no beginner
—being thirty-two years of age—and had for years been
acting in the provinces and at the fairs. He knew his
own mind and his capacities. His stage name was
Préville.[1]

It was in Regnard's merry *Légataire universel*, a
genuine Crispin-part, that he appeared for the first time
before the audience of the Théâtre Français, and the
regular playgoers were most astonished when, instead
of the jovial drunkard-face and projecting stomach of
François Arnould Poisson, which always called forth
laughter as soon as he appeared on the stage, and which
had come down from father to son through three generations, they saw a handsome young face and a light,
graceful, slender figure ; instead of the half-delirious,
stammering and jabbering, with strange distortions of
the face, which for a century had been considered irresistible, they heard clear, nicely pointed speeches, assisted
by a pleasant natural smile and a pair of bright, frank eyes.

At first people were put out ; they thought the new
man doll-like and insignificant compared with his big
bubbling, alcoholic predecessor.

But taste soon changed. People saw that Préville
was no comic actor of the usual kind, but something
quite by himself. To put Poisson into an ordinary play
would have been like letting a bull loose in a china shop.
Nobody would have thought of doing such a thing, and
he would certainly have excused himself emphatically
if it had been suggested to him.

[1] His real name was Pierre Louis Dubus, the son of a paperhanger ; he
was born in Paris in 1721, and died in 1799.

Préville, on the contrary, who in his childhood had passed through many vicissitudes and enjoyed little happiness, who had seen much of the world, and who above all possessed a very sensitive artistic temperament, could not easily content himself with being a mere jester, in spite of his exuberant and playful humour.   He wanted—quite contrary to custom in those times—to extend his field all round.   During the first few years, it is true, he adhered essentially to the old *répertoire*, and accustomed the audience to his graceful and quiet comic art ; but by and by, when sure of his popularity, he undertook half or wholly serious parts, acted fathers, financiers, soldiers, even lovers ; in short, he became the first comic character actor on the French stage, and, what was more, he was the first real interpreter of human character since the classical period.   And all the characters he represented were tinged with the grace and amiability, the humour and delicacy, that were natural to him, and made him the idol of the public. He formed, indeed, a school, and there can scarcely be any doubt that the actors of comic parts in the nineteenth century, whether pathetic, burlesque, droll or touching, men like Régnier, Bouffé, Got, or—to draw parallels from our own (Danish) theatre—C. N. Rosenkilde and Phister, are the direct descendants of Préville.

At his time, when each actor mostly played on one string, the protean power which Préville possessed was a source of the greatest astonishment.   To see him one day as the smart, powdered, affected wit Beaugénie, the next as the outspoken Miller Michau (in *La Chasse de*

Henri IV.) ; now as the nimble, witty, sneering Figaro, then as Goldoni's rough blusterer of a benefactor ;[1] and again as the sneaking hypocrite Stukely (in the fashionable drama *Beverley*[2]), or as the frank, dutiful Prussian soldier Paul Werner, seemed almost like magic to the public of those days.

In private life Préville was as amiable and fascinating as on the stage. Far from being a *poseur*, like so many of his colleagues, he was good-natured, but impatient, unsteady and impulsive, full of fancies, now for painting, now for carpentering or other artisan's work, always incredibly careless and irregular in money matters. His less gay-living, bitter and prudent colleague Lekain frequently reprehended his carelessness, and said to him, " Don't rely on the public ; it is always ungrateful. They won't care in the least if you ruin yourself. The pit, which apparently idolises you, will cry in an ecstasy of delight, ' First amuse me, then you may die ! ' You must secure a respectable living for yourself, in case some day you should think of retiring from the stage."[3]

These admonitions, however, did not affect Préville in the least, and indeed he never suffered from want, but continued to live in comparative competence and high esteem.[4]

About the same time another actor made his *début* ;

---

[1] Géronte in *Le Baurru bienfaisant*.
[2] A mixed tragedy by Saurin after Moore's English original, *The Gamester*.
[3] *Mémoires de Préville*, éd. Barrière, p. 153.
[4] He was the first actor who as a teacher at the newly-established school of declamation became a member of the Institut de France.

his name was Molé,[1] and he was as much idolised as
Préville, though in a different way.   But he had rather
more difficulty in gaining his position.   When, on 24th
November 1754, at the age of twenty, he tried his luck
for the first time at the Théâtre Français, he was not
accepted.   His line, the lighter lovers, was already
occupied by Grandval and Bellecourt, both fine and
elegant *petits-maîtres*, and for six years Molé had to
travel about in the provinces before, after a fresh *début*
in 1761, he was accepted as third lover in the *genre*
called *Molière-lovers.*

The new literature also came to his assistance.
Young Molé, whose beauty was at the same time more
gentle and more robust, more pathetic and more manly
than that of the elegant *viveur* Grandval and the somewhat dry "*bellâtre*"[2] Bellecourt, found a field for himself
in the sensitive, broken-hearted hero who dominated the
new mixed drama.   The desperate gambler Beverley
became his crowning performance, and in this branch
he entirely distanced his predecessors, not merely as an
actor, but—a most important thing for the *prestige* of a
lover—in the favour of the fair sex.   He was idolised
by the ladies to a marvellous degree, and even men
shared in the idolatry.   When in the autumn of 1766
he fell seriously ill of inflammation of the lungs, and his
life was in danger, his admirers—consisting, so to speak,
of all the regular playgoers—showed the most touching

---

[1] François René Molé, a son of the sculptor and painter Molé, born in
1734.

[2] "Would-be beauty"—a term applied to Bellecourt by Voltaire (who
did not like him) in a letter of 10th April 1754.

51

53

52

Marquise de Villette.   Brizard.
Voltaire.   Mme. Denis.

54

—Préville as Mascarille in *L'Etourdi* (p. 297).   53—Brizard as King Lear (p. 303).

52—Molé (p. 298).   54—Crowning of Voltaire in the Théâtre Français (p. 304).

sympathy with him in his illness.   Night after night the
actor who according to old custom announced the next
performance, was asked by the pit how Molé was going
on ; daily bulletins were issued from the house where
he lived ; Court and town spoke of nothing but Molé's
illness ; and when at last he began to recover, and
people heard that his physician had recommended him
to drink plenty of good old claret with his meals, every
wine-cellar was ransacked, and on one day Molé received
two thousand bottles of wine of all the choicest vintages.
A sum of money was collected for him, and when at last
the beloved actor was restored to health, a benefit was
granted him, at which the theatre was overcrowded, but
the enormous proceeds of which he instantly spent on
jewels for his mistress.

In short, Molé was a power, and turned the *blasé*
capital upside down.   Of course the sceptics thought
this idolatry ridiculous, and the wits aimed their shafts
at the hysterically enthusiastic fits of the Parisians.   In
his *Secret Memoirs* Bachaumont reprints a long libel
about the history of Molé's illness, which, by the by,
shows better than anything else to what fantastic heights
actor-idolatry could rise.   Some of the verses may be
quoted here.

> " Généraux, catins, magistrats,
>   Grands écrivains, pieux prélats,
>   Femmes de cour bien affligées,
>   Vont tous lui porter des dragées ;
>   Ce ne peut être que Molet,
>   Ou le singe de Nicolet.

Si la mort étendait son deuil
Ou sur Voltaire ou sur Choiseul,
Paris serait moins en alarmes
Et répandrait bien moins de larmes,
Que n'en ferait verser Molet,
Ou le singe de Nicolet."[1]

On the whole the theatre was the fashion now ; it was frequented and discussed and had an importance never before attained.   First nights were events at which all who wanted to count for something desired to be present.   And not only the plays, but the quality of the acting was discussed, disputed, debated by tongue and pen, in pamphlets, letters and journals, at literary suppers, in the famous Café Procope, at Court festivals and in the salons of the *haute finance*.

Regarded from the outside the theatre and its art had never occupied so prominent a position as during these decades of the middle of the century.   And never during this century had the Comédie Française possessed such a glorious staff of players ; in tragedy the three shining names of Dumesnil, Clairon, and Lekain ; in comedy the admirable Préville, the idolised Molé, Grandval, and Bellecourt, and the enchanting actresses Gaussin and Dangeville, besides many smaller male and female stars.

---

[1] "Generals, *cocottes*, magistrates, great writers, pious clergy, Court-ladies deep in grief, all go and bring him sweets ; it can only be Molet or the monkey of Nicolet.   If death spread its gloom over Voltaire or Choiseul Paris would be less alarmed and shed far fewer tears than over Molet or the monkey of Nicolet."

Nicolet, to whose monkey Molé is compared, was a noted stage manager of the fairs.

This company, essentially homogeneous in method of acting, building on the same traditions, trained in the same *milieu*, always judged, applauded, laughed with or wept with by the same public, obtained a firmness of style, a uniformity of conception, a self-assurance in acting, which had the result that in the eyes of the world the Théâtre Français ranked as the first of all stages, the theatre *par excellence*, the model, the ideal, to all other theatres.   There may have been other stages on which genius burst out more quickly into flame, others where poetry displayed itself more independently, but there was absolutely none where dramatic art could muster at once so many well trained, uniformly disciplined star companies, every member of which could boast of having issued from the academy of the old general, Moliére.

However, this glorious period did not last long.   In 1778 Voltaire, at the age of nearly eighty-four, after many years' absence from Paris, made up his mind to revisit the capital and his dear Théâtre Français, for which he had sacrificed so many years' work.   Even at that time much was altered.   His favourite actress, Mlle. Clairon, had left the theatre as early as 1766, in just anger at the shameless and tyrannical reign of the ruling noblemen.   Afterwards she had led a sort of princely life in Germany as the mistress of the Margrave Alexander of Ansbach.   Lekain, Voltaire's dearest and most gifted pupil, had died at the beginning of the year in which his great master was to revisit the theatre; Grandval, Mlles. Gaussin and Dangeville had retired long ago.   Mlle. Dumesnil had persevered longer,[1] but, as Voltaire said, during the last years she had only been fit to represent bacchantes.

Those who replaced them could not equal these great players. The handsome Mme. Vestris was ambitious, but of mediocre gifts ; she imitated the masterfulness of Mlle. Clairon,[2] but entirely lacked her energetic will-power in acting. Brizard was a sympathetic and tasteful tragedian, whose lot it became to introduce some of Shakespeare's characters, especially *King Lear*, in the shallow adaptation of Ducis, and whose tame acting was quite in harmony with the adapter's intentions, whereas his noble appearance and agreeable voice gained him favour and popularity in patriotic parts, such as Henry IV. in the famous play by Collé. La Rive was a young man who attempted, quite in vain, to enter into the heritage of Lekain. Tradition was kept up to a certain extent, but the glory was gone.

And—what would have enraged Voltaire most of all—the professional liberty, the republican solidarity, of which something was still left in the middle of the century, had now almost entirely disappeared under the arrogance and tyranny of the nobles of the Court. Though the theatre still belonged in part to the actors, they were virtually deprived of all liberty of action. And the irresponsibility which resulted from this state of things led to unparalleled indolence and indifference. Their daily bread was secured to the players by privi-

[1] She remained at the theatre till 1776.

[2] She succeeded in driving away the much more talented but ugly Mlle. Saint-Val, which caused a theatrical scandal of long duration, during which Mme. Vestris could scarcely appear on the stage without being insulted by the pit, which even at that time showed revolutionary tendencies.

lege, so they neglected their professional work with the greatest carelessness. Collé (in 1780) states it as an absolute fact that the plays, even the new ones, were not properly rehearsed, and that the *sociétaires* no longer consulted the authors or asked for their views and opinions concerning their own pieces. And he adds : "These good qualities, combined with their negative talents (*leurs métalents*), must, if matters are not mended, necessarily lead to the decline of the theatre, taste, comedy, and actors." It is clear that the *ancien régime* even of the theatre stood in need of being reformed by a revolution.

However, all these defects and shortcomings were not supposed to be noticed, and were ignored by Voltaire, when once more, shortly before his death, as the intellectual King of France, he visited its capital. The physical monarch, Louis XVI., had refused to see him, because, as he said, he neither respected nor liked him, and he thought that, after all, Voltaire might be contented with his shutting his eyes to his presence in Paris.

But so weakened was the King's power already that, in spite of this distinctly outspoken Royal displeasure, all Paris exerted itself to offer the old author a homage of which no king during the last century had been the object. And the culminating act of this almost idolatrous apotheosis was to take place in the Théâtre Français, the establishment to which Voltaire had devoted the greater, if not the better, part of his gifts.

In spite of his ill-health, the infirm old poet had been induced to honour the theatre once more by the prospect of seeing some of his plays performed on its stage. It

was the 1st of April 1778, and the plays which were
to be acted were his tragedy *Irène* and his comedy
Nanine.

From the moment when his well-known sky-blue
coach, decorated with golden stars, rolled through his
gateway, all the streets surrounding the theatre were
filled with waving crowds, and endless shouts of
"Voltaire!" sounded like smouldering cries for liberty
on his way. When he alighted before the theatre, the
most elegant ladies flocked round him to touch his
clothes, as if he were a saint ; and in the theatre the
spectators were going out of their minds with suspense
until they saw him appear in the box reserved for him,
in which his niece, Mme. Denis, and the Marquise de
Villette were already seated.

The audience had scarcely caught sight of him when
they burst into deafening cheers ; the actor Brizard
entered his box and placed a laurel-wreath on his head.
The old man shed tears of joy, and said, " Ah, God! are
you going to kill me?" after which he took off the wreath
and gallantly offered it to " Belle-et-Bonne," the Marquise
de Villette.

At last the curtain rose on the tragedy, which calmed
the minds of the audience and laid a suitable restraint on
the enthusiasm. But after the interruption the festivities
were resumed. The curtain rose again, and in the middle
of the stage a pedestal had been placed, on which stood
the new bust of Voltaire which shortly before had been
acquired for the hall. The bust was crowned with a
wreath, and surrounding it in a large semi-circle, holding
garlands and palms in their hands, stood all the actors

and actresses, while trumpeters were playing enthusiastic
fanfares.   Then Mme. Vestris came forward and recited
with immense pathos a poem that ended with these
lines :—

> Voltaire, reçois la couronne
> Que l'on vient de te présenter ;
> Il est beau de la mériter,
> Quand c'est la France qui la donne.

After this, amid deafening cheers the actors laid
their crowns and wreaths round the bust, which some
of the ladies kissed in their ecstasies of enthusiasm,
while the crowd in a frenzy of delight saluted the idol of
the time, the old champion of liberty, who here received
a homage greater than had ever been paid to an
absolute monarch.

This half-ludicrous, half-imposing apotheosis was a
kind of final tableau to the pompous, luxurious drama
of the eighteenth century.   Two months later Voltaire
was dead, and with his death the curtain fell on one of
the great dramatic epochs in France.

THE BETTERTON PERIOD

I

Court Literature during the Age of the Restoration—Influence of the Court on the Drama—Distinguished Amateurs and Female Wits.

THE Puritan suppression of the theatres during the Civil War and the Commonwealth became fatal in more than one respect to the development of theatrical art in England.

The sudden, absolute, and long-lasting prohibition of all acting [1] not only produced a rupture of continuity which was never quite healed, but, according to a law which seems inevitable in the progress of culture, the narrow, despotic bigotry, when its ties were broken at last, called forth an unbridled licentiousness, a cynical, impudent pleasure in saying and doing all that had been hitherto forbidden, and even much more, which in reality far exceeded the bounds and inclination of the English national character. And as this licentiousness found its best refuge in the theatres, these places were attacked by an alien fungus of which they have never since been entirely cured. The worst, though not the most prominent symptoms of the disease, however, was not its cold cynicism, but its lack of national foundation, its inconsistency with the essential elements of the national character.

[1] See vol. iii. *The Shakespearean Period in England,* p. 239 f.

A very degenerate descendant of the old, simple, and warm-hearted Shakespearean time, whose art had its strongest roots in the English soil, whose full and deep tones harmonised with the best elements of the British popular mind, the drama of the Restoration, when it made its entry on the stage, had picked up from the French their keen wit and bright conversation, though not their gift of handling gallant and amorous subjects with the polished and imperturbable grace which prevents them from giving offence. English people are by nature chaste in their speech ; if they throw off their natural bashfulness and give way to frivolity, they are apt to become coarse.

This was what happened with the drama of that time ; its authors, in the attempt to copy the shuttle-cock playing of the frivolous French writers, tossed out atrocious indecencies among the public, who after the long Puritan abstinence greedily caught at this coarse amusement.

When in May 1660 young King Charles II. landed in England, hailed by the people as its deliverer from the horrors of the Civil War and from Puritan oppression, we may say that the kingly thought which filled the " merry monarch," and which on the whole guided him during his twenty-five years' reign, was to provide amusement for his people and himself—especially for himself.

And round him flocked a host of noblemen, some of whom had been his companions in exile, and who were now determined to support the King in his purpose ; a motley crew whom wars, exile, and a roving life

had marked and branded, so that it was difficult to dis-
cern whether they were adventurers or diplomats, office-
hunters or politicians, bravoes or warriors.   At any rate
they were all libertines and wits, all equally ready to
empty a bottle, seduce a girl, and write a sonnet or a
play ; men like the Earl of Rochester, the very incarna-
tion of the Restoration period, the beguiling Mephisto of
the King, cynical and sentimental, cowardly and violent,
a drunkard and a Don Juan, a thoroughly cultivated
poet, a zealous and enthusiastic patron of art ; or the
jovial Sir Thomas Killigrew, "the King's court-jester,"
who, fat and self-complacent, swallowed all offices and
spent all fortunes that came within his grasp, who with
unshaken good humour bore his permanent financial
difficulties, and who wrote a comedy as easily as he sued
the King for an office or a sum of money ; Sir George
Etheredge, a great gambler, a libertine in thought and
deed, the lover of the beautiful actress, Mrs Barry, and
a very popular playwright ; Sir William D'Avenant, the
ever-enterprising poet, officer, stage-manager, etc. etc.,
whom fate had tossed about far and wide ; George
Villiers, Duke of Buckingham, whose adventurous life
was as full of vicissitudes as one of the long eighteenth-
century novels, the dashing soldier, the spendthrift and
light-living courtier, the witty part-author of the satirical
parody-comedy *The Rehearsal*.

With a Court composed of such men—and the list of
them might be considerably increased—there was no
difficulty for Charles II. in finding what he understood
by royal amusement.   But—as he had seen in France—
one of its elements was the theatre.

The Court of Louis XIV., his theatre, his literature, his glory and splendour, were the unattainable ideal which turned the heads of most European monarchs. But Charles II. was very far from being a Louis XIV. ; he by no means felt himself to be a kind of divine power, in which the forces and aspirations of the whole nation were centred. The capacity to attract and identify himself with all that was valuable in the work of his country, which was the strong point of the " Roi Soleil," was entirely lacking in the reckless and careless Charles.

It was easy enough to create a new theatre—there were plenty of people who were ready to start it—and a new literature as well. But this literature and its stage became a fashionable amusement for the higher classes, especially for those who were connected with the Court, rather than a fruit of the contemporary intellectual life of the nation. It was old-fashioned to take an interest in the plays of the earlier time. The Shakespearean drama was considered by the King, and therefore by "people," as an obsolete remnant of an uncivilised period. After seeing a performance of *Hamlet*, one of the diary-writers of the time puts down in his memorandum book : " I saw *Hamlet*, *Prince of Denmark*, played, but now the old plays began to disgust this refined age, since his Majestie's being so long abroad." [1] In order to refine the old poets, their masterpieces were subjected to a number of mutilations, which have continued with great per-sistency down to our own time. We see a Romeo and Juliet who marry and live happily ever after, a

[1] Evelyn's *Diary*, 26th November 1661.

Macbeth with additions of opera and ballet,[1] and so forth.

But first and foremost the King's French inclinations [2] gave rise to an entirely new Court literature, written for and partly by the courtiers themselves, in which they imitated the style and subjects of the French dramatists to the best of their ability.   The old variegated, strong, imaginative tragedies were replaced by a series of "heroic" dramas with a gallant but interminable struggle between duty and passion, expressed in clumsy rhymed verses, that were very far removed from Corneille's sonorous alexandrines, which they were meant to resemble—an abominable species of plays, because their style was not suited to the English language, nor their subjects to the English character.

Comedy fared better, in so far as the English humour could not be kept out of it.   But, as was said above, not only was frivolity unbecoming to the British author, but he knew too little of his *métier*.   Scenes that in themselves may be amusing and well described characters are heaped together in a dilettante way without a vestige of the architectonic mastership which distinguishes the construction of Molière's or Regnard's comedies.   How enormous, for instance, is the gap between the art of Molière's *Misanthrope* and Wycherley's imitation of it, *The Plain-Dealer*, or between Regnard's *Gambler* and Susanna

---

[1] In the adaptations of the two tragedies by James Howard and D'Avenant respectively.

[2] The Earl of Orrery (Roger Boyle), the father of the English "heroic" drama, writes in a letter that he has adopted "the French Manners, because I heard the King declare himself more in favour of their Way of Writing than ours."

Centlivre's adaptation of the same play. Even the best plays of this period fashioned after the French pattern, if compared with their models, appear like chaotic outlines of dramas.

And, as a characteristic fact, the majority of playwrights were amateurs, men of high rank, courtiers, who occupied themselves with literature during the leisure hours left from their pleasures and official duties. There was Sir Robert Howard, Dryden's brother-in-law ; the Earl of Orrery, the introducer of the heroic tragedy ; Etheredge, Wycherley, Sedley, Congreve, Vanbrugh, those merry and coarse playwrights, whose dialogues are spicy like men's talk after an old-fashioned English dinner, when the heavy port-wine came on the table after the ladies had left the room—all of them amateurs, courtiers, statesmen, civil or military officers, to whom dramatic work was merely an amusement. When during his sojourn in England Voltaire paid a visit to Congreve, the most popular and noted of all, and complimented him on his plays,[1] Congreve thanked him for the honour, but added that he had no desire to be regarded as an author, but as a private gentleman, and in this latter capacity only did he wish to receive visits. To this Voltaire replied very rightly, that if Congreve had never been anything but a private gentleman, he would probably not have been troubled with his visit.

The Court amateurs impressed their stamp on the

[1] William Congreve wrote but five plays in all, besides a masque and an opera, and during the last twenty-eight years of his life he wrote no plays at all. It was during this period that Voltaire paid him his visit.

theatrical literature of the time. A considerable number
of their plays had real and lasting success, which continued far beyond the lifetime of their authors, especially
Wycherley's *Country Wife*, an imitation of Molière's
L'Ecole des Maris and *L'Ecole des Femmes* ; Congreve's
Love for Love and *The Way of the World*, the witty
dialogue of which may still be read with pleasure ; Vanbrugh's *The Relapse, or Virtue in Danger*, whose ludicrous
Lord Foppington became a celebrated type on the
stage.

Besides these gentlemen-authors, of course, a large
number of professional writers wrote for the stage.
Dryden is the leading literary name of the time ; yet he
was no real leader. Though his pen was much more
fluent than any of those of the distinguished amateurs—
so fluent that it easily adapted itself to all *genres* and all
convictions—his art was much more tinged by his Court
surroundings than they were influenced by his personality. His plays—he wrote twenty-seven in all, heroic
dramas in rhymed verse, tragedies in blank verse,
comedies in prose and verse, and operas—are so many
sacrifices to the varying times and to the tastes of the
changing Courts ; some are intolerable, nay, ridiculously
bombastic, several of them are written with ease and
effect, but none of them bears the stamp of a truly
poetic mind.

And what is said here of the most fluent and gifted
writer of the time applies to the many smaller stars.
None of them, whether siding with or against Dryden
in the always inevitable literary quarrels, left a memorable dramatic work of his own ; none found other paths

than those once marked out by the Court amateurs. Several of them, nevertheless, obtained very considerable and lasting, though nowadays incomprehensible, successes, thus especially, George Farquhar, whose *Constant Couple* with its sequel, *Sir Harry Wildair*, and *The Recruiting Officers*, became as popular on the Continent, in Germany and Denmark,[1] as in the country of the young author.

Amidst all this smooth, elegant mediocrity we discover the emaciated, tortured faces of two men, endowed with genuine poetic gifts—Nathaniel Lee, the poet of horrors, whose wild dramas point towards the past and turn our thoughts to Christopher Marlowe, and "tender Otway," whose sensitiveness and choice of subjects foreshadow the future. His *Venice Preserved* and *Don Carlos* show him as an embryonic Schiller. But these two *raræ aves* only give golden promises, which are not redeemed by any mature masterpiece, perhaps, among other reasons, because misfortune and misery carried them off too soon. Lee died insane in his fortieth year, Otway at an even earlier age from distress and starvation.

A characteristic feature in the dramatic and literary physiognomy of the time are "the female wits," as they were mockingly called. Quite unknown in the time of Shakespeare, the English authoress, who in later times is seen frequently enough, makes her first appearance under Charles II. But the blue-stocking of the Restoration differs very much indeed from the respectable lady novelist of the nineteenth century.

[1] See above, p. 169.

A showy adventuress, half courtesan, half political agent, as light in her morals as free with her tongue and with her pen—such was the typical authoress of the time ; such was Mrs Manley, noted for her novel of scandal, *Secret Memoirs from the New Atalantis*, as well as for her plays ; such was Mrs Aphra Behn, who gave the theatre no less than eighteen witty and very immoral comedies ; such was to a certain degree Mrs Susannah Centlivre, among whose plays *The Busy Body* in particular became a popular play in all *répertoires*.

Witty amateurs of high rank, witty ladies of the *demi-monde*, who lived by their pen as well as by their other gifts, fluent writers of loose morals, were the types that formed the literary background of dramatic art during the Restoration.

II

Revival of the Theatre under Charles II.—The Two Patented Managers, Sir Thomas Killigrew and Sir William D'Avenant—Old and New Actors—Thomas Betterton and his Fellow-Actors.

THE theatre was soon as far removed from the old time as literature, and the Shakespearean period, with its strong national, but distinctly artistic, theatre, soon was seen by the eye of the times as if far off in a strange mist.

As soon as the Puritan repression was thrown off with the death of Cromwell and the retirement of his son, while General Monk, who had no Puritan tendencies, dominated London with his 7000 soldiers and

prepared the entry of Charles II., a former stage ward-
robe - keeper, now bookseller, named John Rhodes,
applied for permission to play comedy in the old
Cockpit Theatre,[1] in Drury Lane. He obtained the
licence about the beginning of 1660, and began his
performances in the little playhouse with, for the most
part, fresh, untried players, the one who became most
noted of them being a colleague of Rhodes, the bookseller,
young Thomas Betterton.

However, the old actors of the time before the Civil
War were not all dead. Royalists—necessarily, we may
say—nearly all of them were ; some of them had fought
bravely for the Stuarts, as much from the instinct of self-
preservation as from loyalty to their King. After being
scattered far and wide, a number of them now reappeared,
some of them provided with military titles, such as the
popular character-actor Major Mohun, and assembled in
the well-known theatre, The Red Bull.[2]

Finally, Beeston, former leader of the company
called the "Beeston Boys," received a licence from the
old censor, Sir Henry Herbert,[3] to act in the Salisbury
Court Theatre (Whitefriars).

All these three stages were opened in 1660, even
before Charles II. made his entry into London.

But as soon as the King felt himself firmly seated
on his throne, matters assumed a different aspect.
Charles certainly did not dislike the theatre ; on the

[1] One of the closed private theatres. See Vol. iii. *The Shakespearean Period in England*, p. 92 ff.

[2] The Red Bull (see vol. iii. *The Shakespearean Period in England*, p. 92 ff.), with the Cockpit and Salisbury Court, was still standing.

[3] For Herbert, see vol. iii. *The Shakespearean Period*, p. 129 ff.

contrary ; but it was to become a Court amusement according to Royal taste, and could not be allowed to remain loose and develop itself independently. For this purpose the existing theatres were abolished, Sir Henry, the old Censor and Master of the Revels, lost his power, which was a real reform, and two new Royal patents were granted to Sir Thomas Killigrew and Sir William D'Avenant, favourites of the King, and particularly well qualified for the position.

Both were typical men of their time. Killigrew, who was about fifty when appointed to the office of Royal theatre manager, had been honorary page to Charles I., and had afterwards accompanied his son into exile. He enjoyed great favour with the latter ; he even had some influence over him, since with his jovial, always cheerful humour, he could induce the monarch, who was supremely indifferent to State affairs, to do things which no serious argument from anybody else could make him do. During his exile, Killigrew had been occupied in different ways. He had been the ambassador of young King Charles in Venice, and occupied this post so conscientiously in the spirit of his master, that he had been obliged to leave the town on account of his vicious behaviour ; he had cultivated poetry and written half a score of plays, which, however, do not show much of the wit which he really displayed in his talk. It was said of him, and the poet Cowley, who wielded a very witty pen, but was exceedingly dull in conversation :

Had Cowley ne'er spoke, Killigrew ne'er writ,
Combin'd in one, they'd made a matchless wit.

Such as he was, and having made it his principle to apply for all the appointments that yielded any income and did not necessarily require over-exertion of effort, we cannot wonder that it was Killigrew who was entrusted with the task of transforming the English theatre into an instrument for Royal amusement. For Killigrew's stage became the specifically Royal playhouse. It was situated first in Vere Street, in a former tennis-court that had been reconstructed for the purpose, afterwards in a new building in Drury Lane, and was called " The King's Theatre," and the company, as in former days, was styled " His Majesty's Servants."

He formed his company, for the most part, of the old players of the time before the Wars, and, as far as can be seen, left the artistic and administrative leadership to the best among them, while he himself attended to his Court offices—he was a gentleman of the bed-chamber, and at the same time, in reality, a kind of official Court-jester—and to his diverse private amusements.

The leading actors at the Theatre Royal were, above all, Major Michael Mohun and Charles Hart, and of these two again it was the latter who, as a matter of fact, ruled the theatre. Hart had famous stage-blood in his veins, as he was a grandson of Shakespeare's sister Joan. As a boy he had acted girls' parts at Blackfriars, and was now a popular lover and character player. Othello, Alexander the Great (in Lee's *The Rival Queens*), and Amyntas (in Beaumont and Fletcher's *The Maid's Tragedy*) are mentioned as his best *rôles*. He was a fine, stately, serious man, who, with pedantic severity, watched over the dignity of the stage, and, as

far as possible, respected the old traditions.   Like his
colleague, Major Mohun, Hart had served as an officer
in the Civil Wars—where, however, he had only risen to
the rank of a lieutenant—and both these men, with the
fidelity of veterans, served their King's amusement as
well-trained soldiers in the small irregular force of actors,
though, from the very scanty information we possess
about them, it is impossible to form an idea of the
nature of their art.

And we know scarcely as much about the other
members of the company, though a few of them, like
Clun, enjoyed great consideration among the older
generation of spectators, whereas the modern taste half
despised these old-fashioned actors, and acknowledged
none but the comic actor, John Lacy, as a really first-
rate player.   Lacy, by the by, also belonged to the old
school of comedians, though he was a somewhat refined
specimen, half dancer, half court jester.   Originally a
dancing-master, he afterwards served as a lieutenant,
and seems to have used his physical advantages with
much gracefulness in the service of dramatic art.   His
wit and fashionable elegance rendered him a great
favourite with the King, who even had him painted in
three of his parts in a full-size picture, which is still to
be seen at Hampton Court.[1]   There he appears as a

[1] Not in Windsor Castle, as is stated in biographical handbooks.   The
picture is by Michael Wright, and represents Lacy as the low comedy Irishman, Teague, in Sir Robert Howard's polemical comedy *The Committee*, as
Scruple in John Wilson's *Cheats*, and Galliard in a play by the Duke of New-
castle (*Variety*).   So these three characters must probably be considered as
Lacy's principal parts.   A copy of Wright's picture is to be found in the
unique collection of pictures of theatrical history belonging to the Garrick
Club.

handsome, well-shaped man, with an expressive and amiable comedian's face. He was also the author of some witty comedies.

One of the younger generation was Kynaston, who, nevertheless, must be classed with the older school in so far as he still represented the female lovers, though his time required ladies to act women's parts. But as he was very young and very handsome, and from his childhood had been trained for his special line, he competed successfully with the new rising actresses, and many spectators thought that no woman came up to him in his strong part, that of pathetic, tragic, young women. However, he soon passed over to the male character, in which he also became an actor of note.

The actresses at the Theatre Royal became better known for their beauty and light morals than for great artistic gifts. The King's predilection for these stage beauties is well known, best of all perhaps his relations with the merry, impudent, and very good-looking Nell Gwynn, who from the position of orange-girl had risen to the stage, where she attracted greater attention by her coarse humour and captivating appearance than by any kind of talent. Though she swore like a trooper, and neither respected nor cared to adopt refined manners, the merry King thought it a good joke to make her both Lady of the Bedchamber to the Queen and his own acknowledged mistress, which so tickled her humorous fancy that she composed the following poetic epitaph on herself:—

Here Nelly lies, who, though she lived a slattern,
Yet died a Princess acting in St Cattrin.

Among the other ladies of this theatre the most noted
were Mrs Hughes, who was formerly wrongly supposed
to have been the first English actress who appeared on
the stage after the Restoration ; Mrs Knipp, whose
name is especially remembered because she was the
favoured friend of Samuel Pepys, the well-known
" theatrophile " and diary writer ; finally, the two fashionable and light-living daughters of a clergyman, Ann and
Rebecca Marshall.[1]

The second theatrical lessee and manager, Sir William
D'Avenant, was also a man of advanced age, even older
than Killigrew, and experienced in stage matters.   Sir
William was no born aristocrat, but had risen from a
lower rank by his ability and his fidelity to the Royal
cause.   His father had been landlord of " The Crown,"
an inn at Oxford, where, according to an old tradition,
William Shakespeare had frequently lodged, quite as
much for the sake of handsome Mrs D'Avenant as for
that of the good wine.   And, rumour added, it was not
by chance that little D'Avenant bore the same Christian
name as the great poet.   Sir William did not contradict
this myth, which might explain his strong inclination for
poetry, but which, on the whole, seems quite without
foundation.

His life was full of variety, divided between literature,
politics, and theatrical work.   He rose by means of his
pen, won favour with the distinguished wits, and at a
very early age obtained the very lucrative court appoint-

---

[1] English actresses, even if unmarried, always used to be called " Mrs,"
unlike the French, who continued to be addressed as " Mademoiselle " long
after having lost every claim to the title of virginity.

ment of *Poet Laureate*, in succession to no less a person
than Ben Jonson. He got into the good graces of the
Queen—the wife of Charles I.—and accompanied her
into exile in France; he fought as an officer for the
cause of his King, and was knighted for his valour; was
despatched from France as the leader of an expedition
that was to introduce French artisans into Virginia, but
was picked up on the way by ships of the English Commonwealth, imprisoned, and on the point of being hanged;
continued and published while in prison a long epic
poem, *Gondibert*; was pardoned, and—all the time under
Puritan rule—in order to make money, with inconceivable
skill obtained permission to perform a new kind of plays,[1]
which he masked under the name of "operas"—patriotic
spectacular pieces with music, performed with modern
Italian scenery, which was also quite new to the English
public. And now, in his fifty-sixth year, by Royal
licence, he established a new theatre, which became the
principal stage of vital power during this period, and
for which he wrote a number of fluent plays in the taste
of the time.

D'Avenant was not a great, not even a genuine poet,
but he was a wonderfully inventive, enterprising man,
constantly planning new things. And it was essentially
due to him that theatrical art advanced and was led into
new channels. At the same time he took as good care
as possible to keep up the connection with old art, by
somehow or other securing for the theatre the monopoly
of acting no less than nine of Shakespeare's plays, some

[1] The author's authority is among others *Biographia Dramatica*, by
Arth. Davenant.

of the best and easiest to perform among the number, such as *Hamlet, King Lear, Macbeth, Romeo and Juliet, The Tempest,* and *Twelfth Night.* It is true he ill-treated these priceless heirlooms of his supposed father's by "reforming them, and qualifying them for the company which stood under his command and leadership." However, so much at any rate was left of these rich works that the actors could learn from them and grow by them.

Characteristically enough, it was the young actors who flocked round the aging leader, and the young section among the public who appreciated his stage. At its beginnings the theatre, which opened in 1661 in Portugal Row, Lincoln's Inn Fields, was scarcely considered equal in rank to Killigrew's Royal Playhouse. It was under the patronage of the Duke of York, and therefore bore the title of "The Duke's Theatre." And the older generation of playgoers looked with a certain contempt on the unknown names of this company. Who knew anything of Thomas Betterton, James Nokes, Cave Underhill, or Henry Harris ? Among the ladies, it is true, Mrs Davenport was known from earlier appearances in Sir William's operas, nor were beautiful Mrs Davies, and young, talented Mrs Saunderson (afterwards Mrs Betterton) quite unknown ; but taken altogether, the young company consisted of obscure names.

But very soon the tables turned. Under the expert and keenly interested leadership of D'Avenant these unknown young people rapidly became the favourites of London playgoers, while owing to Killigrew's happy-

55

56

57

59

55—Nell Gwynn (p. 319).
57—Thomas Betterton (p. 326).

56—Mrs Davies (p. 324).
59—Colley Cibber as Lord Foppington (p. 352).

go-lucky indifference the Royal actors in the same measure lost their *prestige*. Even the Court favoured the younger stage, and the King showed his interest in his own particular way by including beautiful Mrs Davies in his gallery of lady-loves.

However, D'Avenant was not for long allowed to manage the theatre, which evidently had become very dear to him. He died as early as 1668, at the age of sixty-two. But in the course of the seven years during which he ruled The Duke's Theatre, he had accomplished very considerable work; he wrote fifteen plays,[1] trained a new company, which at his death had obtained a safe and noted position in the favour of the public; he also introduced innovations in scenic art as well as in outward theatrical arrangements, and before his death he planned the construction of a new, entirely modern, up-to-date playhouse, which, however, he did not live to see.

This new theatre was built in a place called Dorset Gardens, near Salisbury Court, Fleet Street, and therefore took the title of "Dorset Garden Theatre." It opened on 9th November 1671, and took the London public entirely by surprise by its extraordinary architectonic and picturesque magnificence, which far surpassed anything that had been seen in other contemporary playhouses. It is true, the expense had amounted to the then enormous sum of £5000, collected by a sort of company of shareholders.

---

[1] The complete number of his plays is twenty-five, ten of which, however, were written before the Restoration. The most noted of them are: *The Siege of Rhodes*, *The Cruelty of the Spaniards in Peru*, the comedy *The Playhouse to be Let*, and his adaptation of *Macbeth*.

But the real leadership of this splendid house, which had been equipped with all the acoustic and mechanical refinements of Italian theatrical technique, was entrusted to D'Avenant's son, Dr Charles D'Avenant, together with the two leading actors of his company, Thomas Betterton and Henry Harris.[1]

These two actors—at times keen rivals—formed a great contrast.

Henry Harris was a genuine type of the Restoration, a half dilettante *élégant*, who dabbled a little in all arts ; he was an able painter, a musician of ability, had much desultory knowledge, was able to talk literature with men and love with women, led the life of a *grand seigneur*, was a modern tenor spoilt by the public. His tiring-room was the meeting-place of wits, who assembled there to discuss the play and current events, and to pour out their latest love-adventures. But all this fashionable life in the world to a certain extent over-shadowed his art on the stage. He was the modern ladies' actor ; we know that he played Romeo and other lovers to great admiration ; otherwise his art seems to have been ephemeral, sensational, and superficial like his character. He was one of those who attract great attention at the moment, but are soon forgotten. The facts of his life are not known, but after 1681 his name had disappeared from all casts ; so he must either have died or left the stage.

Of a very different and much weightier calibre was Thomas Betterton. The artistic value of Harris was

[1] Henry or Joseph Harris ; his Christian name is not exactly known ; at the time, as a rule, he was only called Mr Harris.

short-lived, brilliant, and dazzling like the tail of a comet, but equally without a solid kernel. Betterton, on the other hand, stands in the firmament of art like a solid planet, whose quiet light remains undimmed throughout the ages.

It was the firmness, solidity, and genuine art of Betterton that centred the dramatic art of the time round him as its natural point of support, and caused the period to be called after him. Not that Betterton was a typical son of his age ; on the contrary, he attained great importance chiefly because he staked all his weight and serious art against the reigning levity and shallowness.

He was not trained to be an actor, like so many of his colleagues who from childhood had been attached to the theatre. His father, who was chief of the Royal kitchen, had apprenticed him to a bookseller, and he was an independent publisher before he became an actor.[1]

It was probably his older colleague, formerly a stage manager, now a bookseller, John Rhodes, who won Betterton over to dramatic art. At any rate, it was under the leadership of this man that Betterton at the age of twenty-five found his first engagement at the Cockpit Theatre in Drury Lane. And at this short-lived theatrical institution he was already the un-questioned first lover and hero, with young, handsome Kynaston in the leading female lovers.

He continued to occupy the leading position, which

[1] It seems that he continued his old business some years after having entered on the theatrical career. Two books of 1660 and 1661 bear the name of his publishing firm on their title-pages. Comp. Lowe's *Thomas Betterton*, p. 58.

he seems to have acquired very easily and naturally, after John Rhodes had passed out of theatrical history, and Sir William D'Avenant had engaged most members of his company for his new theatre.

Here also he took his place, unshaken and unopposed, as first tragedian and lover, only now and then eclipsed by Harris, who was more airy, light, and elegant than the somewhat heavy Betterton. The rivalry between the two heroes was sometimes bitter enough, but, in the long run, Betterton was sure to gain the victory on account of his greater power and enduring love of his art. In reality their fields were, or ought to have been, very different. If Harris beguiled the heart as the impulsive Romeo, Betterton captivated mind and feelings by his Hamlet or Macbeth. While Harris, as far as we know, played exclusively heroes and lovers in tragedy and comedy, Betterton was the pronounced character actor, he was equally good whether representing the drunken joviality of Sir Toby Belch, and later of Sir John Falstaff, or Lee's deeply pathetic characters, such as Alexander—one of his leading parts.

All the chief characters in the Shakespearean as well as in the contemporary *répertoire* fell to the share of Betterton. Thus, besides the parts already mentioned, he played Richard III., King Lear, Othello, Timon of Athens, Henry VIII. ; in Otway's *Venice Preserved* Jaffier was one of his celebrated parts ; as Oedipus in the ghastly Greek tragedy of that name by Dryden and Lee, he affected the audience to the highest degree.

Betterton was probably the first theorist among English actors, unless we count Shakespeare in memory of the ever valid little catechism of acting which he has left us in the well-known and often quoted speech of Hamlet. Betterton, however, had made a more special study of histrionic theory. He was not without knowledge, had acquainted himself with ancient classical dramatic art, is said to have been sent to Paris by King Charles in order to study French theatrical art, which at that time was in full flower, and has left his reflections and experiences in a series of rules for acting, especially for dumb show, which, though not equal to those of Shakespeare in spirit and general importance, are very sensible, and must have been of great use to a generation of beginners, who lacked fixed method, tradition or school. He treats in detail the movements of head, eyes and hands, and their importance to scenic art. Though he constantly appeals to nature, it is clear from his dissertation that in his time plastic attitudes and movements and facial play were much more systematised and fixed in a certain style than we approve of nowadays.

As stage manager, too—a function which he combined with that of general manager—he had sound and comparatively advanced views. He had acquired a dim conception of the picturesque and plastic grouping of masses, which has become a principal feature in the work of a modern stage manager, by comparing the effective arrangements of contemporary historical pictures with the prevailing impassiveness and mechanical grouping of the performers on the stage. Thus he writes somewhere : " All the slaves in Lebrun's *Tent of Darius* participate of the grand Concern of Sisigambis.

Statyra, etc.   This w^d render the Representation
extremely solemn & beautiful, but on the Stage not
only the Supernumeraries, as they call them, or Attend-
ants seem regardless of the great Concern of the Scene,
and [but?] even the Actors themselves, who are on the
Stage, & not in the very principal Parts, will be
whispering to one another, or bowing to their Friends in
the Pit, or gazing about." [1]

The picture of the famous actor, painted by Kneller,
which is in the National Portrait Gallery in London,
shows Betterton as a stately and fine man, with a somewhat heavy but very expressive face, a full, flexible
mouth, a large, powerful chin, a marked nose, and
steady but not hard eyes.   The face expresses power
and feeling, combined with no small amount of dignity.

His contemporaries, however, did not consider him
good-looking ; his figure, especially, is described as
rather bad.

A younger colleague of his, Anthony Aston, gives
a vivid, though not flattering description of him in
later years.   He writes : " Mr Betterton (although a
superlative good actor) labour'd under ill Figure,
being clumsily made, having a great Head, a short
thick Neck, stoop'd in the shoulders, and had fat
short Arms, which he rarely lifted higher than his
Stomach—his Left Hand frequently lodg'd in his Breast,
between his Coat and Waist-coat, while with his Right,
he prepar'd his Speech.—His Actions were few, but just.
—He had little Eyes and a broad Face, a little Pock-
fretten, a corpulent Body and thick Legs, with large

---

[1] *History of the English Stage*, p. 51.

Feet. He was better to meet than to follow, for his Aspect was serious, venerable & majestic ; in his latter time a little paralytic.—His voice was low and grumbling, yet he could Tune it by an artful *Climax* which enforc'd unusual Attention, even from the Fops and Orange-Girls." [1]

This description, of course, dates from a time when the great actor was no longer in his full bodily vigour. Betterton continued acting up to old age, and playing parts for which his outward appearance was no longer suited ; thus, at the age of sixty-seven, he undertook the part of Bassanio, the young lover, which he had never played before.

But even apart from the infirmities of age, Tony Aston's words contain sufficient hints to give scope to fancy, and to enable us to imagine what the art of Betterton and his contemporaries was like.

Like everything at this period, the style of Betterton was influenced by France. During the last part of the reign of Louis XIV. a solemn dignity in private life as on the stage had become fashionable. The enormous wigs, the heavy velvet dresses, the quantity of lace and the high heels favoured slow, restrained and measured movements—we have seen that in tragedy running on the stage was unknown in France, even late in the eighteenth century. The attitude of Betterton, his left hand steadily held against his breast, his right hand accentuating his speech with quiet gesture, but never

---

[1] A brief supplement to Colley Cibber, Esq. His *Lives of the late famous Actors and Actresses*, by Anthony, vulgò Tony Aston. The rare little pamphlet has been reprinted by Robert W. Lowe in his edition of Colley Cibber's *Apology*.

moving above the level of his well-rounded stomach, is typical of the conventional representation of dignified deportment which remained customary far later than his own time, and even during a considerable part of the nineteenth century.

But in Betterton this French dignity was seasoned with other genuinely British ingredients. Under the daintily frilled lace and gold-trimmed stiff garments the blood flowed heavy and hot in the veins. At that period people ate much, drank heavily, and took too little exercise. The warm blood was up on the slightest occasion, and the sword sat very loose in its sheath. English theatrical history about the beginning of the eighteenth century abounds in duels, murders, and assaults. Several actors had their careers cut off by a violent death, and even a larger number had more than one manslaughter on their conscience.

But it was not considered the proper thing to represent seething and bubbling passions on the stage as they display themselves in real life ; they had to be transformed, submitted to conventional rules, clothed in rhetorical speech and plastic dignity ; like the horrors of French tragedy, the scene of passionate deeds had to be laid off the stage.

The left hand is pressed against the heart to prevent it from overflowing, while the elegant movements of the right hand are allowed to indicate deep feelings, and well-cadenced speech swells like a broad stream through a large field. This method, which in the young and gifted actor was an artistic principle, became a habit and a routine in the old and mediocre performer.

If we want to form an idea of the dramatic art of Betterton, and thereby of that of his contemporaries and immediate successors, we must understand this duality ; a violent, heavy, and full-blooded passion covered by a fashionable, conventional, somewhat slow dignity.

The great characteristic of Betterton's art must have been the ponderous, swelling passion under the clear and simple form.   The ideals of the time differed so much from our own that we can scarcely understand how he could win his greatest fame by his Shakespearean characters.   He doubtless neither had the power, nor made the attempt to throw the half naturalistic, half fantastic light over these figures in which we like to see them. His time, though comparatively near to that of Shakespeare, was exceedingly far removed from the Renaissance, especially in its conception of art, and what might be called historical imagination was quite unknown in the dramatic art of the time.   All that did not bear the modern stamp in costume, behaviour, speech, and manners was barbarous and unacceptable.

So we may be sure that Betterton produced his great effect by the oratorical power and general feeling which he was able to infuse into his play by staking his own powerful personality, not by efforts to represent his character in a picturesque or naturalistic psychological form.

This supposition indeed agrees with the otherwise rather scanty information we possess about his acting. Colley Cibber, for instance, his younger colleague and afterwards manager of Drury Lane Theatre, writes of his Hamlet in the ghost scene :—" . . . [This was the Light into wh. B. threw this scene] ; which he open'd

with a Pause of mute Amazement! then rising slowly to
a solemn, trembling Voice, he made the Ghost equally
terrible to the Spectator as to himself! and in the
descriptive Part of the natural Emotions which the
ghastly Vision gave him, the boldness of his Expostula-
tion was still governed by Decency, manly, but not
braving, his voice never rising into that seeming Out-
rage, or wild Defiance of what he naturally rever'd." [1]

It has been asserted, by the bye, that this very
character of Hamlet, as performed by Betterton, had
come down by tradition from Shakespeare's own days,
as D'Avenant, his manager, had rehearsed the part with
him ; D'Avenant, again, had seen Taylor in it, who had
been instructed by Shakespeare himself. But this means
at most that Betterton may have inherited some pieces
of business, for there can scarcely be any doubt that his
method of acting differed exceedingly from that of the
Renaissance.

In Betterton's younger years Hamlet was his crowning glory, and all testimonies are unanimous in pointing
out the unique power he exercised over his audience by
his affecting, yet well controlled delivery, and his most
expressive facial play.[2]

---

[1] *An Apology for the Life of Mr Colley Cibber*, ed. R. W. Lowe. London,
1889, i. 101.

[2] About the latter a famous contemporary pamphlet has the following
note :—"I have lately been told by a Gentleman who has frequently seen
Mr *Betterton* perform this part of *Hamlet* that he has observ'd his Counten-
ance (which was naturally ruddy and sanguin) in this Scene of the fourth Act
where his Father's Ghost appears, thro' the violent and sudden Emotions of
Amazement & Horror turn instantly on the Sight of his Father's Spirit, as
pale as his neckcloth, when every Part of his Body seem'd to be affected
with a Tremor inexpressible ; so that, had his Father's Ghost actually risen
before him, he could not have been seized with more real agonies ; & this
was felt so strongly by the Audience that the Blood seemed to shudder in

In 1662 Betterton married Mrs Saunderson, at the time leading actress at the Duke's Theatre; she was serious, somewhat melancholy of temperament, a pleasant, intelligent actress, whose Ophelia, Juliet, and Queen Katherine (in *Henry VIII.*) were very popular, and whose cultivated, quiet manners caused her to be the favoured teacher of princely amateur actresses. Their married life was childless, but happy.

His favourite partner, however, was Mrs Elizabeth Barry, who possessed greater talent as an actress, and was decidedly the first female player of this period. Born in 1658, she was much younger than Mrs Betterton, and—contrary to the rule in those days—of good family, her father being a lawyer, afterwards Colonel Barry.

She was far from handsome, and as on account of her defective musical ear it was impossible for her to learn the conventional chanting delivery, which had been cultivated after the French pattern, she at first had great difficulty in making her way. However, her lover, the clever scoundrel the Earl of Rochester, is said to have taught her acting in his own way.[1]

And she really seems to have become something unique. Even her appearance was out of the common. Her figure was full and middle-sized, her eyes were light, her hair and eyebrows dark. She had large, irregular and striking features, a big expressive mouth,

their veins likewise, & they in some Measure partook of the Astonishment & Horror, with which they saw this excellent actor affected." From a libel on Colley Cibber, *The Laureat*; quoted by R. W. Lowe, *Thomas Betterton*, p. 86 f.

[1] Th. Davies, *Dramatic Miscellanies*, iii. 209 ff.

which was drawn much to the right when she smiled. This uncommon exterior combined with a peculiar, very varied mode of acting and strong, vivid facial play, gave her a solitary but prominent place among her female colleagues.

Among these, however, the charming Mrs Bracegirdle possessed a most fascinating talent. Widely differing from Mrs Barry, who was most successful in tragedy, and whose best parts were in Otway's exciting and passionate plays,[1] Anne Bracegirdle was the lover born of Congreve's pieces, light, piquant, merry and witty, with a slender elegant figure and a regular handsome face. And with Congreve—whom she is said also to have preferred off the stage—her professional name is essentially associated. She created the two female lovers Angelica and Millamant in two of his plays, which were immensely famous at the time, *Love for Love* and *The Way of the World*. The career of Mrs Bracegirdle was but short. She retired from the stage as early as 1707, when only thirty-three years old.[2]

Among the male colleagues of Betterton, Sandford was a characteristic type of his time. He was the villain *par excellence*, "the best villain in the world," as Charles II. called him. And nature itself had created him for this line. He was not a scoundrel by choice, but by

[1] Monimia in *The Orphan* and Belvidera in *Venice Preserved*, by this author, were among her best performances. She was also successful, however, as the coquettes in comedy, such as the frivolous Mrs Fraile in Congreve's *Love for Love*.

[2] She was born in 1674, so was much younger than Mrs Barry, and died in 1748. She was unmarried, and though surrounded by swarms of love-making men, she preserved an exceptionally good reputation. Congreve is the only man whom she seems to have favoured.

necessity, as Cibber says.   His figure was small and bent, his face lean and gloomy, his arms long and thin, and the public was so accustomed to see him commit all kinds of villanies that they could not imagine a rascal except in the shape of Sandford, or Sandford except in that of a rascal.

Once, it is related, an author had been inconsiderate enough to provide him with the part of an honest man, but this quite put the audience out.   During the first act they fully enjoyed Sandford's excellent simulation of honesty, and anticipated in suspense his being unmasked, but when the last act came, and Sandford continued unshaken in his honesty, they were indignant and hooted at the play.

A very talented lover in tragedy as well as comedy was William Mountfort, a tall, well-shaped, handsome young man, who with his fine voice and powerful capacities might have become a worthy successor to Betterton, if he had not while still a youth been murdered in the street outside Mrs Bracegirdle's house.

Moreover, the stage had pillars of support in the inevitable, indispensable professional low comedians, on whose appearance the audience were as sure of amusement as they were of wickedness at the appearance of Sandford.   This irresistible trio consisted of James Nokes, Anthony Leigh, and Cave Underhill.

Of these Nokes was by far the most distinguished, especially because his humour was of the truly British sort.   He was one of those sepulchral, grave comedians, whom the French call *pince-sans-rire*, and who even now have irresistible representatives among English low comedians.   Their comical personality excites the mirth of the audience at their first entry, and calls forth outbursts of laughter.   But the more people laughed the graver became Nokes.   " And, sure, the ridiculous Solemnity of his Features were enough to have set a whole Bench of Bishops into a Titter, cou'd he have been honour'd (may it be no Offence to suppose it) with such grave and right reverend Auditors." [1]

Strangely enough, his most celebrated part was Sir Martin Mar-all, the principal character in Dryden's adaptation of Molière *L'Etourdi.*

Less original, less peculiarly English, was Anthony Leigh.   His comic art seems to have been more influenced by the Franco-Italian style ; though more of a mask, more outwardly gay, less true to nature than Nokes, he was on the other hand more lively and more varying.   His name is particularly associated with his performance of the merry Father Dominic in Dryden's *Spanish Friar.*

Cave Underhill belonged to the same generation, and was essentially of the same type as Nokes, but his appearance was less comical in itself, and he was less eccentric in his originality.   As he was physically stout and heavy, had a monkey-face, a large, broad mouth, and a small, flat nose, so his art was dry, heavy, simple, entirely impliable.   Outside his very limited comic line he was quite useless, and, on the whole, his humour was of the sort that amused the actors more than the audience, especially when they were seated together in a tavern, and Cave told them

---

[1] *An Apology for the Life of Mr Cibber*, i. 144.

stories while they were consuming many cups of " Bristol milk," as he called the golden sherry.

This period of the history of English theatrical art is remarkably mixed. It still lives a little on the remainder of the heritage from the great, rich Shakespearean period, but is trying at the same time to strike new coin of the light French gold. People are heavy and full-blooded, fashion is light and shallow, passions are strong and coarse, outward form is required to be smooth and polished. The result is inconsistency, uncertainty as to ends and means, which finds a firm point of support only in Betterton's solid, powerful, and manly art.

THE CIBBER PERIOD

I

DURING this period the outward shape of the theatre showed a considerable difference from the old national Shakespearean stage. In the first place, after the Restoration the playhouses were always constructed as closed, indoor theatres. The old arena-form was entirely abandoned, and the stage was arranged with painted wings and back-curtains, after the Italian style—in short, in a style essentially like that of a modern theatre. As a remnant of the old platform-shape, the stage still projected in an oval into the pit, thus forming a kind of platform in front of the scene.

This projecting oval disappeared at the beginning of the eighteenth century, or was limited to a gentle curve, while the proscenium continued to be very deep, richly ornamented with gilt pilasters, with latticed boxes for spectators above and doors leading on to the stage below. Thus the drop-curtain and the scene of action were tolerably far removed from the spectators, but, in order to be seen and heard, the actors had frequently to come forward from the stage proper, and act a great part of the play in the proscenium. In some old or old-fashioned theatres—for instance, our own [Danish] Royal Theatre—this arrangement is still seen. Modern

338

stage - technique limits the proscenium to the smallest possible space, to a mere frame, within which the stage and all that passes there is seen like a picture.

The orchestra now had its place in front of the stage, no longer in a box or gallery above or beside it.

The auditorium consisted of a pit, with seats—not as in France, exclusively with standing-room for gentlemen —and of three rows of boxes.   The bottom row was quite low, at such a level to allow the gentlemen in the pit, leaning against the balusters, to converse easily with the fashionable ladies, who preferred to occupy these seats.   There was also the Royal box, and, contrary to the custom in France, the King and Queen frequently visited the theatre.   Charles II., in particular, was a constant visitor there, and memoir-writing playgoers tell us of his difficulties in distributing his Royal favours among his different jealous lady-loves present.

The middle row was considered less *comme il faut,* as its boxes were occupied by the genteel courtesans ; they were masked, and therefore went by the name of vizard masks.   In former times it was customary for all ladies to wear masks in the theatre, and under this disguise to carry on flirtations with their acquaintances among the gentlemen who did not recognise them.   But by an edict of Queen Anne, in 1704, ladies were forbidden to wear masks in the theatre.

The upper gallery was the cheapest and least genteel place, where the lower classes went.   Moreover, for a long time it was the custom to allow lackeys free admission to these seats during the last act of the play, which was a great nuisance to the actors, as this impudent and

turbulent folk caused much disturbance at the performances.   And it was the cause of great battles when, far
on in the eighteenth century, the managers abolished
these free places.

There were no longer, as in the time of Shakespeare,
seats for spectators on the stage itself, but distinguished
playgoers, who could pay for the privilege, might constantly be admitted behind the scenes.   During the
Restoration it was even customary for noble *beaux* to
haunt the tiring-rooms of the actresses, to be present
at their dressing and undressing, and to talk in such
a way that the actresses who were not quite devoid of
shame had to send their young servant - girls away.
However, on account of the great scandals made by
the coarse noblemen, Charles II., though he was by no
means prudish, forbade all admission to the tiring-rooms
of the actresses.

Another custom, however, continued to exist, which
was, that the wits assembled after the performances in
the green-room, discussed the events of the day, and
planned nocturnal expeditions.

When, in 1732, the harlequin - player, John Rich,
opened his new fashionable theatre in Covent Garden,
he fixed the admission fee to the stage at 10s. 6d., "in
order to prevent the wings from being overcrowded."
But even this high price, which would equal about thrice
the sum in our days, was no sufficient obstacle.   It was
Garrick who first succeeded in putting a stop to this
distracting nuisance by resolutely giving up this not
inconsiderable income, and forbidding admission to the
stage to all outsiders.

The prices of admission on the whole were high. As early as the Betterton period, a place in the pit cost 2s. 6d., in the ground-floor boxes 4s., in the middle gallery 1s. 6d., and in the upper gallery 1s. These prices probably corresponded to three times their value nowadays. In 1732 a ticket to the pit or lowest boxes cost 5s., to the middle gallery 2s., while the high gallery maintained its comparatively cheap price of 1s. At first-nights and new performances of particular attraction these prices were even considerably raised.

And on these occasions, when all tickets were sold, the proceeds might amount to such considerable sums as £500 or £600.

In spite of the large sums that might be gained, the playhouse at the time of Betterton found it difficult to keep itself going. The reason partly lay in the fact that the expenses of a theatre had very much increased. The scenery, which during the Shakespearean period had cost nothing to speak of, now, with all the devices of Italian machinery, transformations, and various new-fashioned means of effect, swallowed up so much of the proceeds that very little was left for the actors and the manager.

Moreover, a large section of the public held aloof from the theatre, because the auditorium was dominated to so great an extent by the masked, but on that account none the less shameless, "girls," and the bad-mannered young cavaliers, the so-called *beaux*, who between them rendered the place intolerable to decent people.

These *beaux* were of somewhat different characters. There was the mere *beau* without any admixture of the wit, who went to the play for the sole purpose of showing himself and his smart clothes and trifling with the girls ; there was also the mere wit, who was not a *beau*—the literary man, who went there in order to discuss the merits of the author and actors ; and finally, the attractive combination of *beau* and wit.   This leading party had its place in the pit close to the stage in the so-called "fops' corner," whence they decided the success or failure of the performance—that is to say, if they chose to remain in the theatre.   But this they frequently did not.   Owing to the remarkable custom that spectators, if they left before the end of the first act, could have their money returned, there was a constant running in and out of these fops, who came in smelling of orange flower and jessamine, examined the boxes while combing their large curly wigs, whispered a few words to a friend, cocked their hats rakishly on one side of their heads, and strode away to another theatre.

A characteristic feature in the playhouse of those days was the orange-women, a body of handsome young girls, who, under the leadership of a somewhat maturer woman, the so-called Orange Moll, offered the—in those times expensive—golden fruits for sale to the spectators, and at the same time carried on much flirtation with the flippant *beaux*.   It was considered a delicate and fashionable courtesy to offer such a fruit from the basket of the orange-woman to one's lady, or even to an unknown lady as an introduction before speaking to her.

The English audience, then as now, was a motley, lively, impulsive flock, but in those times it was far from being so easily and naïvely amused as in our own days.

58—Spectators in a London theatre.   In the box *beaux* and orange girls (p. 343).

In spite of the apparently cordial relations between the two worlds on each side of the footlights,[1] a pitiless, mocking censure was always ready to laugh at stilted and false tragic art, and at times there were sudden outbursts of coarse excitement which, especially when the rioters were the worse for drink, would degenerate into excesses that far surpassed the worst scandals among the hot-tempered French audiences. Fights, even on the stage, between actors and noblemen, which sometimes resulted in manslaughter, occurred not infrequently; and when in one way or another the passions had been roused, the auditorium looked like a battlefield, where the combatants fought with chairs and benches, where swords were drawn in earnest on the stage, and where scenery and material worth thousands of pounds were destroyed, to the despair of the unfortunate manager.

On the whole, however, the relations between the actors and the public were kindly enough, even though the tolerably free intercourse had disappeared which existed at the time of Shakespeare, when playhouses served for general popular amusement, and were managed partly after a republican shareholding system without much interference from higher quarters. The actors were now not merely in name, but in reality, the " King's Servants "; the upper ten members of the King's Theatre belonged to the Royal household, were called Gentlemen of the Great Chamber, and wore a uniform of scarlet cloth with gold

---

[1] There was, by the way, no row of footlights (*rampe*) before the time of Garrick, after his great tour abroad; the stage was lighted by large chandeliers.

embroidery, the material of which was presented to them.   The actors belonged to " His Majesty's Revels," with which no interference was allowed.   Thus when in 1670—under Charles II.—Parliament intended to impose a tax on the theatres, they met with strong resistance from the court party, who maintained the view that the actors were the King's servants and part of his pleasure.   Then Sir John Coventry, M.P., asked maliciously whether His Majesty's pleasure was to be found among actors or actresses, a playful remark, however, which was not well received.   The merry monarch hired some bravoes to attack Sir John, and they disarmed him and cut off his nose.

On the whole, this Royal patronage, which entailed a great deal of restraint, was not favourable to theatrical development, except in so far as it rendered theatrical performances very fashionable, and thus sent high class people to the theatres.

This fashion, however, did not last long, not far beyond the reigns of Charles II. and James II., as it had sprung up in imitation of French custom.   Under William III., when England received liberty of the Press, and especially after the accession of the Hanoverian dynasty, under the long and peaceful ministry of Walpole, the theatres, though still nominally dependent on Royal patents, were in reality allowed to manage themselves and to develop with the business-like liberty that suits the English people best.

The outward vicissitudes in the history of the London theatres during these periods are numerous and very intricate; it would scarcely be worth while or answer the purpose of this book to pursue them all.

It may just be mentioned here, that in 1682 Charles II. made an attempt to amalgamate the two playhouses into one single Court theatre, probably in imitation of Louis XIV., who two years previously had done something similar in Paris. But what proved to be a successful proceeding in France did not suit the much more independently inclined English people. In France, the Royal command produced a centralisation which lasted for a century; to a certain extent its influence is even still at work. In England no more than thirteen years elapsed before the union was broken. The privileged Royal Theatre at once came into the hands of skilled men of business; it became a kind of shareholders' enterprise, which was dominated by a particularly ill-natured leader, the pettifogger Christopher Rich, a name which became most obnoxious to all actors, but which nevertheless for many years continued to be attached to theatrical management in London. Christopher Rich was a man without a vestige of artistic scruples, a man to whom it made no difference at all whether he exhibited elephants or Shakespeare plays, provided he made money by it, but a crafty and persevering man of business, who saw and profited by all chances; a queer and original person, who had a mania for building, altering, and arranging theatres, but was perfectly indifferent as to the performers or performances on their stages. There are constant revolts against him, everybody leaves him, his licence is withdrawn; but he always turns up again with new handsome theatres and acquires new licences for acting in them. On his death he left to his son, John Rich, the harlequin player and introducer of the Italian pantomime into England, a new theatre and the means to build another one shortly after : Covent Garden Theatre, one of the two principal playhouses in London, which, though it continued to be a few degrees inferior to the Drury Lane Theatre, nevertheless maintained its rank as a refined and fashionable stage.

But before the point was reached when the drama was firmly rooted in these two historic houses there had been constant changes and much flitting about.   In 1695 the old staff of actors, with Betterton and Mrs Barry at their head, for the first time revolted against Christopher Rich, who had cut down their salaries, and in general, when he felt himself in sole possession of the field, treated them in a disgracefully stingy manner.

Then they induced King William III., who as a rule did not take great interest in the theatre, to come to their assistance, and he allowed them to leave Rich and build their own playhouse in Lincoln's Inn Fields.   So the principle of absolute power was broken, and London had two stages : Drury Lane, under the management of Christopher Rich, and The New Theatre, or The Theatre in Lincoln's Inn Fields, which was the enterprise of a company of shareholders, with Betterton as artistic leader.   The New Theatre had a glorious start (30th April 1690) with the first performance of Congreve's *Love for Love*, which was one of the most popular, and remained one of the wittiest comedies of the time.

But the brilliancy of the beginning did not last.

The two theatres kept up a sharp competition ; they tried to tempt players away from one stage to the other, and to annoy each other in every way. Rich had succeeded in engaging some clever young performers, and these new members ridiculed the old ones at The New Theatre, especially Betterton, who insisted on continuing to act lovers' parts. Bitter prologues and epilogues on both stages testify to the heat of the battle.

Both theatres momentarily suffered great damage from the sensational attacks which a High Church clergyman, named Jeremy Collier, directed in 1698 against the immorality of the English stage. Clerical attacks of this kind mostly remain without effect, because they generally aim at wrong points and come at the wrong time. But in this case it was different, not only because the onset was so unusually violent, but even more because it could not be said to be quite unjust.

Though the authors [1] attacked gave sharp replies, a momentary slackness set in. The authors suspended writing, and people stayed away from the theatres. And when things came into a regular course again, the tone on the stage had certainly become less gross. There is an evident difference between the plays written before and those written after the attacks of Collier.

However, as stated above, the instantaneous effect was economically ruinous to both theatres. In their difficulty both Betterton and Rich had to take refuge in French and Italian ballet-dancers, which made no

---

[1] Congreve and Vanbrugh wrote pamphlets against Collier, but Dryden, who was severely attacked, did not ; afterwards he even openly confessed that the clergyman had been right.

difference to Rich, but to Betterton and his colleagues was, no doubt, most humiliating.

When new plays were again forthcoming, Rich was fortunate enough to get hold of an author, Farquhar, whose *Constant Couple* and its sequel *Sir Harry Wildair* became immense successes, and whose characters rendered the names of the young actors popular.

In the same proportion as Drury Lane under the financial leadership of Rich, and with its talented young players, rose in distinction, all went down-hill with the stage in Lincoln's Inn Fields. The theatre was too small and inadequate; the good old actors were now too advanced in age; Betterton had become tired of the management, and the discipline in the republican theatre was very bad.

Thus the very popular dramatic author and highly respected architect, Sir John Vanbrugh,[1] started a company of shareholders, who built a large new theatre in the Haymarket. And here the old actors made their entry—in 1705—under the leadership of Vanbrugh, Betterton being engaged merely as an actor. This new theatre in the Haymarket, however, did not answer the expectation formed of it. It was fine to look at, but very bad from an acoustic point of view. Not very long after it was converted into an opera-house, in which

[1] Vanbrugh, a friend of Congreve's, like the latter was one of the wittiest, but also one of the most immoral dramatists of the time. He wrote altogether ten plays, among which *The Relapse* and *The Provoked Wife* were the most popular. The latter play, in which a wife punishes her brutal husband (Sir John Brute) by cuckolding him, especially roused the anger of Jeremy Collier. Some of Vanbrugh's plays are adaptations of Molière, Boursault, and Dancourt.

Nicolini's celebrated company of singers reaped great successes.

After incredible confusion, intrigues and quarrels behind the scenes, during which new managers were appointed and again dismissed ; after a new but vain attempt to collect the actors into " Her Majesty's only Company of Actors " ;[1] when Rich had been driven away from Drury Lane by brute force, and every licence for theatrical management had been withdrawn from him, when he had immediately after rebuilt the old Lincoln's Inn Fields from the foundations, and having by inconceivable artifices acquired a fresh licence, had died before this new theatre was opened, the conditions in the year 1714 were as follows :—

The old Drury Lane was now the best and leading stage, the proprietors and managers of which were the trio Cibber, Wilks, and Booth, whose work will be described more in detail in the following chapter.

The most important rival of Drury Lane was the new theatre in Lincoln's Inn Fields, owned and managed by Rich, junior,[2] the harlequin John.   Young Rich differed very much from his father, being a born acrobat, quite illiterate, but an excellent harlequin, with Franco-Italian nimbleness, and very expressive in his gestures.   He was exceedingly plain, talked and wrote badly, and was as inferior an actor as he was an excellent pantomimist. His private character—unlike that of his father—was kind-hearted and amiable.   The attraction of Rich's theatre, hitherto unknown in England, was pantomimes

[1] Under Queen Anne in 1708, or rather on 31st December 1707.
[2] With his brother, Christopher Mozier Rich.

with metamorphoses, flying devils, dancing tables, mechanical statues, etc., which he set up at great expense, and which drew such crowds to the theatre that Drury Lane had to adopt the same *genre*, in order to tempt people to attend its performances.

Finally the theatre in the Haymarket continued to maintain itself as an opera-house, with foreign and native singers.

These were in the main the theatrical conditions throughout what is usually called the Cibber Period.

II

Colley Cibber, his Art and that of his Contemporaries—Wilks, Dogget, and Booth—Addison's *Cato*—Mrs Oldfield and Mrs Porter.

IN the year 1690 a young man made his *début* on the stage of Betterton. He was nineteen years of age, an enthusiastic admirer of the theatre, but somewhat confused in his manners : his name was Colley Cibber. He was both well educated and of good family, which was not exactly the rule with actors. His father was a highly-respected sculptor of Danish birth, Caius Gabriel Cibber,[1] his mother, Jane Colley, of good old English lineage.

The *début* of the young man was not glorious, but in a certain way, nevertheless, brought him luck. He had

---

[1] Caius Gabriel Cibber was born in Flensburg in 1630. He went to England some time before the Restoration and worked his way upward, so that he was mentioned as the first sculptor in England at that period. Among his works the most noted are the bas-relief on the Monument in the City, and the two figures of " Fury " and " Melancholia," originally in Bedlam Lunatic Asylum, and now in the South Kensington Museum.

to bring a message to Betterton on the stage, but was so horror-stricken by stage-fright, that he broke down entirely, and brought general confusion into the scene. In those times the rehearsals were exceedingly defective, everything was left to chance, and Betterton did not even know the name of the young man. After the close of the act he asked the prompter who the silly young man was. Downes replied, " Master Colley." " Master Colley!—then forfeit him." " Why, Sir," said the prompter, " he has no salary." " No," said the old man, " why then put him down ten shillings a week, and forfeit him 5s." [1]

Just as in this instance, Colley Cibber's faults frequently turned out profitable to him. His gifts were neither deep nor extensive ; nature had not particularly qualified him for stage-work, nor did he ever become a great actor or a great character, but he was an amiable man with great pliancy and elasticity of mind ; he came at the right moment, made the right use of his chances, and—most needful of all to a theatrical manager—he was successful.

When he started on the boards he was a small, fair-haired, pale, and slender young man. His voice was feeble and apt to become shrill when he forced it. On the whole, he seemed to be ill suited for the lovers' and tragic parts he wanted to play.

But, opportunist as he was, he knew how to turn his natural defects to artistic account.

He early displayed a somewhat small, but ever

---

[1] The anecdote is reported after a verbal tradition by Thomas Davies : *Dramatic Miscellanies*, iii. 445.

readily flowing poetic and dramatic vein,[1] and even as a young actor, he began to write plays.   In the first of these, *Love's Last Shift*, or *The Fool in Fashion*, of 1696, he created a part for himself which gained him a signal success.   This was a sarcastic description of the latter day dandy, a ludicrous fop, with nicely curled and powdered wig, cocked coat-tails, and enormous lapels, with his snuff-box and perfumed lace-trimmed gloves, named Sir Novelty Fashion ; he became immensely successful with the public of the time, who constantly met with his prototype in real life.   When (with much difficulty by the bye), the young actor had succeeded in getting his play acted ; this character became so popular that Sir John Vanbrugh, for the subsequent season, wrote a sequel to it with some of the same characters, only that, Sir Novelty had become Lord Foppington, as which he became fixed as a classical stage figure.

For this type all Colley Cibber's shortcomings became advantages ; the lively, impudent face with the upturned snub-nose, the little mouth with the vapid smile, the slender figure, the thin, shrill voice.   And it was this type, indeed, which created his name as an actor.

On the whole, in comedy Colley Cibber became an able and popular player, though probably none of his

[1] He wrote and adapted altogether thirty plays, among which, besides *Love's Last Shift*, the most popular were : *The Careless Husband*, *The Provoked Husband* (together with Vanbrugh), *The Nonjuror* (a free adaptation of *Tartufe*, in which the principal character was a Jacobite priest), as well as his adaptation of Shakespeare's *Richard III.*, which was used all through the eighteenth century, and even far on in the nineteenth.   Besides this he composed fluent, but very shallow verses, and in 1730 was made poet laureate.   His best literary production, however, was the autobiography, which he published under the title of *An Apology for the Life of Mr Colley Cibber*, *written by himself.*

other parts had the original and personal stamp of Lord Foppington and similar characters.   Colley Cibber possessed great talent for mimicry, and as he had made good use of his eyes he was able to give most vivid imitations of the famous parts of old comedians.

His tragic parts, on the other hand, were merely tolerated by the public; in reality they were very bad. He had no voice to speak of, and his gestures were fidgety and inexpressive; frequently he did not even seem to know what he was doing or saying.   His favourite parts were Richard III. and Iago.

Cibber obtained his firm footing as an actor in Drury Lane, when Betterton and the old noted actors had left this stage and established their own.   As a young and scarcely known man he had remained with John Rich, and here he and several of his colleagues worked themselves up to become players of solid ability.

When the old actors left him, Rich had been obliged to recruit his staff from the provinces.   Among the provincial theatres the one in Dublin, ruled at the time by the noted manager Ashbury, was considered the best. From that stage now Rich first of all received Robert Wilks, who was to become of great importance to the London theatre.

Wilks was an Irishman by birth, and, like Cibber, of a good family.   Born about 1665, he was a few years older than the latter, and before becoming an actor he had held an appointment in a government office.   When as a man of some thirty years he came to London, he was a fully developed actor, and even at his *début* as Palamede, the lover's part in Dryden's *Marriage à la mode*, he eclipsed his predecessor George Powel, who was a clever actor, but coarse and given to drink.

With Powel, to begin with, he had a hard fight—even a physical fight—for the leading part of lover and *élégant* at the theatre, a struggle, however, in which he was sure of victory, both on account of his natural gifts and because he had the advantage over Powel of being a very diligent and accurate actor, who always studied and knew his parts to perfection, while Powel was negligent and, owing to his drunken habits, had a failing memory.

Wilks was exactly the elegant, graceful, arrogant *beau* created for the light, insinuating eighteenth-century lover. " To beseech gracefully, to approach respectfully, to pity, to mourn, to love, are the places wherein Wilks may be made to shine with the utmost beauty," says Steele[1] in speaking of him.

Wilks absolutely preferred comedy, and his proper typical part was probably the amiable, seductive, madcap Sir Harry Wildair in Farquhar's plays already mentioned. He, however, rose even higher than in these very popular pieces. Thus his Prince Henry in *Henry IV.*, Part II., was a model performance.

In tragedy his uneven and jerky delivery was against him, nor was he well suited for strong passions or high pathos, but he could give fine expression to grief, tenderness, and resignation.

---

[1] Sir Richard Steele, in his triple quality as critic—editor of the well-known periodicals, *The Tatler* and *The Spectator*—as playwright (he was the real creator of " sentimental " comedy) and as stage-manager (as which it cannot be said that he worked, for he never did anything but receive the salary), had intimate knowledge of actors.

In private life Wilks was naïvely selfish, very arrogant, and exceedingly touchy with regard to his professional reputation ; he obtained a great deal for himself, but alienated many people by his uncontrolled off-hand manners.   However, behind his arrogance there was much good nature, amiability, and gentlemanly large-mindedness.

Another distinguished actor Rich had acquired from Betterton's New Theatre in Thomas Dogget, according to unanimous testimonies, the most original comic actor of this period.   As far as we can see, Dogget broke away from the old comic school, and he did not content himself with being merely droll, like the old English clown nor had he adopted the conventional masks of the Franco Italian school.   Dogget returned to nature, and tried to characterise each of his figures with naturalistic precision in dress and speech.   Above all, he was successful in reproducing the ways and manners of the lower classes. Therefore the tough mariner Ben, in Congreve's *Love for Love*, became one of his crowning glories.   Congreve on the whole, was a great admirer of Dogget, and in his pieces this peculiarly and originally-gifted actor won several of his greatest victories, such as in the old love-sick Fondlewife in *The Old Bachelor*. Shylock, too, who in those times was represented merely as a low-comic character, was one of his most famous parts.

Thomas Dogget was an exceedingly queer, obstinate curmudgeon, a great financier, an eager speculator on the Stock Exchange, very close in money matters amidst his extravagant colleagues.   But when his obstinate and grasping tendencies did not render him sulky, his humour,

even in everyday life, would sparkle through his somewhat gloomy exterior.

These three were the main pillars in the *répertoire* of
old Rich, and they soon felt strong enough to break with
the unreliable pettifogger. The final result of the excited
struggle over the leadership of the theatre was that the
triumvirate, Cibber, Wilks, and Dogget, became proprietors and managers of the Drury Lane stage. Betterton died in 1710, at the age of about seventy-five, and in
him the last great man of the old generation departed.
Thus the triumvirate had a comparatively easy game as
managers of the only high-class playhouse, as Rich was
never able to restrain his low inclinations towards variety
entertainments. However, the union of the three leaders
did not last long ; a new man was to bring disturbance
into it.

On 14th April 1713 Joseph Addison's tragedy *Cato*
was performed for the first time at Drury Lane, with
Barton Booth in the title *rôle*.

That first-night was an extraordinary event. Nowadays *Cato* would be quite incapable of stirring up the
passions. Its sonorous speeches, full of noble feelings
and sublime thoughts of liberty, but entirely devoid of
dramatic fire, have caused it to be relegated to the book-
shelf, whence it is probably seldom removed, and will
never be brought on the boards. But in those times it
was different. This drama, or rather poem, on Roman
patriotism and political freedom deeply affected not only
literary taste, but also political feeling. And, strangely
enough, Tories as well as Whigs appropriated the piece.
Naturally the speeches on liberty in general gained the

warm approval of the Whigs. But on account of the peculiar conditions of the moment the Tories might equally turn them to account against their opponents. The Duke of Marlborough, who now belonged to the Whig party, had coveted the post of commander-in-chief for life, and this the Tories, headed by Bolingbroke and Harley, considered as an attempt to usurp the permanent authority of a dictator.

The fluent verses of this noble tragedy contains many unintentional but striking allusions to actual conditions, which were each time greeted with frantic applause, first by the Whigs, who wanted to show their love of liberty, then by the Tories as a manifestation of their opinion that liberty was in the wrong hands with the ambitious Whigs, and was rather to be found within their own ranks.

The result of all this sensation was an extraordinary success for the theatre and for the actor who night after night recited the beautiful phrases about liberty, so as almost to be identified with the noble Cato, and to be treated, especially by the great gentlemen of the Tory party, as if he were one of themselves.

Barton Booth was not quite a new-comer. He was some thirty-two years of age when he played Cato, but the year before he had already reaped great success by his noble dignity, his handsome appearance and voice, and his refined bearing as Pyrrhus in *The Distrest Mother*, a tragedy by Ambrose Philips.[1] He began his career in Dublin, and afterwards acted in different places among others under Betterton as well as under Rich.

[1] Adapted from Racine's *Andromaque*.

He was now immediately established as the first tragedian in England, the successor of Betterton, supported by Bolingbroke, who at the time was the most powerful man in Queen Anne's government. No wonder, then, that his ambition rose high, and his first object was to get a share in the theatre together with Cibber, Wilks, and Dogget. During the last few years the management had proved very lucrative to the three partners, so lucrative that two of them readily yielded to necessity and thought there would be enough for four. But the third, Dogget, who was an eager Whig and at the same time very grasping and still more obstinate, thought it so disgraceful, so absurd and so unjust, that Booth, who was supported by the Tories, should be pushed on by Royal favour to take his share of the proceeds, that he sold his share, and with his usual obstinacy never more set foot in Drury Lane, either as manager or as actor.

So the triumvirate now consisted of Booth, Cibber, and Wilks, a partnership which was more suitable than the union with Dogget, in so far as the three new partners possessed the same degree of culture, were all of good family and good breeding, and all, professionally and privately, had in the main the same tastes. Under these three refined, cultivated, well-bred managers the theatre had a smooth and bright course, which raised it to a state of prosperity and stability which it had not known since the Restoration.

Each of the three managers had his little foibles. Wilks could not help boring his companions with his uncontrolled vanity, and he mostly vented his ill-humour on Booth, who sometimes thwarted him in the matter of parts. But his excitement was partly subdued by the dignified indolence of Booth or by the even tempered Cibber, who acted as mediator.

Booth, it must be said, could not maintain in his other parts his great reputation as Cato. He was entirely devoid of humour and constantly played in the same sepulchral, pompous and somewhat apathetic fashion. His sublime indifference on the stage occasionally became all but offensive, and one evening it happened that an indignant spectator sent up a messenger to ask him if he played for his own amusement or for that of the audience.

Cibber was a passionate gambler, and this mania took away a good deal of his thoughts from the theatre especially from his work as actor. However, he was not much affected either by gain or loss. He would go straight from the coffee-house, where he had lost a considerable sum, to the performance, humming an opera tune, dress and go on to the stage absent-minded and without the slightest idea what he was going to say. But he had a very cool manner of concealing his absence of mind, which even in parts he had played a hundred times was so great that it often put him into serious difficulties. Thus, when he was playing one of his dandy parts, he would make a deep and very long bow to the lady present, drawling out "Your humble servant, madam," to an extraordinary length, then taking a pinch of snuff, strutting deliberately across the stage he gravely asked the prompter "what is next?"[1]

[1] Thomas Davies, *Dramatic Miscellanies*, iii. 480 f.

However, in spite of some friction, defects and absurdities, the theatre prospered better under this triumvirate than it had ever done before.

And this was due in no small measure to the two excellent actresses the theatre possessed in Mrs Oldfield and Mrs Porter.

Anne Oldfield was the more interesting of the two, and on the whole the most talented player of this period. Contemporary accounts of her are unanimous in speaking of her uncommonly great gifts as an actress, especially in the most fashionable character, the highly intelligent, graceful, witty, and slightly affected lady. Though risen from low origin—the author Farquhar had discovered her dramatic abilities when, quite as a young girl,[1] she was serving as barmaid in the tavern called "The Mitre," St James Market, which was kept by her aunt—her womanly adaptability rapidly acquired all the fashionable light and airy brilliancy of mind and exquisite well-bred manners. And it was just this captivating wit, this refinement which became the strong points of the young barmaid, both on and off the stage. Her somewhat precocious and coquettish form of conversation was dubbed "Oldfieldismos," by Pope.

She had splendid physical qualifications for the stage. Very beautiful and sparkling with life, she attracted attention at once. Her eyes were most expressive, and her whole figure, which was of medium height, possessed a peculiar charm, which was equally removed from the somewhat depraved type of earlier days as from the

---

[1] She was born about 1683 and made her *début* in 1699, but during the early part of her career she attracted little notice.

prude. Her voice was soft yet full, and her delivery in comedy always natural and to the point, while her talent was less suited for the pompous, declamatory style of contemporary tragedy.

She was admirably qualified for the style of Cibber, and in his plays she created a number of characters which became classical on the English stage, quite as much, probably, through her brilliant and graceful play as through their own intrinsic value. Among the most famous of her parts were Lady Betty Modish in *The Careless Husband* and Lady Townly in *The Provoked Husband*. Her life was not long; she died in 1730, when only forty-seven years old. But she filled the whole Cibber period with her name, and died in the midst of her fame, which was so great that she—the first actress to be so honoured—was laid with great pomp in Westminster Abbey, a short time after the death of her great French contemporary, Adrienne Lecouvreur, to whose corpse, as was mentioned in a former chapter, even a decent burial was denied.

Mrs Oldfield's proper domain was, as we have said, the contemporary *répertoire*; and though the public also liked to see her in tragedy, she only played tragic parts when compelled, as they seemed to put her under restraint and to prevent a free display of her powers. "I hate to have a page dragging my tail about," she said; "why do they not give Porter those parts? She can put on a better tragedy-face than I can." Mary Porter was indeed the leading *tragédienne* of the theatre and of her period, the only successor of Mrs Barry, though scarcely so distinguished. She possessed some of the same qualities as her predecessor—an expressive, though not a handsome appearance, and a strong, but coarse and rough voice; but she was at the same time more massive and more effaced.   Her play was at times very monotonous, influenced as it was by the contemporary bad French school of rhetoric, with its chanting, cadenced delivery.   In violently passionate scenes, however, she was able to rise to great heights of power and ardour, which carried away her audience to irresistible enthusiasm.   Unlike Mrs Oldfield, she became very old—her death did not occur till 1762—but her career was interrupted for several years by the fracture of one of her legs, caused by a carriage accident, and her work was essentially connected with the Cibber period.

Without being deep or rich, this period is not quite without importance to the English theatre.   Besides procuring for the actors a financially and socially settled position, it led dramatic art into channels which allowed of further development.   It could boast of no great geniuses either among actors or dramatic authors, but it brought with it a peaceful, pleasant calm after the riotous confusion of the Restoration.   Tragedy ran in a somewhat dull strain; it was penitently moralising and rhetorical; comedy abounded in comparatively innocent playfulness, mixed with a small dose of sentimentality, calming the nerves like a cup of tea after many strong drinks.   The comedies of the time, though now lost in oblivion and never likely to be revived, rose above merely ephemeral value, in so far that some of them lived throughout the century, not only on English but on European stages.

Light and superficial, like Cibber's Lord Foppington himself, well-dressed and well-bred, with a ready smile and a nascent tendency towards sentimentality, without ardent longing for higher ideals, without bitter opposition to old traditional forms, but quite contented with its present conditions, the dramatic art of this period glided smoothly over the boards.

III

Last Years of the Cibber Period—James Quin, Charles Macklin, and Mrs Clive.

ABOUT the year 1730 the good days of the Cibber triumvirate drew to a close. In this year the great ornament of the stage, Mrs Oldfield, died. Booth, who had been ailing for some years, played for the last time in 1728.[1] Wilks passed away in 1732. Mrs Porter, who, as we mentioned above, was injured by being thrown out of her carriage in 1731, became an invalid for a tolerably long time. So Cibber alone remained of the leading staff of actors who had impressed their stamp on Drury Lane. He was now a man past the sixties, and had made much money as a shareholder in the theatre. So it was natural enough for him to retire. In 1733 he sold his share to a new theatrical amateur named Highmore.[2] However, he lived for many years after having retired, acted off and on as a guest, occasionally appearing in

[1] He died in 1733.

[2] How largely the value of the theatre had increased under his management appears from the fact that in 1714 Barton Booth paid £600 for his share ; Cibber, nineteen years later, received more than five times that sum viz. 3000 guineas, for his.

his old leading parts, among which the comic ones still
afforded amusement, while his tragic characters were in
sharp contrast to the new school that had arisen.   With
his smooth and even temper, Cibber remained brisk and
cheerful up to old age.   When past seventy he had a
sensational literary quarrel with no less a person than
Pope, in which he acquitted himself with wit and good
humour, and teased the irritable satirist considerably.
At last he died in 1757,[1] at the age of eighty-six, pleased
with himself and all the world to the last.

Almost immediately after the dissolution of the triumvirate and the retirement of Colley Cibber, the theatrical
world became the scene of disturbances and confusion,
the like of which had scarcely ever been seen, and which
proved better than anything else by what a firm hand
this stage had been managed by the three able actors,
especially Cibber.

Highmore, the new proprietor of Drury Lane, a vain
young man of the world, who possessed some money and
fancied himself a great expert in theatrical matters, was
at once ruined.   He had no sooner bought the theatre
than nearly all the actors left him and established a new
stage, guided and incited by Theophilus, the impudent
and utterly dishonourable son of Colley Cibber.   The
actors maintained that they could not be sold with the
theatre like slaves on a negro-plantation, and as they
had no written contracts—which were not in use in the
patriarchal days of the triumvirate—they simply left
without notice.   This revolt, by the bye, occasioned

---

[1] He was buried in the Danish church, which his father had built in 1696
by order of the Danish King, in Wellclose Square, Whitechapel.

the introduction of minute contracts for the actors, the so-called *articles*, by which, as in our own days, they are engaged for one or more years.

The successor to Highmore was Fleetwood, also a young *viveur*, quite ignorant of stage matters. And if he remained longer in his position it was not due to his greater skill, but in the first place to the fact that he was richer, and in the second to his seductive amiability, which in difficult situations disarmed indignation at his carelessness and disability. He succeeded in collecting some of the old players and a few new ones, but though the theatre prospered financially, in art and discipline he brought it down to such a low state of decadence that his leadership must be mentioned only as a warning example to show how rapidly such amiable amateurs can interrupt and destroy a development which has grown in spite of difficulties through a number of years.

Thus while Drury Lane was losing its old reputation as the first and most refined London stage, new theatres had grown up. Besides the magnificent Covent Garden, built by Rich in 1732, and the previously mentioned Opera House in the Haymarket, a new theatre, the so-called Little Theatre in the Haymarket, had been built almost opposite the Opera. This was the place to which the Drury Lane staff went after their revolt against Highmore, and during the prevailing friendly relations with France, French companies also acted on that stage. The Lincoln's Inn Fields Theatre, built in its time by old Rich, was also in use. At the great annual fairs plays were performed by permanent and comparatively good companies, and finally, of late a new little stage had been added, the theatre in Goodman's Fields,[1] whose career did not last long, but was very turbulent.   It was for the Little Theatre in the Haymarket that Henry Fielding wrote his sensational political satires, which were a thorn in the flesh to Sir Robert Walpole, England's wise and powerful leader during many years.

Fielding's political plays drew crowds of people to the new theatre; the performances caused enormous tumult, and frequently stormy applause, when some welcome blows were directed against the Government.

Walpole, however, put a stop to these unpleasant performances in an ingenious, though scarcely honest, way, if we may credit the reports of contemporary theatrical chroniclers.   Giffard, who was then manager of Lincoln's Inn Fields Theatre, received an anonymous satirical play, *The Golden Rump*, which was so bold and so open in its attacks on the Government that he felt prompted to apply to the minister, with the question whether it would be allowable to have this play acted.

Now, according to the Bill of 1693, which granted liberty to the press, dramatic pieces could no longer be censored.   But on the ground of this libellous play, *The Golden Rump*, Walpole requested a limitation of theatrical liberty, and in spite of great opposition he succeeded in carrying the so-called Licensing Act (of 21st June 1737), according to which all stage per-formances were submitted to censorship.   However, the whole story of this terrible play, *The Golden Rump*,

---

[1] It was opened in October 1729 by the dramatic author Thomas Odell, who soon, however, left it to the actor Giffard.   Giffard rebuilt it in 1732, in a much more magnificent style.

which was never performed, never printed, and whose author was never known, is asserted to have been a made-up affair between the minister and the manager, and the former was even supposed to have helped in composing the criminal play as a reason in support of his request for censorship.   So it was by a crafty manœuvre that England received this blessing, which entailed a restraining power over the theatres, that under this form lasted for about a century.   The first consequences of the Licensing Act were that the two "minor" theatres, the Little Theatre in the Haymarket and Goodman's Fields, were momentarily closed, and the control over literature was manifested during the following season by the prohibition of the performances of *Gustavus Vasa*, a tragedy by Brooke, which, when printed afterwards, won great appreciation, and of Thomson's *Edward and Eleonora*, because these pieces contained some sentences in praise of liberty which did not please the authorities.   Both these plays were almost ready for performance in the two theatres, Drury Lane and Covent Garden respectively, and thus the prohibition caused an immediate and irreparable loss to the theatres.[1]

While national art was hampered in this way, favour was shown to French actors and dancers, who were not supposed to do political harm.   However, this untimely protection called forth violent political demonstrations against the French players.   A hostile audience filled

---

[1] The authors, on the other hand, found compensation in publishing the plays, and the public, with a solidarity of opinion characteristic of the English, demonstrated so powerfully by subscribing, especially to *Gustavus Vasa*, that Brooke gained over £1000 by his play.

the whole theatre in which they acted, hooted and cat-called when they attempted to play, threw peas on the floor to prevent them from dancing, made speeches against the magistrates, drove away the soldiers who were summoned to keep order, and on the whole, by persevering in their riot, gained a bloodless victory over the anti-national Government party.

If this transition period, therefore, abounded in external and political events, from an artistic point of view it was poor and dead.

The leading stage-name of this time is that of Quin. James Quin was the last off-shoot of the Betterton school. In him we still see some of the weighty, dignified pomposity which was one of Betterton's characteristics. But what in the latter was penetrated with spirit, in the former was not much more than flesh. Cumberland, a younger contemporary and dramatic author, gives a very graphic description of his tragic "epigonic" style; he says: "With very little variation of cadence, and in a deep, full tone, accompanied by a sawing kind of action, which had more of the senate than of the stage in it, he rolled out his heroics with an air of dignified indifference that seemed to disdain the plaudits that were bestowed upon him. Unable to express emotions, whether violent or tender, he was forced or languid in action and pon-derous and sluggish in movement. In the great characters of tragedy he was lost, and the most trustworthy of con-temporary critics declares that people will remember with pleasure his Brutus and his Cato, and wish to forget his Richard and his Lear."[1]

[1] Joseph Knight, *David Garrick*, p. 62.

However, Quin was by no means a dull actor, as might be supposed from the descriptions of his play. This monotony was, so to say, founded on system. Like his predecessor Barton Booth, he considered imperturbable dignity, regular declamation, never interrupted by a smile or an impulsive movement, the only admissible style in tragedy. And this taste was shared by the public. Cumberland belonged to another generation, and when he drew his sharp satire, the style of Quin had long ago passed out of fashion.

But in his days of vigour Quin was unquestionably the first leading actor who, though never himself a manager, had a most powerful position as leader of the rehearsals in the theatres to which he belonged.

Outside tragedy, in comedy, and especially in private life, Quin was most jovial and humorous. Very fond of a good table and a bottle, Quin possessed the genuine, old-fashioned, broad English humour, which can neither be taught nor imitated, the same humour which renders Falstaff an incomparable and inimitable character to us ; and it must not be forgotten that, though Quin's name is essentially attached to a dull period of decline, his performance of fat Sir John was, according to all *connoisseurs*, a masterpiece of natural comic art.[1]

[1] This was the last part he played after having—in 1748—retired from the theatre. It was his custom every year to come up from Bath, where he lived, and play his crowning part at the benefit performance of his old friend, the actor Ryan. But when in 1754 he lost two front teeth, he did not want to do so any more, and he wrote to Ryan in apology : " My dear friend, there is no person in the world whom I would rather serve than Ryan, but, by God, I will whistle Falstaff for no man." In compensation he made Ryan a present of £1000, which otherwise he would have left him in his will. On the whole he was very good towards those whom he liked, and in spite of his sharp tongue he was good-natured towards his enemies.

The years of Quin's youth had been turbulent
enough, and he had acted in many different theatres;
his chief work, however, was connected with Covent
Garden, where, under the management of John Rich,
he was absolutely dominant, and received the largest
salary ever paid to an English actor.[1]

In every way differing from James Quin, was Charles
Macklin, a queer and not very sympathetic character,
but in certain respects an actor with creative talent.
As Quin was the last link in one chain of development, Macklin was the first link in the next, or at least
the transition link between the two.   That he did not
become the main support of a new movement, was due
to the peculiarities of his whole personality.   Coarse
and angular in appearance as in character, sour and
unmanageable, untidy and incapable of consecutive work,
Macklin was much better suited for opposition than for
leadership.

He and Quin were born and sworn enemies, and
nothing, indeed, could be more irritating to Macklin than
Quin's conventional grandeur, or more disgusting to
Quin than Macklin's unsavoury naturalism.

Both were almost of the same age,[2] and both educated in Ireland.   But Macklin only was of Irish descent
—his real family name was M'Laughlin—and his hot,

---

[1] Quin died in 1766, at the age of about seventy-three.   He spent his
last years in Bath, where he was a very popular person.

[2] The year of Macklin's birth is unknown.   Some authorities assert that
he was born in 1690, others in 1699.   At all events he lived to a great age.
Quite towards the end of the eighteenth century he was still seen as a
regular frequenter of his coffee-house, a living treasury of anecdotes of past
theatrical experiences, which he poured out to eager young chroniclers.
He died in 1797.

60

61

60—Anne Oldfield (p. 361).   **61**—Quin as Coriolanus (p. 370).

quarrelsome Irish blood played him many tricks throughout his life. With a youth even fuller of vicissitudes
than that of Quin, Macklin had begun his professional
career as the harlequin of a small company of jugglers,
and on the whole he worked essentially as a low-comic
actor, in which branch he displayed bizarre and coarse
humour mixed with crude naturalism.

But, strangely enough, while Quin, who considered
himself a tragedian, and only against his proper
inclination used his rich humour in refined comic
parts, won his greatest artistic victory as Falstaff, the
great histrionic achievement of Macklin was that, contrary to conventional taste, he gave a serious stamp to
Shylock.

That the part of Shylock was given to Macklin as
a low-comedy actor was not astonishing, for from the
beginning of the century it had been the custom to
include this part in the *répertoire* of the leading comic
actor.   Doggett played the part in 1701, though not in
the original Shakespearean form, but in the adaptation
of Lord Lansdowne under the title of *The Jew of Venice*.
Afterwards this adulterated form had been extensively
employed, until in 1741 Macklin—who at that time was
working at Drury Lane and had great influence with the
leader—proposed to the manager, Fleetwood, to perform Shakespeare's own play with himself as Shylock,
at the same time declaring that he would represent the
part in a manner very different from the usual
style.

Macklin's experiment created a great sensation—the
interest in the theatre was now so high that an actor's

conception of a classic figure roused attention [1]—and it became a success.   Instead of the traditional ludicrous Jew, who was the butt of endless jokes and buffoonery, what people now saw with increasing wonder was the display of an uncanny, hard and obstinate passion, which was exactly the strong point of Macklin. [2]

Macklin's Shylock marked a new epoch in the conception of this character, and it was the climax of his own art.   Though he continued acting till he was past eighty, and after this momentous success recast a number of other Shakespearean parts—such as Iago, Touchstone, Macbeth—he never succeeded in concentrating his powers to such an intensity as in Shylock, of whom it was said—

> This is the Jew
> That Shakespeare drew.

By his rough and coarse half-naturalism Macklin stands remarkably isolated in this polished time.

Another player of this period, who possessed an original and peculiar talent, deserves to be mentioned, and that is the somewhat coarse-grained, grotesquely

---

[1] As regards Shylock, the tradition does not go back as far as the Shakespearean time ; nothing is known about the manner of acting this part in those days.   However, as that period knew nothing of a sharp distinction between the divisions "comic" and "tragic," between which a strongly marked line was drawn in the eighteenth century, Shylock in those times was probably acted as it was written, neither comically nor tragically, or, we may say, both comically and tragically, in one word, humanly.

[2] In everyday life it might rather be called his weak point.   His unbridled, violent temper frequently brought him into difficult situations. Once he killed a young colleague in a fury because he had taken one of his wigs.   The law courts, however, treated crimes of this kind with leniency ; otherwise the staffs of the theatres would have been excessively reduced. Quin also had manslaughter on his conscience.

62

63

62—Macklin as Shylock (p. 371).   **63**—Mrs Clive as Mrs Heidelberg (p. 373).

comic actress, Mrs Clive, *née* Raftor.   Kitty Clive, as she
was usually called, was the freshest and most talented exponent of the specially English *genre* called the "singing
chambermaid," or "leading comic."   She made her first
master stroke as Nell in Coffey's very popular little
opera *The Devil to pay*, partly by her splendid singing
voice, but particularly by her exceedingly taking humour
and her very prominent talent for comic parody and
caricature.   Nor was she long in acquiring an absolute
power over the audience, not only in the leading parts
of her particular style, but even in parts that were not
suited to her, but which she transformed according to her
own nature, such as Portia, whom she represented in a
broadly comic manner, parodying well-known advocates
in the law courts.

Like most comic character-actresses she imagined
herself to be a *tragédienne*, and played by preference
Ophelia and other delicate poetic female characters ; and
as she was very rough, physically and mentally coarse-
grained, her dream of course was to act the most refined
and elegant female parts.   In all such characters she
was painfully inadequate ; the audience, however, tolerated her with resignation, as she was so incomparably
amusing in her own domain.   Dr Johnson said of her :
" Mrs Porter in the vehemence of rage and Mrs Clive in
the sprightliness of humour I have never seen equalled.
What Clive did best she did better than Garrick,[1] but
could not do half so many things well."

It cannot be said of Mrs Clive that she was parti-

[1] Mrs Clive continued acting far on in the Garrick period, and was by
turns his worst tormentor and his good friend.

cularly typical of this period, as a sparkling and healthy humour belongs to all times ; and so this actress glided smoothly into the new time, to which, also by her age she essentially belonged.[1]

---

[1] Catherine Clive was born in 1711 ; in 1733 she married a lawyer of a very good family, from whom, however, she was divorced soon after. She retired from the stage in 1769 and died in 1785.

DAVID GARRICK

I

Garrick's *Début*—His Qualifications for Histrionic Art—The New Elements
in Garrick's Acting.

WHEN the New Theatre in Goodman's Fields had been closed in consequence of the Licensing Act of 1737, there was silence about it for some years. But at last it seemed that the manager Giffard found ways out of the difficulty. He gave paid concerts in the "former" theatre, as he called it, and as a "gratis" addition some play was acted.

For 19th October 1741 we possess a play-bill,[1] which is interesting in several respects ; it runs as follows :—

October 19th, 1741.

Goodman's Fields

At the late Theatre in Goodman's fields, this day, will be performed a Concert of Vocal and Instrumental Music, divided into Two Parts

Tickets at three, two, and one shilling.

Places for the Boxes to be taken at the Fleece Tavern, next the Theatre

N.B.—Between the two parts of the Concert, will be presented an Historical Play, called

The Life and Death of

King Richard the Third

Containing the distress of K. Henry VI.

The artful acquisition of the Crown

by King Richard.

---

[1] Joseph Knight, *David Garrick*, London, 1894, p. 22 f.

The murder of young King Edward V.
and his brother in the Tower
The landing of the Earl of Richmond; and the death of King
Richard in the memorable battle of Bosworth field, being the last that
was fought between the houses of York and Lancaster.
With many other true Historical passages.
The part of King Richard by a Gentleman (who never
appeared on any Stage),

.   .   .   .

With entertainments of Dancing
By Mons Froment, Madam Duvall,
and the two Masters and
Miss Granier.
To which will be added
A Ballad Opera of One Act, called,
The Virgin Unmask'd,
The part of Lucy by Miss Hippisley.
Both of which will be performed gratis, by persons
for their diversion
The Concert will begin exactly at six o'clock.

The exciting item of this circumstantial play-bill
which was to draw people to the theatre, was hardly
the concert or the dancing entertainments with which
Shakespeare's tragedy had been smartened up, not even
Henry Fielding's farcical *operetta* ;[1] it was hidden in the
little parenthesis about the gentleman, who had never
yet appeared on any stage. This was in reality a
manager's trick. The initiated knew well that this
mysterious gentleman, under the assumed name of
Lyddal, had acted several times both in London in the
same theatre and, under the same manager, at Ipswich.

[1] *The Old Man taught Wisdom, or The Virgin Unmask'd*, of 1734,
remained in the répertoire throughout most of the century.

They also knew who this amateur really was ; it was no secret in theatrical circles that it was a wine merchant named David Garrick.

On the whole, the young business man was well known among stage people. Four years previously he had opened his wine stores in Durham Yard, one of the by-streets off the Strand, not being far from Covent Garden. He was an eager play-goer, was not long in making acquaintance with several of the actors, which in those times, when admission to the wings could be bought, was not difficult, made friends in particular with Macklin, who was considerably older than himself, became the declared lover of one of the most popular actresses, wrote little love poems in *The Gentleman's Magazine,* and even a short dramatic work, *Lethe,* a kind of satirical *revue.*

So now in his twenty-fourth year [1] he had made up his mind to take the decisive step from man of business to actor, and in doing so he followed a desire which had always burned in him. He writes to his brother Peter : " My mind (as you must know) has been always inclined to ye Stage, nay so strongly so that all my Illness and lowness of Spirits was owing to my want of resolution to tell you my thoughts when here. . . . Finding at last both my Inclination and Interest requir'd some new way of Life, I have chose ye most agreeable to myself, & though I know you will be much displeas'd at me, yet I hope when you find that I may have ye genius of an Actor without ye vices you will think less severe of me, & not be asham'd to own me for a Brother."

[1] David Garrick was born at Hereford on 19th February 1717.

Certainly Garrick had not inherited his inclination
for the stage from his family.   His father was an officer
and belonged to a recently immigrated Huguenot family,
and his mother the daughter of an Irish clergyman.   An
uncle, in whose house he had stayed as a boy, trying to
learn his business, and who had left him £1000 in his
will to start a business of his own, was a wine merchant
in Lisbon ; in short, no theatrical ancestors whatever can
be traced in his family.

Nevertheless he was particularly well qualified for
dramatic art.   Perhaps it was the mixture of French
and Irish blood which produced these exceptional qualifications ; as a matter of fact, Garrick was equipped for
his art in a unique degree.   " Nature," says the author
Cumberland, " had done so much for Garrick that he
could not help being an actor."

He was of medium height,[1] a size which is particularly well suited to character players, as it adapts itself
easily to all figures.   Among the tall Englishmen he
was probably considered short, and his adversaries
always attacked him on this score, if they could find no
other fault with him.[2]   But his body was exceedingly

---

[1] According to a little verse which he wrote himself on the occasion of a
competition with his much taller colleague Spranger Barry, he was about
sixty-four inches high.   The verse runs as follows :—

> Fair Juliet at one house exclaims with a sigh,
>   No Romeo's clever that's not six feet high ;
> Less ambitiously, t'other does Romeo adore,
>   Though in size he scarce reaches to five feet four.

[2] The comedian Foote, once the bitter enemy of Garrick, when chaffed
about his puppet show with full-size dolls, replied that they were by no
means natural size, only as high as Garrick.

well formed and possessed an ease and grace of movement which may have originated in his French lineage,
and which at any rate were uncommon in his somewhat
heavy colleagues.

Of the same origin, no doubt, were his large, brown,
sparkling eyes, which were celebrated for their beauty,
and his very flexible brows and forehead.   His nose was
rather large, straight, and noble in form, his chin round
and strong, his mouth full of life and delicately curved.

The general impression he gave was that of an alert,
lively, graceful, and charming, but not typically English
personality.

So, endowed with all these physical advantages, with
an impressionable mind, a quick wit, and great courage
in showing off his capacities, young Garrick began his
histrionic career in 1741 at the little Goodman's Fields
Theatre.

To say that his *début* was successful would be to
place him on a level with a thousand other beginners.
It frequently occurs that persons of really great talent
have a difficult start, that at the outset their peculiarities
repel or irritate the spectator.   This was not the case
with Garrick.   From the very first evening, when he was
indicated on the play-bill as an unnamed "Gentleman"
personating Richard III., it was clear to experts and to
the general public that here was something new, something rare and masterly.

Lovers of the theatre left Covent Garden and Drury
Lane, and crowded night after night into the hitherto
little esteemed Goodman's Fields to admire the new
tragedian and comedian ; for immediately after Richard

he attemped one of Cibber's fops.[1] Not long after he
produced his own farce, *The Lying Valet*, with himself in
the leading part as Sharp.   Then he played a celebrated
Lovelace part, Lothario, in Rowe's moral tragedy, *The
Fair Penitent*, then the Ghost in *Hamlet*, with the
manager, Giffard in the leading part ; and besides these
a number of comic characters, such as Fondlewife in
Congreve's *The Old Bachelor*, and the ludicrous poet
Bayes in the old parody-comedy, *The Rehearsal*, not to
mention many others, all during his first stage season.
Next year, at the age of twenty-five, he acted King Lear,
and though he did not at once entirely master this
colossal task, he soon worked himself up to it.

Such versatility, such mastery in all branches of
dramatic art was unique, a phenomenon which everybody wanted to see.

Garrick himself describes with naïve joy all the homage of which he is the object in a number of letters to
his elder brother, Peter, to whom he has constantly to
excuse the disgrace he has brought on his family by his
deep fall from the position of a bad wine merchant to
that of a great actor.   He says in one of them : "The
favor I meet with from ye Greatest men has made me
far from repenting of my choice.   I am very intimate
with Mr Glover, who will bring out a Tragedy next
winter upon my acct.   Twice I have sup'^{t} wth ye Great
Mr Murray, Counsell^r, & shall wth Mr Pope, by his
introduction.   I sup't with Mr Littleton, y^e Prince's
Favourite, last Thursday night, & that with y^e highest

---

[1] Clodio in *Love makes a Man*, by Colley Cibber, after Beaumont and
Fletcher.

64

65

64—David Garrick (p. 380).　　　65—Garrick as Richard III. (p. 383).

Civility and complaisance. He told me he never knew
what Acting was till I appear'd, & said I was born to
act w^t Shakespear writ. These things daily occurring
give me Great Pleasure. I din'd with Ld Halifax &
Ld Sandwich, two very ingenious Noblemen, yesterday, & am to dine at Ld Halifax's next Sunday with
Ld Chesterfield. . . . In short, I believe nobody (as
an Actor) was ever more caress'd, & my Character as a
private Man makes 'em more desirous of my Company.
(All this *entre nous*, as one Broth^r to another.)"

This was no exaggeration on Garrick's part; London
was, indeed, "hornmad after him," as another letter-
writer confesses. Even people who were never in the
habit of going to the play wanted to see the young
magician. Pope, who had not been in the theatre for
several years, went and declared that there had never
been the equal of that young man, and never would be.
Even clergymen, such as Thomas Newton, afterwards
Bishop of Bristol, sought his acquaintance, and encouraged him eagerly to continue the histrionic career
for which he was born, and which would make his fortune without hurting his character.

Of course, there were heretics who did not want to
swear allegiance to the new prophet, and these were mostly
among his own colleagues of the old school and their
adherents. When Quin went to see his young rival for
the first time, he shook his head and said : If this young
fellow was right, we are all wrong. And this was the
exact truth. Garrick's art was a renovation, therefore it
created a unique sensation, and therefore the opposition
against it came mostly from his elder colleagues. Among

these Quin was the hitherto infallible pope, and he considered Garrick as a modern sectarian, who for a time
drew people to his false doctrine ; but ere long, he
thought, they would come back to the one saving church.
Such and similar utterances reached the ears of Garrick,
and he wrote the following epigram, which shows that
he was conscious of the renewal he had brought about :—

"Pope Quin, who damns all churches but his own,
   Complains that heresy corrupts the town:
   That Whitefield Garrick has misled the age,
   And taints the sound religion of the stage;
   'Schism,' he cries, 'has turned the nation's brain;
   But eyes will open, and to church again!'
   Thou great Infallible, forbear to roar,
   Thy bulls and errors are rever'd no more!
   When doctrines meet with gen'ral approbation,
   It is not heresy, but reformation."

In what, then, did this revival, this reformation
consist? As far as I know, Garrick himself has not
explained it, nor his contemporaries.   But with the
knowledge we possess of the style of acting which prevailed at the time of his appearance, it is not difficult to
see what he demolished and what he built up.

First of all, it must be accentuated that the regeneration he introduced affected the representation of serious
characters, not—at least not in nearly such an important
degree—that of comic parts.   This was chiefly due to
the fact that comic art was not corrupted in the same
way as tragic art, but—through Nokes, Doggett, and to
some extent Cibber and Quin, as well as Mrs Clive—
had remained fresh all the time.

But what had become of tragic representation we have seen. Influenced by the roaring style of Beaubourg and Duclos, tragedy had been turned into this indolently-dignified, monotonous declamation that was represented by Quin among others, a manner which did not distinguish one tragic character from another except by costume, and which allowed the verses to roll on in a certain fixed cadence, with now and then an outburst of unwarranted fury. It was, as Dr Johnson described it afterwards,[1] the declamation which roared while passion slept.

With this school Garrick's acting was a decided and probably a quite conscious rupture. In those times people were not wont to theorise about dramatic art, except in a general way about its *raison d'être* and its usefulness. But surely Garrick and his friends among the actors, before he himself entered their ranks, had discussed many an artistic question, found out many a new principle, and overthrown many old rules. And we can hardly be mistaken in supposing, though there is no positive fact to prove it, that his old friend Macklin, the queer original with the new ideas, gave many an impulse to his reforming efforts.

So much, at any rate, is certain: that the new, or relatively new, element in Garrick's art, what distinguished it from the prevailing style was, that he intro-

[1] In a famous prologue written for the opening performance of Garrick's management of Drury Lane. The passage in question runs as follows :—
"Then crushed by rules and weaken'd as refin'd,
For years the power of tragedy declin'd ;
From bard to bard the frigid caution crept,
Till declamation roar'd while passion slept."

duced the varied representation of tragic character instead of the conventional rhetorical technique of which tragic art had hitherto consisted. The strong point in Garrick's powers was variety and many-sidedness, and it was quite natural that he should soon turn this mental and physical capacity into a principle. In a letter to Garrick his friend already mentioned, the clergyman, afterwards Bishop Newton, wrote some observations which throw a clear light on this conception of his art: " The thing that strikes me above all others is that variety in your acting, and your being so totally different a man in Lear from what you are in Richard. There is a sameness in every other actor. Cibber is something of a coxcomb in everything; and Wolsey, and Syphax, and Iago all smell strong of the essence of Lord Foppington. Booth was a philosopher in Cato, and was a philosopher in everything else. His passion in Hotspur and Lear was much of the same nature, whereas yours was an old man's passion and an old man's voice and action; and in the four parts wherein I have seen you, Richard, Chamont,[1] Bayes, and Lear, I never saw four actors more different from one another than you are from yourself."

Garrick's renewal of dramatic art was exceedingly important in so far as he was the real creator of character-play, or at least the re-creator at a time when, as a matter of fact, this art did not exist in other civilised countries no more than in England.

What Ekhof about the same time began to carry out in Germany was Garrick's achievement in England, and

[1] In Thomas Otway's tragedy *The Orphan, or The Unhappy Marriage*.

66

67

68

66—Garrick as Lear (p. 384).

67—Margaret Woffington (p. 387).   68—Mrs Pritchard (p. 388).

he became of so much greater importance, first, because England in itself was much more important than Germany, but also because his ambitious nature, which aspired to power, money, and general consideration, raised him to high spheres of society and culture, whence not only his fame as an actor but also his ideas could spread over almost the whole world, whereas Ekhof was contented to remain within a much more limited circle.

II

Garrick's Fellow-Actors—Peg Woffington and Mrs Pritchard—Garrick's Fight for the Management—The Old and the New Styles.

GARRICK'S start was modest enough in so far as his *début* took place in such a third-rate theatre as Goodman's Fields. However, his ambition did not allow him to remain long under such modest conditions. Outward circumstances, moreover, came to his assistance, as the sorely-tried theatre was closed again in 1742—during Garrick's second season there—after which he at once received an engagement at Drury Lane, the leading theatre of London, with the comparatively large salary of 600 guineas a year.

Before his new engagement, however, he made a professional journey to Dublin, together with his declared mistress, Margaret Woffington, a journey which became a true triumphal expedition to both, though especially to Garrick, who stirred up the audiences of the Irish capital to even madder enthusiasm than those of London.

It was not only in his art and in his intercourse with the public that Garrick exercised such a charm; in private life he was quite as captivating, not least to women.   Like a little pasha he only needed to throw his handkerchief among the handsome actresses and they were all his obedient slaves.   At the beginning of his career, however, Margaret, or Peg Woffington as she was usually called, was his chosen favourite.   It was to her that he was said to have written [1] the charming song about " Lovely Peggy," of which the following verses may be quoted here:—

> " The Sun, first rising in the morn,
>   That paints the dew-bespangled Thorn,
>   Does not so much the day adorn,
>   As does my lovely Peggy.
>
> " While bees from Flower to Flowers rove,
>   And Linnets warble through the Grove,
>   Or Stately swans the waters love,
>   So long shall I love Peggy.
>
> " And when Death with his Pointed Dart,
>   Shall strike the blow that rends my heart,
>   My words shall be when I depart,
>   Adieu, my lovely Peggy."

Peg   Woffington   was   exceedingly   popular,   but scarcely very prominent as an actress.   Being a few

[1] The authorship has been contested, though, as it seems, without sufficient reason. It is true, the whole poem in its graceful poetry is essentially superior to the other poems Garrick wrote; but, as Mr Joseph Knight, one of his biographers, justly remarks, from early times love has produced similar miracles.

years older than Garrick,[1] she had begun her professional career much earlier than he, even as a child at
a play-booth in Ireland, where she was born. Like
Mrs Oldfield, she had risen from a very low station, but
though she may to a certain extent be considered as
Mrs Oldfield's successor, she never equalled her in refinement and elegance. She was certainly very handsome
and very charming, but there was a touch of masculine
rakishness in her manners, and especially in her voice,
which was rough and unpleasant. She had, indeed, a
predilection for playing male parts, and had a real and
lasting success in Sir Harry Wildair, formerly Wilkes's
great part in Farquhar's frequently-mentioned plays, in
which she so successfully produced the illusion of a man,
that an enthusiastic lady spectator, who was ignorant of
her disguise, offered to marry her.

Her morals were exceedingly light, and though she
lived for a time in a matrimonial way with Garrick, she
was anything but faithful to him, which, however, did
not prevent her from becoming furiously angry, when he
afterwards made up his mind to marry another woman.
Her career was not very long, and it had a sad end. In
1757, when she may have been 44, while reciting the
epilogue after acting Rosalind in *As You Like It*, she
was seized on the stage with an apoplectic fit that
paralysed her tongue and her legs. In this sad state
the formerly buoyant and brilliant favourite of the public
lived on for three years longer.

Among other actresses who were playing at Drury
Lane when Garrick joined it there was first of all the

[1] The year of her birth is supposed to be 1713, and she died in 1760.

excellent Kitty Clive, who has been mentioned before, and further Mrs Pritchard, who was to become his principal fellow-player.

Mrs Pritchard, *née* Vaughan, the leading performer in high tragedy, differed from her famous colleague in so far as she played solely and purely from natural inspiration. She simply learned her part and then acted it ; that was all. Of reflection over her *rôle*, of studying it, of following any school old or new, there was no question at all. She just acted her part and, what is most important, generally did it well, sometimes with sublime power. It is asserted that of Macbeth she only knew the scenes in which she acted, yet Lady Macbeth was the character in which she rose highest, and had moments of the most admirable effect.[1] Johnson aims not far wide of the mark in calling her "an inspired idiot" ; at any rate her ignorance was boundless, nor did she care in the least to acquire any knowledge. This, however, is certain that she had great natural gifts for dramatic art. But, characteristically enough, her fame was greatest in the parts which she acted together with Garrick. The nights when they played Macbeth and Lady Macbeth, Hamlet and Queen Gertrude, Benedick and Beatrice, were celebrated. So we may suppose that the clever little man imperceptibly turned her heavy talent just in the direction where it would display itself to greatest advantage and correspond well with his own artistic conception.

[1] She did not play it till 1748, when Garrick himself as manager gave it to her ; formerly he had been obliged to play with several inferior actresses.

Mrs Pritchard was excellent also in broadly comic parts, intriguing or jovial ladies, and similar characters, and in these as well as in her tragic *rôles* she maintained her popularity as long as she remained on the stage,[1] whereas the younger heroines, whom she of course continued acting, no longer suited her when her natural tendency to stoutness had increased beyond proportion.

On the male side Drury Lane was very badly equipped under the management of Fleetwood. Besides Macklin, whose peculiar characteristics as an actor have been mentioned before, Delane was the only actor of any distinction. He was popular as hero in the affected "French" style, and Garrick while at Goodman's Fields had parodied his absurdities on the stage. He was an easy and well-bred lover in comedy, in which branch he was able to assert himself, whereas in tragedy Garrick of course crushed him entirely. On the whole, as might be supposed, it was Garrick who had to support Drury Lane during the coming years, as far as this declining theatre could be supported. He acted a number of his afterwards most glorious parts, such as Hamlet, Abel Drugger in Ben Jonson's *Alchemist*, Macbeth, Othello, etc. Still the conditions were unsatisfactory because Fleetwood's management was so bad and dull. With this amiable amateur matters had gone more and more down-hill. Though the theatre always gave good receipts, he was over head and ears in debt because of his disorderly life and his passion for gambling. Garrick

---

[1] She retired on 24th April 1768, and died a few months later. She was born in 1711.

naturally burned to be enabled to carry out his own ideas, and a year after his new engagement he attempted a revolt against Fleetwood's impossible management. Hoping that the authorities would not refuse him and his colleagues a licence to play somewhere else on their own account, he induced the whole staff, including his friend Macklin, who hitherto had been Fleetwood's trusted man, to leave Drury Lane.

But Garrick's hope was disappointed. The authorities sided with the incapable but licensed manager, and refused to allow the actors on strike to play on their own account. Thereupon Garrick, with his prudent, commercial nature, entered on fresh negotiations with Fleetwood and induced the manager, who had now entirely the upper hand, to re-engage the whole company except one, Macklin, with whom Fleetwood was so furiously angry that he would on no account have any more to do with him. The actors had pledged themselves not to accept a re-engagement with Fleetwood unless all were agreed. Garrick now offered Macklin to pay him a considerable portion of his own salary until the conditions should change, but this proposal the irascible Irishman refused with contempt, and broke entirely with Garrick. The latter, as negotiator, now found himself in the dilemma of having either to sacrifice his friend or to leave the whole staff— who with that one exception all desired re-engagement— unprovided for. To a perfectly independent character there would have been no choice, but, opportunist as he was, Garrick would naturally choose to save the many.

And so he did, but he was punished by experiencing for the first time the displeasure of the public. When reappearing on the boards after this affair, he was literally hooted off the stage without being allowed to say a word, and this was repeated for several nights, till Fleetwood, who occasionally had an idea of his own, and also had extensive acquaintance in the lower sporting world, continued to distribute several hundred tickets among boxers and prize fighters, who were willing to adopt a summary means of convincing Macklin's adherents that they were wrong.

For some years now all went on in the old grooves at Drury Lane. But it could not last long. In great displeasure with the prevailing conditions Garrick went to Dublin in 1745, where with Thomas Sheridan [1] he for a time managed the Smock Alley Theatre at the head of an excellent company, among which were the fine, tender and fascinating lover, Spranger Barry and the afterwards very popular and most captivating Miss Bellamy.

On Garrick's return to London after this successful period in Ireland, where he entirely spoiled the market for Quin, who had formerly reaped much honour and gold in that country, he found that Fleetwood had at last succumbed to his creditors, and had fled to France. Then Garrick accepted an engagement with Rich at

[1] Thomas Sheridan, b. 1717 in Dublin, d. 1788 in Margate, was the father of the noted author, manager and politician Richard Brinsley Sheridan. He was a many-talented and many-sided man : M.A., actor, playwright and teacher of rhetoric. He was less gifted as an actor than as a manager, in which latter position he raised the Irish theatre far beyond what it had been before.

Covent Garden, where, besides the pantomimes, the old
school of acting had its principal seat, with Quin as
leader ; and now a constellation was formed of old and
new elements, which was hailed by the public with
impartial enthusiasm for both parties, and which was a
source of amusing reflections to *connoisseurs*.   One of
these, Cumberland, has written down his impressions,
thereby giving us a most graphic picture of these remarkable theatrical nights.   On 14th November 1746 a
performance was given of Rowe's well-known tragedy
The Fair Penitent, in which, as stated before, Garrick
acted the seducer Lothario while Quin was Horatio.
The female lover's part was acted by Colley Cibber's
daughter-in-law, Susannah Maria Cibber, *née* Arne, a
very talented actress, who afterwards, under Garrick's
influence, developed into marked distinction, while the
husband, Altamont, was represented by Quin's good
friend Ryan, a very sympathetic man and popular
second-rate player.

" When Rowe's ' Fair Penitent ' was being performed,
Quin (says Cumberland, who was present) presented
himself upon the rising of the curtain in a green
velvet coat, embroidered down the seams, an enormous full-bottom periwig, rolled stockings, and high-
heeled, square-toed shoes, with very little variation
of cadence, and in deep full tones accompanied by a
sawing kind of motion which had more of the senate
than the stage in it, he rolled out his heroics with an
air of dignified indifference that seemed to disdain the
plaudits bestowed to him.   Mrs Cibber, in a key high
pitched, but sweet withal, sang, or rather recitatived,

69

71

69—Thomas Sheridan as Oedipus (p. 391).
71—Garrick and Mrs Pritchard in *Macbeth* (p. 401).

Rowe's harmonious strain somewhat in the manner of the improvisatore's. It was so extremely wanting in contrast, that though it did not wound the ear, it wearied it; when she had once recited two or three speeches, I could anticipate the manner of every succeeding one—it was like a long legendary ballad of innumerable stanzas, every one of which is sung to the same tune, eternally chiming to the ear without variation or relief.

" Mrs Pritchard was an actress of a different cast, had more nature, and of course more change of tone, and variety both of action and expression. In my opinion the comparison was decidedly in her favour. But when, after long and eager expectation, I first beheld little Garrick, then young and light, and alive in every muscle and in every feature, come bounding on the stage, and pointing at the wittol Altamont (Ryan), and heavy-paced Horatio (Quin), heavens, what a transition! It seemed as if a whole century had been stepped over in the changing of a single scene—old things were done away, and a new order at once brought forward light and luminous, and clearly destined to dispel the barbarisms and bigotry of a tasteless age too long attached to the prejudices of custom, and superstitiously devoted to the illusions of imposing declamation."

At Covent Garden as in every other place where he had been, Garrick soon became the first man. He further increased his popularity by a new little piece he wrote, *Miss in her Teens*,[1] which became an immense success, and in which he himself and the elegant, witty

[1] A free adaptation of Dancourt's *La Parisienne*.

actor Woodward created the two characters which to the public were irresistibly amusing, the mincing Fribble and the swaggering Captain Flash.

Garrick was a ruler born. Wherever he went, it was his will that became dominant, and so it happened also at Covent Garden, where Quin had hitherto been omnipotent. But, naturally enough, he was ever on the alert to find a domain of his own. And in this he was now to succeed. After the collapse of Fleetwood Drury Lane in its fearful state of decadence had come into the hands of two men of business, one of whom, James Lacy, at this period had the ruling power. His partner having failed, Lacy proposed to Garrick to undertake the theatre with him, Lacy managing the accounts and the business, while Garrick was to undertake the artistic and administrative leadership.

Garrick was now thirty years old. He had received a large salary, had always been economical[1] and had saved enough, or at any rate, had sufficient credit to buy half a share of Drury Lane for £8000.

And thus, after a career of only six years as an actor, he stood at the goal of his dreams: he was the generally acknowledged leading actor in England and the head of the theatre which for a long time was

[1] Many stories are told about Garrick's parsimony. While he and Peg Woffington lived together, they were to supply the expenses for housekeeping in turns month by month. But their guests noticed a considerable difference between the Woffington and the Garrick periods. The former were extravagant, abounding in feasts with plenty of good food and wine, whereas the latter were distinguished by a Spartan frugality, which was no doubt more wholesome, but not so amusing to the guests. This economical tendency, by the bye, was of the kind which on solemn occasions may spend large sums, but is close in the details of everyday life.

considered the chief theatre of the town. Here, as his own master, he was enabled to carry out what he had been hitherto obliged to see other managers neglect.

III

Garrick as Theatrical Leader—His Company—His Relations to Literature.

GARRICK at once showed his natural gift for leadership in the combination of the staff he engaged, and most of all by taking no heed whether they were his friends or enemies, rivals or not, his only aim being to create a company as full and as excellent as possible. Thus, in spite of old enmity, he at once engaged Macklin ; he further unhesitatingly acquired his most important rival in popularity as hero and lover, the "silver-tongued" Spranger Barry, an uncommonly fine and tall young man, with whose splendid outward qualifications Garrick could not in the least compete ; moreover, the fashionable and witty comedian Woodward, and as good second-class players — Delane, Yates, Havard, and others—as could possibly be obtained.

His female staff was particularly brilliant. Besides the acknowledged first-class performers, Mrs Pritchard, Kitty Clive and Peg Woffington, he engaged Susannah Maria Cibber, with whom he had acted at Covent Garden, and who had not avoided becoming his mistress. This very sensitive, but perhaps slightly affected actress, who had been unhappy in her married life, but now lived separated from Cibber's abominable son Theophilus, was, except Mrs Pritchard, from whom she differed

exceedingly, the best female tragedian.   Her part was
that of the tender lover ; she played Juliet, Rutland (in
Jones's *Earl of Essex*), Constance in *King John*, Zara,
that is, Zaïre (in Aaron Hill's adaptation of this tragedy
by Voltaire), and similar characters.[1]

A somewhat later addition was the handsome,
coquettish George Anne Bellamy, who, though she never
became a great actress, was always in favour and sometimes created a sensation, besides good secondary
players, such as Miss Hippisley (Mrs Green), Mrs
Macklin, and others.

So admirably composed a company had never been
seen in London.   Garrick might be quite at his ease in
beginning his long and glorious leadership, and was able
to gain an easy victory in his competition with the other
London theatres.

Garrick had won his signal artistic success almost at
a blow, and to all connoisseurs his creative talent had
been manifest from the beginning.   His great object
now was to get the new school firmly established, to
subdue the other actors to it, so that he might no longer
shine like a lonely star among the others who had been
moulded on the principles of the old conventional style,
but might create a fresh unity, a harmony of concerted
acting, which alone can satisfy the sensitive artistic
eye.

Ensemble of acting must needs be the artistic goal

---

[1] Susannah Maria Cibber, b. 1714, d. 1766, was originally a singer ;
and long after having taken up dramatic art and left the operatic career
because her voice was too small, she roused the enthusiasm of Handel by her
deeply pathetic singing in the *Messiah*.   Her health was delicate and she
died comparatively young.

of a stage-leader, but only very few have a gift of creating
it or calling it forth. Garrick possessed this capacity.
It is true, they called him "the little tyrant"; but a
stage-manager must be something of a tyrant if he is to
carry out to any extent what he has at heart. And
Garrick, morever, exercised his tyranny in a pleasant
manner.

From the beginning his object was to restore the
external order and discipline which during the preceding
period of decline had been slackened to an alarming
degree. Order, decency and decorum were the watch-
words, characteristic of the time, which Garrick had
chosen for his motto in his stage leadership. For this
purpose one measure he took was to expel spectators
from the stage, one of Garrick's first exploits, and by no
means one of those which required least courage.[1] A
matter of equally great importance, however, was to
give proper attention to the rehearsals, so as to render
them artistically effective. It is always an unmistakable
token of decline when rehearsals are neglected and slurred
over, and when the actors cannot be made to "play out,"
as it is called in technical language, which means rehearsing in such a way as to give the leader a real idea of the
intentions of the different players, so that he may be able
to time them together to a harmonious union.

This practice had for a long time fallen into disuse
because there had been no competent stage-leader. But

[1] "As the admittance of persons behind the scenes has occasioned a
general complaint on account of the frequent interruptions in the performance, 'tis hoped gentlemen won't be offended that no money will be
taken there for the future"; so it was printed at the foot of the play-bill,
courteously but decisively.

Garrick very decisively made a point of it, and the actors who did not comply with his rules were excluded from the new *répertoire*.

As to the literary side of Garrick's leadership, it was naturally thrown somewhat into the shade. In the eighteenth century it was dramatic art which held the leading position at the theatre. The new dramatic literature was not very strong, and was at any rate exclusively calculated for stage success. This theatrical era, so glorious in other respects, could boast of no great poetic event.

Garrick himself was a fertile playwright. His name is attached to no less than some forty plays; a large part of these, however, are merely adaptations of older plays, and none of them is of particular value, though he wielded a very fluent pen, and among other things wrote a number of the prologues and epilogues inevitable at that time.

But besides these works of his own, which he by no means unduly pushed forward, he presented on his stage nearly all that his time produced of any importance; but this, however, as we have said, was not much, and neither the names of the authors nor the titles of the plays mean much to the modern reader.

Who in our time has heard of Dr Hoadly's *Suspicious Husband*, of Arthur Murphy's *The Way to Keep Him?* Who remembers the humorous or serious comedies of George Colman or Edward Moore? Someone or other, perhaps, recollects Beverley, the gambler,[1] or may have

---

[1] In Moore's pathetic mixed tragedy *The Gamester*, which was played all over Europe.

seen portraits of Garrick as Lord Ogleby,[1] but in a literary sense it is dead as well as the great majority of the numerous dramatic pieces of the eighteenth century.

However, Garrick may be reproached with one real error of literary judgment, namely, that he rejected Oliver Goldsmith's first dramatic attempt *The Good-natured Man*, not because this play, when acted at Covent Garden became a great success, but he ought to have been able to see that Goldsmith possessed the kind of talent which it is the duty of a powerful and wealthy theatrical manager to protect.

Garrick's relations to Shakespeare were of a peculiar kind. It is, at any rate outside England, a general and popular mistake that the resurrection of Shakespeare is due to Garrick, that he imparted to the people, who had forgotten the great poet, fresh knowledge of his dramas, and called forth a new fashionable taste for his art.

This is quite a mistake. Shakespeare had never for a moment been forgotten by the English public, and had at no time been omitted from the *répertoire*. During the first period of the Restoration the taste for what came from abroad had caused people to look upon national poetry with a little insincere contempt. But, in the first place, these times were long gone by, and secondly, this tendency of public taste had not prevented the actors from constantly having the name of Shakespeare on their play-bills. At the time of Garrick's

---

[1] In Garrick and Colman's play, *The Clandestine Marriage*, founded on Hogarth's well-known series of pictures, *Marriage à la Mode*. [This play was recently revived in London, and acted with great success.— *Translator*.]

appearance Shakespeare's plays were at any rate acted quite as much in London as they are now, and the great generally known characters, such as Hamlet, Richard III., King Lear, Shylock, Othello, Falstaff, etc., belonged to the permanent *répertoire* of every distinguished actor.

A very different point is that Shakespeare was mostly acted in a very adulterated form. We have seen that *Macbeth* was turned into a kind of opera, *Romeo and Juliet* into a comedy, *The Merchant of Venice* into a farce, and so on. And the honour is attributed to Garrick of having brought back the great plays to their original form. But not even this honour is due to him entirely. Certainly, he himself thought that he had considerably raised Shakespeare, and it is quite true that he eliminated the most tasteless passages from some of the plays ; but he, no more than other adapters up to our own days, could forbear introducing new tasteless elements of his own invention, and especially cutting and rearranging in a most undue and irreverent way.

Public taste at the time had arrived at the sort of literary refinement which loses the sense for every kind of artistic production which does not bear its own stamp. And the fact was that from mere over-refinement the most awful excesses of tastelessness were committed. Garrick's adulterations of Shakespeare are not worse than many of those of the nineteenth century, yet they were bad enough and mark no real progress from the periods immediately preceding. His remodellings of *A Midsummer Night's Dream* and of *The Tempest* were simply crimes. His abridgments and textual alterations in *Hamlet*, on which he congratulated himself highly, were silly and inadmissible ; on the other hand, he improved the text of *Macbeth* and brought it so close to that of Shakespeare that the older generation of actors, who were accustomed to D'Avenant's abominable adaptation, could not recognise the play at all. So great was the general ignorance that when Garrick announced his intention to play the *Macbeth* of Shakespeare Quin exclaimed in astonishment : "Don't I play *Macbeth* as Shakespeare wrote it?" And when he heard Garrick speak the powerful words of the real play he burst out indignantly : Where in the world did the fellow get that from?

The real revival of Shakespeare, however, did not consist in the literary form employed by Garrick, but in his way of acting. And yet we must beware of thinking that Garrick's representation was even an attempt at returning to the variegated, ardent, at once naturalistic and fantastic style of Shakespeare's own time. It was far from being so. It was an enormous progress in so far as it replaced the conventional, measured, chanting declamation and the stiff regular action by a varied, lively delivery, really characteristic acting, expressive movements of the face, in short, by fresh life instead of dead form. It seized the generally human and dramatic elements of Shakespeare's figures and rendered them with a hitherto unknown life and emotional expression. But it was scarcely capable of, nor did it aspire to, the reproduction of individual character, much less historical colour and the peculiar style of the Renaissance.

We need only cast a glance at the pictures of some

of Garrick's most celebrated Shakespearean characters to understand better what is meant by this.

The first thing that strikes us is the costume, which to our eyes appears so absurd and unpoetic. English historians of the theatre have wondered that Garrick did not reform the tragic stage-costumes simultaneously with the tragic mode of acting. But this was exactly what he did. Just as he broke with the bombastic declamation, he abolished the absurd hero-costume which we know from the French theatre. He replaced the flying feathers and festooned skirts by a simple modern costume, which in its way harmonised well with the style of his art. Nobody had done this before him, and we need only compare the tragic costumes of Quin and Sheridan,[1] to understand that even in this domain Garrick introduced a reform.

Macbeth, who in our eyes resembles Cassander,[2] to people in those days looked merely like an everyday gentleman of high rank. To act Hamlet and Romeo in powdered bag-wig, lace cuffs and square-cut coat was just like playing them nowadays in a dress-coat and a white tie. There is nothing ludicrous and tasteless in it, if all historical or romantic colour is dispensed with, so that only the general human elements remain. To us, who value picturesqueness on the stage so highly, it is not the form under which we wish to see Shakespeare represented, but in themselves Hamlet's melancholy, Romeo's love, Macbeth's horror, from a general dramatic point of view may as well be represented in a modern as

[1] Comp. pp. 370 and 391, figs. 61 and 69.
[2] One of the characters in the Italian pantomime : a ludicrous old man.

in a historical costume, and at all events better than in a ludicrous and grotesque one, such as was the fashion before Garrick's time.[1]

At all events Garrick's great capacities succeeded in turning people's attention quite away from the costume and in making them think exclusively of his acting. It was only in his later years that the thought arose how absurd it was to act the old legendary characters in quite modern attire. The sensation and enthusiasm created by his Macbeth, for instance—who, such as we see him in the pictures, looks almost like a parody—was absolutely undisputed at the time.

His younger contemporary, Thomas Davies,[2] says among other things, in speaking of this part, " Before Mr Garrick displayed the terrible graces of action from the impression of visionary appearance, the comedians were strangers to the effects which this scene[3] could produce. Macbeth, they constantly exclaimed, was not a character of the first rate ; all the pith of it was exhausted, they said, in the first and second acts of the play. They formed their judgement from the drowsy and ineffectual manner of Garrick's predecessors, who could not force attention or applause from the audience during the three last acts. When Roscius[4] was informed what judgement the players had conceived of Macbeth,

[1] In a few parts, such as Richard III., Garrick, as seen in Hogarth's picture, used a kind of historical attire, an Elizabethan Knight's dress. At a later period he also seems to have altered the costume of Macbeth ; at any rate there exists a picture in which he wears a similar, but incorrect dress.

[2] *Dramatic Miscellanies*, ii. 167 f.

[3] The Banquet scene where Banquo's ghost appears.

[4] A surname by which Garrick was generally called, and which had been given him at his first visiting performances in Dublin.

he smiled, and said he should be very unhappy if he were not able to keep alive the attention of the spectators to the last syllable of so animated a character.

" This admirable scene was greatly supported by the speaking terror of Garrick's look and action.   Mrs Pritchard showed admirable art in endeavouring to hide Macbeth's frenzy from the observation of the guests, by drawing their attention to conviviality.   She smiled on one, whispered to another, and distantly saluted a third ; in short, she practised every possible artifice to hide the transaction that passed between her husband and the vision his disturbed imagination had raised.   Her reproving and angry looks, which glanced towards Macbeth, at the same time were mixed with marks of inward vexation and uneasiness.   When, at last, as if unable to support her feelings any longer, she rose from her seat, and seized his arm, and, with a half-whisper of terror, said, ' *Are you a man ?*' she assumed a look of such anger, indignation, and contempt, as cannot be surpassed."

The same overwhelming expression of the horror which he called forth in Macbeth both as an actor, and evidently also in others as a stage-manager, in a hitherto unknown degree and one which was obviously most astonishing to the spectators, was also his strength, both in Richard III. and in Hamlet.   Characteristically enough, the artists who have pictured him in these three parts have all chosen this motive of horror for their representation, and the literary memorials of his acting point in the same direction.[1]

[1] See, for instance, G. Chr. Lichtenberg's detailed description of Hamlet's first meeting with the Ghost, *Auserlesene Schriften*, p. 82 ff.

But Garrick had many more strings to his bow. His strength lay precisely in the versatility and remarkable elasticity of his capacities. His mastery was, like that of Schröder in Germany afterwards, nearly all-embracing. It went even further in one way, though it may not have dived so deep ; for Garrick played lyric lovers, like Romeo, a branch which was not in Schröder's time, with grace and warmth, though he did not attain the summit of his art in these characters.[1]

Among his Shakespearean *rôles* experts put the highest value on his Lear. It lay in the nature of things that he did not draw this character on a gigantic scale, with monotonous declamations like his recent predecessors, Quin, Booth, and a certain Boheme, who is said to have been the best of them. These three were all tall, stout men, who adhered to the principle of one-stringed pathos. Garrick's rendering of Lear was much more complicated. It was said of Barry and Garrick, who acted the part simultaneously, that Barry was indeed "every inch a king," but Garrick was "every inch King Lear," which indicated clearly enough the difference between the two methods of acting. Garrick in this part again revealed his masterly power of characterisation by depicting the whole scale of Lear's vivid sentiments, his violent, easily roused, but senile passion, his madness, his touching love for

[1] He acted Romeo at a time when Spranger Barry and several of his best actors had left him in order to go to Covent Garden, and he did it chiefly on purpose to defy that theatre. The town for a time was divided in an artistic struggle over the two Romeos, Barry and Garrick, and the two Juliets, Mrs Cibber and Miss Bellamy. Most of the combatants, however, probably sided with the perfectly beautiful Barry and the pathetic Mrs Cibber.

Cordelia, his kingly pride, with a stamp of individuality, which his predecessors and many of his successors lacked.

Though these great Shakespearean figures stand as landmarks in Garrick's art, he was no less admired in modern parts.   Mixed tragedy and sentimental comedy possessed a perfect exponent in him, and his Beverley was probably the most admired of all.   The general public perhaps loved him best in his comic parts, such as Abel Drugger, the foolish little tobacconist in Ben Jonson's *The Alchemist*, the smart, airy valet Archer in Farquhar's *The Beaux' Stratagem*, or the low-comedy libertine Sir John Brute, in Vanbrugh's *The Provoked Wife*.   Of the latter part a contemporary play-goer[1] gives a most graphic description, which shows Garrick's power as a comic actor of drawing a character in the minutest details.   " Sir John Brute," he says, " is not only a lewd dog ; Garrick also shows him as an old fool.   On a wig which is tolerably suitable to his age, he has placed a small fashionable gold laced hat so negligently that it does not cover more of his forehead than the part already covered by the wig.   In his hand he holds one of these oak canes with a hammer-like knob, such as young fops generally use in their morning walks in the Parks (morning means here the time between ten and three), and which makes them look like devils of fellows, a kind of cudgel which shows but slight traces of art and culture, just like the majority of human cads who use them.   This cane is used by Sir John to accentuate his words with a bang, especially where only

---

[1] G. Chr. Lichtenberg's *Auserlesene Schriften* (iv. 228).

72

73

72—Garrick and Miss Bellamy in *Romeo and Juliet* (p. 405).
73—Garrick and Mrs Abington in *The Suspicious Husband* (p. 410).

women are present, or now and then to slash about with in his fury when nobody is present who might take it amiss . . .

" Nearly every theatre possesses an actor who is tolerably capable of playing a drunken man, for the simple reason that there is ample opportunity of studying this part . . . Nevertheless Garrick acts the ludicrous Sir John in such a way that I should certainly have discovered his extraordinary talent, even if I had heard nothing of him before, and even if I had seen him only in one scene of this play.

" At first he wears his wig straight, and you see his round, full face.   Afterwards when he comes home quite drunk, his face looks like the moon a few days before its last quarter, as nearly half of it is dimmed by his wig The uncovered part is bloody and shining with sweat, yet most benevolent, so that it entirely compensates for the loss of the other half.   The waistcoat is open from top to bottom ; his stockings hang in wrinkles ; the garters are loose and—very significantly—are not a pair. It is a wonder that Sir John has not put on shoes of different sex ?

" In this sad state he enters his wife's room, and to her anxious question what is the matter with him (and she has good reason enough for her question) he replies: ' Sound as a roach, wife ! '   Yet he does not move away from the door-post, against which he leans as heavily as if he wanted to rub his back against it.

" Then he becomes alternately brutal, drunkenly wise and again kindly, all amid the loud applause of the audience.   In the scene where he goes to sleep he astonishes me. The way in which, with closed eyes, swimming head and pale face, he quarrelled with his wife, and mixing up his r's and his l's to a kind of inarticulate sound, now scolded, now babbled out scraps of moral sentences with which his own state contrasted most abominably ; then the way in which he moved his lips, so that you were at a loss to say whether he was chewing or tasting or speaking—all this surpassed my expectations as much as anything else I have seen this remarkable man do. You should hear him pronounce ' prerogative ' in this part. It was not till after two or three efforts that he was capable of getting to the third syllable."

It was very seldom indeed that Garrick made a mistake, was inadequate or unsuccessful in a part ; but then he had the sense, and as a manager also the power, to spare himself and only to undertake parts for which he felt inclined and which he felt himself capable of fully mastering. Compared with the *répertoire* of many other great actors, the number of his parts is very small, as far as we know, not much over a hundred ; this was to a certain extent due to the fact that he soon—as early as at the age of forty-six—stopped learning new parts, which, of course he could permit himself only on account of being a manager as well as an actor.

His private life, like his artistic career, was unusally happy, leading ever upward to increased power, greater wealth and higher esteem, but, as a natural consequence of never-failing success, without considerable vicissitudes.

At the age of thirty-two Garrick married the handsome Eva Maria Violetti, a dancer of Austro-Italian origin, and the marriage seems to have put a sudden and definite stop to all *amourettes* with actresses. Several of the old "flames" left the theatre in their jealousy, but repented afterwards and returned to their positions. As far as we know Garrick's married life was extremely happy. The couple were always together, travelled together, and went out together; Garrick had even no difficulty in introducing his wife into the highly aristocratic circles which he was fond of frequenting— otherwise an unheard of thing for actors. His circle of intercourse was very heterogeneous—statesmen, sports- men, painters, poets and prose writers, besides his colleagues, but it was a principle of his always to seek the best in every branch. On the whole, he cannot be acquitted of a certain snobbishness.

He managed his theatre undisturbed and without many ups and downs for twenty-nine years.

Like all stage-managers, of course, he had to put up with annoyances, with some discontent on the part of the actors, with revolts and desertions of slight consequence, and he always managed these affairs with great wisdom and discretion; there was the unavoidable leading lady chicanery and the caprices of the actresses, pretences of illness, complaints, tears, and all the rest of it, to which numerous letters, classified and endorsed by Garrick himself, bear amusing witness; [1]

[1] According to himself his worst tormentor was Mrs Abington, who first joined his theatre in 1756, and indeed, her letters are, if not uncommon, yet always astonishing in their hopeless pretentiousness and absurd loquacity. Otherwise Mrs Frances or, Fanny Abington, *née* Barton, was one of the most popular, and in spite of her obscure origin, most elegant actresses

but taken all in all, his management was uncommonly cloudless and brilliant.

It had but one interruption, the great tour abroad undertaken by Mr and Mrs Garrick from September 1763 to April 1765, a journey which turned out quite a triumphal procession for the great actor, and spread his fame, which was as great as it could be in England, over the whole of civilised Europe. Not that he made one of the artistic tours now common; he did not act in public at all on this journey; but by his exceptionally polished social capacities and his unfailing talent for making his way he gained so many admirers and powerful friends in all high circles that his fame spread like that of a king. In Paris he came into close contact with the greatest authors, especially in the sphere of the *philosophes*; his visit was the indirect occasion of Diderot's well-known pamphlet *Paradoxe sur le Comédien*, and the periodicals of the time are full of enthusiastic eulogies[1] of the brilliancy of the great Garrick, and the wonderful capacities for dramatic art which he had displayed in private circles.

On his return from this triumphal journey he intended to retire from the stage at once. Being already very rich he bought a magnificent country seat, Hampton House on the Thames,[2] where he lived in princely style.

Later it was she who created Lady Teazle in Sheridan's famous *School for Scandal*, and this part was typical of her talent.

[1] As an exception from the rule, Charles Collé's well-known Diary contains a furious attack on Garrick, whom the ill-natured author, probably without much reason, accuses of conceited arrogance and unbearable *grandeur.*

[2] It still exists under the name of Garrick Villa, and is situated near Hampton Court.

However, he was so much missed both as actor and leader (perhaps he himself also missed the suspense and exciting applause of theatrical life) that it was a boon to all parties when George III. by his Royal authority commanded him to take up his position again.

Then for half a score of years he again managed the theatre of Drury Lane, which through him gained historical fame, without new, great epoch-making events —after his return he himself played no new parts—but with undiminished power and unchangeably brilliant success, so that in the season of 1776, after a series of farewell performances, which spread over a period of several months, he was able to retire with a truly enormous fortune [1] and unimpaired honour as an actor. Only for a few years was he allowed to enjoy his leisure. He died on 20th January 1779 at the age of scarcely sixty-two.

In Garrick the dramatic art of the eighteenth century attained its climax. There may have been actors whose art was deeper, whose feelings were warmer, whose soul was richer—such as Ekhof and Schröder—but surely none who rose so high, who climbed to the summit and looked round over such an extensive, self-acquired domain, as this great little man. And surely, none was to such a degree an adequate expression of his own age, while at the same time pointing forward to new eras in art. At Garrick's immensely magnificent funeral it was one of Mrs Garrick's arrangements that some person present should throw *Hamlet* down into his open grave. If this was

[1] He left about £100,000.

meant to imply that Shakespeare and true dramatic art were now buried, the symbol was not correctly chosen. Garrick's death did not close a period except in so far as he was its culminating point. But the great extent of his powers rather opened new channels in the realm of dramatic art, just as it opened the eyes of the world to what this art meant.

Certainly in a general sense no actor—either before or after—has achieved so much for his art and his class as David Garrick, so it is quite just that this name, the only actor's name which all educated people know, should have become the standard of the dramatic art of the eighteenth century.

INDEX